THE
NORTH STAFFORDSHIRE RAILWAY
IN LMS DAYS

Etruria, looking south-east from Wolstanton in 1948, across the main line and the Etruria Up and Down Yards. On the far left, the line curving away behind Etruria Yard signal box is heading towards the slag reduction plant, with St. John's Church, Hanley, in the background. Dominating the skyline to the right are the gas holders of Etruria Gas Works, the first of which (seen here on the right with the nearly empty holder almost in the ground) was built by the British Gas Light Company, established in 1904. The gas works was sold to Stoke-on-Trent Corporation in 1922, after which it became the central gas works for the city. In 1931, the first of the waterless gas holders (the tall holder on the left) was built, with a second being added in 1948. This is under construction and just visible peeping out from behind the first one. A fifth, smaller gas holder can be seen through the framework of the empty one. The central large holder is all that remains of the gas works today. In front of the gas works is a complex of NSR-built workers houses, which in turn face on to Etruria Junction. Finally, crossing the centre of the picture, although barely visible, is the Loop Line, which joins the main line at Etruria Junction, with the signal box also in view on the far right. *E.J.D. Warrilow, Keele University collection*

PREVIOUS PAGE: The Down signal gantry at the south end of Stoke station in 1933, painted in LM&SR style. McKenzie & Holland of Worcester were, for nearly fifty years, the contractors for all signalling equipment on the NSR, until the Company took it 'in house' around 1917. The calling on arm was an essential feature in the working of Stoke station and, before its introduction, an extra distant arm was used. This was worked by the station staff from the platform concerned, and was fixed on the post between the home and ordinary distant arms, which were worked in the normal way from the signal boxes. The pulling off of this extra distant arm indicated that the platform was clear to the opposite end. *G.N. Nowell Gossling*

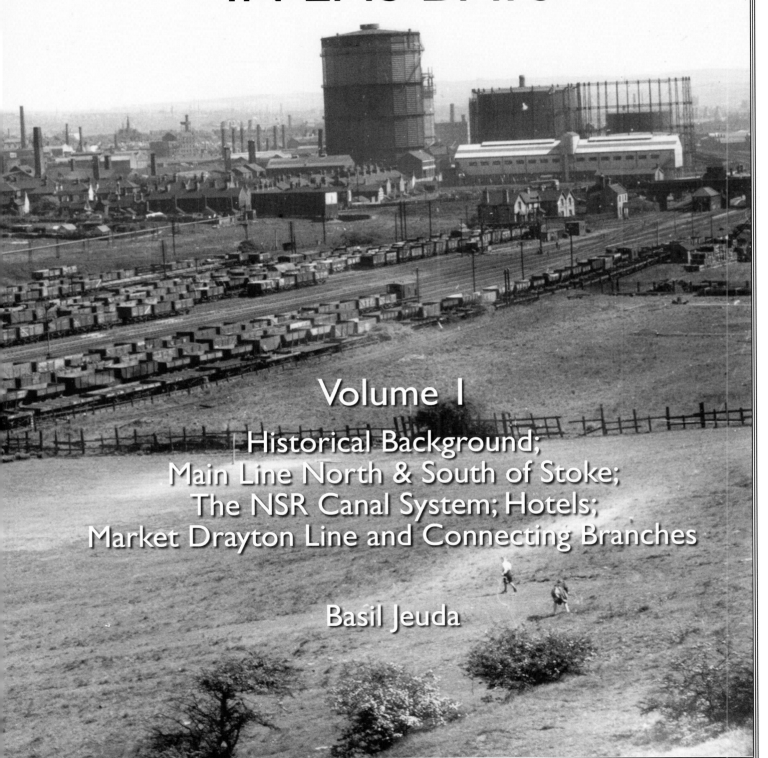

THE NORTH STAFFORDSHIRE RAILWAY IN LMS DAYS

Volume 1

Historical Background;
Main Line North & South of Stoke;
The NSR Canal System; Hotels;
Market Drayton Line and Connecting Branches

Basil Jeuda

VOLUME 1: CONTENTS

Acknowledgements

I would like to thank the following for their information and support: Allan Baker, Paul Blurton, David Bourne, Peter Brown, Robert Cartwright, the late Christine Chester, Mike Christensen, Sheila Cooke, Paul Deakin, Richard Dean, Neville Fields, Chris Fletcher, David Geldart, David Gibson, Alan Faulkner, Mike Fell, Albert Finney, Bob Gratton, the late Clive Guthrie, John Hyde, the late Dr Jack Hollick, Dr David Jolley, the late Robert Keys, David Kitching, Chris Knight, Gerald Leach, Roland Machin, David Moore, the late Claude Moreton, Christine Pemberton, Ian Pope, John Ryan, David Salt, Ron Simpson, Mark Smith, Nelson Twells, the late Gordon Walwyn and Martin Welch.

In addition, I am grateful to the dozens of people who have made time available for me to interview them about their reminiscences and experiences; they are too numerous to name but I hope that they will be able to recognize their individual contributions to the book.

I am grateful for the support given to me by the following organisations: The British Library, British Aerospace, Cheshire Record Office, Keele University Local Studies Library, Manchester Central Reference Library, Manchester Locomotive Society Library, National Archives, National Railway Museum, Newcastle Museum Archives, North Staffordshire Railway (1978) Ltd, North Staffordshire Railway Study Group, Rail Track, the Staffordshire & City of Stoke-on-Trent Archive Services, The Potteries Museum and the Wedgwood Museum.

My thanks go, too, to the many people who have supplied photographs whom I have acknowledged individually in the captions; I apologise for any omissions in this respect. Over the years, I have relied on the traditional photographic skills of Camera Five-Four, Doug Rendell and Tim Shuttleworth but in the digital age I would also wish to highlight and thank Allan Baker, Paul Blurton, David Kitching, David Moore and Christine Pemberton. I am very grateful to Lightmoor Press for agreeing to publish this book and two further companion books, and to one of the co-directors, Neil Parkhouse, for his extremely helpful comments over the years. Finally, to my dear wife Laura for her tolerance and understanding, as ever, as yet another book has altered the landscape of the house for months on end over several years.

Basil Jeuda, Macclesfield, January 2010

1
Historical Background of the North Staffordshire Railway and the Establishment of the LM&SR

The North Staffordshire Railway, or 'The Knotty' as it was familiarly known, was a proud regional railway which, despite the predations over the years of much larger national railway companies, such as the London & North Western, the Midland Railway, and the Manchester Sheffield & Lincolnshire (later Great Central) Railway, was able to maintain its own separate identity until the so-called 'Grouping' of the national railway system between 1920 and 1923. The Grouping was based around four main companies – the London Midland & Scottish Railway, the London & North Eastern Railway, the Southern Railway, and the Great Western Railway.

It would be easy to think of the NSR as purely being a railway system, borne out of the 1840s railway mania and of the three NSR Acts of 1846, which radiated from Stoke and reached out to Macclesfield, Waterhouses, Ashbourne, Derby, Burton-on-Trent, Colwich, Norton Bridge, Market Drayton and Crewe. However, the NSR was much more than that. It owned 119 miles of canal systems and operated nearly all of them – the Trent & Mersey, Caldon, Leek and Newcastle-under-Lyme canals and, for a very short period, from 1847 to 1849, the Uttoxeter Canal; it had its own railway workshops, building and repairing its own locomotives, carriages and wagons; it took over the operating leases in 1847, from the Trent & Mersey Canal, for the working of limestone quarries at Caldon Low in the Staffordshire Moorlands; it owned several hotels, including the flagship North Stafford Hotel directly facing Stoke station, which was set in the midst of Winton Square where also were housed several of the NSR's senior officers.

This book, and the two companion volumes which will follow in due course, specifically look at the changes which occurred in each of the activities that the LM&SR acquired alongside the railway system. These changes took place against the major difficulties that the LM&SR experienced in integrating the various railways it had acquired. This included rationalising the assorted locomotive and rolling stock, and establishing a new locomotive design and build policy; increasing co-operation with its road and rail competitors; reducing its cost base through the closures of branch lines and passenger stations; rationalizing the engine sheds and workshops taken over; attracting new passenger traffic; meeting the threat of competition from buses and road haulage; and in managing the decline of some of its business (such as milk traffic) and canal transport. In addition, the LM&SR had to cope with the fluctuating fortunes of the British economy and the decline of some of the traditional industries, such as iron production and the smaller collieries. The Second World War, whilst damaging the country, provided the railway system with the opportunity to serve new ordnance factories, through the provision of workmen's trains and through the movement of raw materials and munitions in and out. How all of this impacted on the former NSR network, and the industries and communities it served, will be very much the subject of these three volumes.

The core of the NSR network was laid down in the 1846 and 1847 Acts, whose objectives were, firstly, to link the proposed network into those railway lines that were to form the backbone of the national system and, secondly, to meet local needs. The lines, completed in 1848 and 1849, linked Crewe with Derby via Stoke, Macclesfield with Derby and Burton via Uttoxeter, whilst in 1852, the route from Stoke to Newcastle was opened. All these lines acted as spines, with branches built subsequently running off them. The railway from Etruria to Hanley (and subsequently to Kidsgrove), the extension to Market Drayton, the lines from Cheddleton Junction (Leek Brook) to Stoke and to Caldon Quarries and Waterhouses, the line from Rocester to Ashbourne, the railways to Talke and to Chesterton from Chatterley, and the line to Biddulph and Congleton starting at Stoke Junction, were all later extensions of the original network.

These developments of the NSR network took several generic forms. First, there was the linking of the towns in the Potteries and its suburbs, and the provision of passenger stations from the outset. The economics of the Biddulph Valley line rested heavily on the collieries along its length and on the Biddulph Valley Ironworks, with passenger traffic comparatively light. The short Trentham Park Branch provided access for visitors to Trentham Hall, to the emerging suburb of Trentham and, a few years later, to Trentham Park. The opening up of the Leek, Caldon & Waterhouses Railway provided the link to Caldon Quarries and to Waterhouses, where it connected with the separately owned Leek & Manifold Valley Light Railway.

Secondly, mineral lines were developed to serve the coal and ironstone reserves, and their related iron and steel making works. There was also the Wheelock Branch, which served Cheshire's salt and brine deposits to the north and west of Stoke. The Chesterton, Apedale, Talke and Pool Dam lines never had any passenger traffic, whilst the Audley line provided a passenger service ten years after it opened for mineral traffic. Similarly, the short Sandbach Branch, whose commercial importance was disproportionate to its length, opened for passenger traffic in 1893, forty-one years after its opening for mineral traffic.

Thirdly, there was the development of certain small lines to link market and rural towns into the NSR network, such as the Ashbourne Branch and the development of the Cheadle Branch.

ABOVE: The Crest of the North Staffordshire Railway, depicting Stafford Castle and the Staffordshire Knot from which 'The Knotty' derived. It was mounted on a maroon background (here omitted for clarity) and featured on locomotives and coaching stock. *Manifold collection*

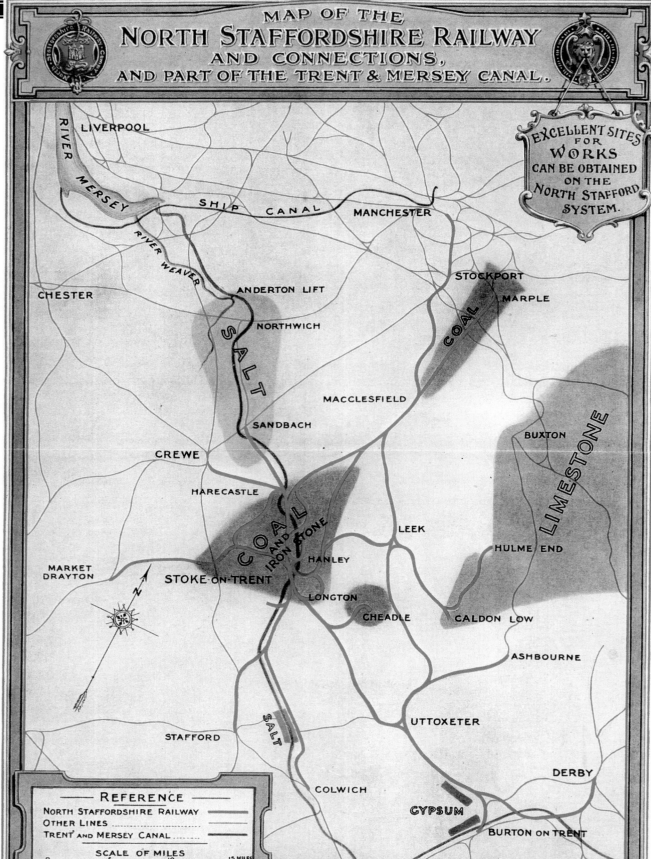

This map of the NSR appeared as an advertisement in the 1912 Year Book of the newly-established County Borough of Stoke-on-Trent Chamber of Commerce. Numerous railway lines radiate out of Stoke, connecting with parts of the national railway system that encircled the NSR. The Trent & Mersey Canal can be traced from Burton on Trent, bottom right, past Colwich to Anderton, top left. Of significance is the presence of large deposits of minerals – salt, coal, ironstone, gypsum and limestone – nearly all of which were transported by the NSR's railway and canal systems; the prosperity of the Company relied heavily on the economic fortunes of their producers. *Author's collection*

Much of the NSR network passed through rural areas and served small village communities. This painting shows an NSR 'C' Class 2-4-0, No. 55 *Colin Minton Campbell*, at Bosley on the Churnet Valley line, five miles south of Macclesfield. This particular class was the mainstay of the NSR's suburban services from the 1880s through to the late 1920s, when they were replaced by the newly-introduced LM&SR classes. In the background is the stone warehouse, the station master's house, the crossing keeper's cabin and the goods office. Milk from the many farms in this area went to Manchester and its neighbouring mill towns. The movement of milk traffic by 'The Knotty' was the lifeblood for numerous villages on the Churnet Valley, Ashbourne, and Derby lines of the NSR. *Alan Turner*

Fourthly, there was the acquisition of, or leasing by, the NSR of certain lines originally promoted and built by others. The Silverdale & Newcastle Railway was leased to the NSR on 31st August 1860 under a 999-year lease and this section remained a leased line into LM&SR days. Similarly with another small line, the Talk o' th' Hill Branch, the lease carried forward into the LM&SR era. The NSR also worked the Manifold line, under an agreement linked to a percentage of gross receipts.

Finally, whilst the location of stations throughout the NSR operating era was largely determined when individual lines opened, the NSR carried out a regular review of the requirement to build at new locations to meet local needs and social changes. There were two main elements to this; first, the NSR needed to respond to the expansions of suburbs to the Potteries towns, and also of Stone and of Burton; secondly, with the emerging competition from trams, the NSR sought to counter this with the construction of halts, wooden platforms long enough for one carriage, coupled with the purchase of three steam rail motors. Most of these halts, as well as all three rail motors, had short lives, with some halts closing in the NSR era. At the time of Grouping, the NSR had ninety-six stations; there were a further two, at Ashbourne and at Macclesfield Hibel Road, that it jointly owned with the L&NWR, and six more on the Great Central & North Staffordshire Joint Railway from Macclesfield to Marple Wharf. The larger stations in the Potteries, as well as those at Macclesfield, Norton Bridge, and Uttoxeter, had both station masters and goods agents. The individual salaries paid to station masters, and to goods agents, reflected the relative importance of the stations – firstly Stoke, next urban stations such as Etruria, Silverdale and Leek, then other urban and important country stations such as Fenton, Cheddleton and Radway Green, and finally minor country stations such as Bradnop, Madeley Road, Great Haywood and Aston by Stone.

The NSR, at 31st December 1922, had issued capital of £10,928,123, with approximately 9,000 shareholders, and was paying a respectable 5% dividend. It was a profitable company. Its recent profits, perhaps a little distorted by certain financial settlements with the Government after the 'European War' and calculated before dividends, were:

31st December	1920	1921	1922
	£439,581	£324,145	£313,672

In 1922, its final year of independent operations, the NSR carried more than 10 million passengers, of which no fewer than 4.1 million were workmen, with nearly all the remaining 6.1 million being Third Class; it also issued over 5,000 season tickets. In addition, the Company carried over 7.3 million tons of goods, 1.7 million of which were classed as merchandise, more than 3.8 million tons were coal, coke and patent fuel, and 1.8 million tons of other goods. It was only a modest carrier of livestock, however, just over 181,000 heads, or 3,300 per week. Special milk trains originated from the NSR network, serving destinations such as London and Manchester.

The NSR operated 220 miles of track, of which it owned 206; it worked eight miles (the Manifold line) and its proportion of the joint line with the Great Central, from Macclesfield to Marple, was six miles. In addition, the NSR had running powers over 329 miles that it used continuously and over a further 83 miles that it used occasionally. Other companies, such as the L&NWR, the GCR, the Midland, and the Great Northern, had running powers over the NSR network and these were reciprocated.

Because the NSR operated a passenger network that linked, mainly, a number of smaller townships radiating out of Stoke, there was very little opportunity for fast train running. The fastest running over the NSR was on the Macclesfield to Stoke working of the L&NWR's mid-day passenger express from Manchester (London Road) to London (Euston); the nearly twenty miles were covered in 27 minutes at an average speed of 44.2mph. The fastest time in 1914 between Stoke and London was on the same train, covering the 145^1/$_2$ miles in 2 hours 41 minutes at an average speed of 54mph.

Over the years, the NSR also provided a wide range of excursion arrangements. Some were on its own network, to places such as Rudyard Lake, Keele and then Uttoxeter racecourses, and Alton Towers, and others further away to destinations such as Blackpool and Llandudno. It provided local cheap travel arrangements for market shoppers, anglers, Sunday School parties and workmen. It appears that Workmen's (weekly) fares were not available during the First World War but, by October 1921, Workmen's Weekly tickets (Third Class) were issued from eleven stations or halts and, from 10th July 1922, this facility was extended to Workmen's Daily Return tickets (Third Class), available from thirty stations. Workmen's fares at Grouping accounted for 40% of all passenger journeys and nearly 14% of all passenger revenue.

The NSR operated numerous through passenger services partly over 'foreign' lines: between Stafford and Manchester; Uttoxeter

LEFT: The changing nature of Edwardian leisure led to the NSR building five locomotives for the crack tourist expresses from Derby/Burton/Stoke to North Wales/ Blackpool. This commercial postcard, from an F. Moore painting, shows 'G' Class 4-4-0 No. 86, one of a class of four built at Stoke Works in 1910. *Author's collection*

BELOW: The First World War demonstrated the benefits of having a national railway system under the integrated control of the Government. This provided the backdrop for the fundamental reorganisation of Great Britain's railway system, later known as the Grouping, and the demise of the NSR. This poster is exhorting the war effort and part of the NSR's Locomotive, Carriage & Wagon Works was given over to the manufacture of munitions. *Imperial War Museum*

and Manchester; Holyhead and Stoke/Derby; Stoke and Liverpool; Derby and Chester; Manchester/Stoke and Wolverhampton/ Birmingham and London Euston; Stoke and Colne/Blackburn; and Brighton/Eastbourne and Stoke. Also during the summer months, there were through carriages between Nottingham, Derby and North Wales, in conjunction with the L&NWR and the Midland.

At 31st December 1922, the NSR owned 192 locomotives, three steam rail motors, and one battery electric locomotive (located permanently at the works of Thomas Bolton & Sons Ltd at Oakamoor). Apart from the rail motors, nearly all these locomotives had been built at the NSR's Locomotive Carriage & Wagon Works at Whieldon Road, Stoke. As a result of the shortage of materials and the use of this works for munitions manufacture during the war, the building of new locomotives between 1915 and 1918 constituted a mere ten. Nineteen new locomotives were built between then and 1923, including the last batch of four 'New L' Class 0-6-2 tank locomotives early in 1923. To overcome a motive power shortage after the war, two 0-6-0 tank locomotives were purchased from the nearby Kerr, Stuart Works in 1919.

The NSR's coaching stock at 31st December 1922 was 534. The works, over many years since 1861, had built carriages but, with the need to build larger vehicles and bogie stock, the underframes had been bought in from the Metropolitan Railway Carriage & Wagon Co. Ltd after 1906. In April 1919, the NSR placed its largest ever contract for coaching stock, to the value of £65,614 for sixteen carriages and underframes. The NSR, in 1920-1, built a further six new coaches and possibly one new train of five coaches.

There was little wagon building during the war because of the shortage of materials. After the cessation of hostilities, there was an enormous backlog of wagon repairs and only a modest amount of new build took place, such as the thirty narrow gauge tippling wagons for use in Caldon Quarries. The stock of merchandise and mineral vehicles at 31st December 1922 amounted to 6,248. There had been little change in recent years – in 1912 the total amounted to 6,338.

In respect of horses and road vehicles employed in the collection and delivery of parcels and goods, the following table shows the growth:

Goods & Parcels Road Vehicles

31st December	1913	1921	1922
Road Motors	3	19	32
Horse Wagon and Carts	216	229	291
	219	248	323
Horses for Road Vehicles	167	155	181
Horses for Shunting	12	7	6
	179	162	187

These figures show a significant increase in the volume of traffic being carried, as well as the rapid expansion in the use of road motors – features that would continue throughout the LM&SR era. The number of shunting horses was in decline and they were probably only in use at Bolton's works at Oakamoor, at Uttoxeter and at the wagon repairing shops at Stoke.

The NSR employed 6,577 staff in March 1921, dropping to 6,360 in March 1922, approximately 0.9% of employees on Great Britain's railways. After the war and with more difficult economic conditions, all railway companies reduced their workforce and nationally the reduction between 1921 and 1922 totalled 59,000. There is no available analysis of the numbers employed in different departments of the NSR but it is known that there were approximately 760 employed in the works, down from 874 in 1913.

The NSR provided for its staff a savings bank and also a Friendly Society, whilst deductions for wages were made for rent (for tenants of NSR houses), the infirmary, health insurance and unemployed insurance. (In 1930 the actuary reported a deficiency in the Friendly Society accounts of £311,941, an enormous sum in those days and steps were taken to run it more prudently). In December 1922,

RIGHT: The last NSR cricket team, in 1923. In 1921, the NSR had significantly expanded sporting facilities for its staff and, after Grouping, it was known as the LM&SR NS Section Amateur Athletic Association. As well as a wide range of sports, activities also included indoor games, ladies' hockey and a choral society. The pavilion was used for badminton, table tennis, whist drives, and dances. *Author's collection*

BELOW RIGHT: A Membership Book for the LM&SR NS Section Amateur Athletic Association, 1928. *Cheddleton Railway Archives*

the NSR owned 371 houses for its employees, compared with 316 in 1913. The NSR ran a miniature rifle club and this was located in Winton Square. There was an NSR Amateur Athletics Association established in 1921, which provided facilities for angling, athletics, bowls, cricket, football, swimming and tennis, and held its own annual sports meeting on the Railway Athletic Ground, adjacent to Winton Square, that it had purchased in 1921; this continued into LM&SR days, though obviously linking into the Company's regional and national sporting initiatives. The Swimming Section was based at Newcastle swimming baths and the Horticultural Society used for its meetings the Ladies First Class Waiting Room at Stoke station. The NSR also supported the Railway Servants' Orphanage at Derby, where there were fifteen children (out of the 280 attendant) from the families of its workforce.

The NSR owned five hotels and public houses. Two of three main hotels, the North Stafford Hotel in Stoke and the Hotel Rudyard at Rudyard Lake, had been owned since 1849 and 1851 respectively, and the Churnet Valley Hotel in Leek since 1900. All these were actively promoted. There were two public houses, the Bull's Head in Hanley and the Yew Tree Inn at Caldon Low, the latter being acquired in late 1922 as part of an NSR policy of buying properties near to the faces of its quarries at Caldon Low. The North Stafford Hotel was leased in 1920 to the Home Counties Public House Trust Ltd (later the Trust House Group).

The NSR worked Caldon Quarries, initially through a 999 year lease obtained in 1769 between local landowners and the Company of Proprietors of the Navigation from the Trent to the Mersey. When the NSR acquired the Trent & Mersey Canal in 1847, the rights to work the quarries passed to them. The lease continued throughout the NSR era, as this enormous limestone hill yielded up its assets (as it still does to this day). From the 1860s onwards, annual output exceeded 180,000 tons. The older quarries were in decline at the time of the Grouping but the new quarry face had produced limestone since 1909 and its output potential was considerable. The following table shows activity at Grouping:

Year	Output Tons	Revenue £	Expenditure £	Surplus £
1913	311,558	29,508	25,630	3,878
1920	224,858			
1921	101,105			
1922	187,692	44,593	43,413	1,180

As mentioned earlier, the total system which comprised the Trent & Mersey Navigation, which was in fact formed by several canals, consisted of 119 miles of waterway. Of the total mileage,

the T&M Canal itself was 93 miles, running from Shardlow (on the outskirts of Derby) to Preston Brook (near Runcorn); the Caldon Canal went from Etruria to Froghall (17 miles) with a short stub of the Leek Canal (3 miles); the NSR also leased the Newcastle-under-Lyme Canal (4 miles) from its shareholders in 1864. Total tonnage carried in 1912 was 1,059,035 but this dropped sharply over the next few years to 534,821 tons. The Caldon Canal was constructed to carry limestone but this traffic stopped in 1920 with the closure of the last of the four incline railways, or tramways, that had linked the canal to the Caldon Quarries since 1778. Traffic on the Leek Canal was small, mainly coal to merchants at Leek Wharf. Traffic on the Newcastle-under-Lyme Canal had all but ceased by 1913, when the NSR, who were contemplating the construction of a light railway from Trentham through Newcastle to Pool Dam and Silverdale, obtained the consent of this canal's shareholders to its partial closure; this was agreed but the railway line was never built. The profitability of the NSR Canals just prior to Gouping was as follows:

Year	Receipts £	Expenditure £	Net Receipts £
1913	57,264	33,205	24,058
1922	57,185	64,257	(7,342)

A sequel to this was the 1921 NSR Act, which authorised the partial closure of the Newcastle-under-Lyme Canal from Trent Vale Bridge to Newcastle Basin, as well as the formal abandonment of the Trentham to Silverdale Light Railway. The significant railway development authorised by this Act was a freight loop line from Shelton, crossing over the main line just north of Etruria, curving round and passing through the goods yard and terminating behind Stoke station. The objectives of this scheme were to divert heavy local freight traffic between the towns on the Loop Line and the marshalling yards south of Newcastle Junction, and to provide Stoke station with four platforms so as to ease bottlenecks; this scheme was not proceeded with by the LM&SR who, in the early and mid 1930s, significantly expanded the marshalling yards at Stoke/Shelton and Cockshute instead.

The origins of the reorganisation of the national railway system

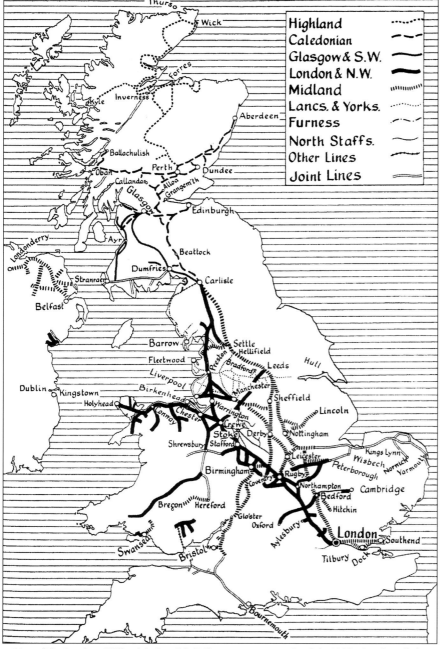

Map of the London, Midland & Scottish Railway system as at 1st July 1923, showing all the constituent companies. This was the date when the NSR and the Caledonian Railway were absorbed into the LM&SR. *The Economist, LMS Supplement, 2nd July 1938*

develop and to improve the internal facilities for transport within the United Kingdom, to secure effective supervision and co-ordination, and to ensure that such developments and improvements shall be adequate and suitable to meet national requirements.' Its preliminary conclusions, reached in November 1918, were firstly, that the organisation of transport agencies of the country, particularly of the railways, could not be allowed to return to its pre-war position; secondly, that the temporary arrangements for the control of the railways and canals during the war would not be a satisfactory permanent settlement; and thirdly, that the unification of the railway system was desirable, under suitable safeguards, whether ownership was in public or private hands.

Following the cessation of hostilities in November 1918, the Government continued to review its options. In August 1919, the Railway Act was passed, giving the Ministry of Transport the control of the railways for a further two years. At the end of 1919, the Railway Executive Committee was dissolved, to be succeeded by the Railway Advisory Committee. In June 1920, a White Paper was published outlining proposals for the future organisation of transport undertakings in Great Britain and their relations to the state. Specifically, it contained proposals for the railways to be grouped into seven systems, one of which was the North Western. This system consisted of the L&NWR, the Midland Railway, the Lancashire & Yorkshire Railway, the NSR and the Furness Railway. There was some criticism of these proposals but agreement was finally reached in May 1921 between the Government and the Railway Companies' Association, representatives of Traders and Trades Unions; this led to the passing of the Railway Act in August 1921. The legislation included the establishment of a North Western Group, consisting of the above-mentioned companies plus the Caledonian, the Glasgow & South Western and the Highland railways; subsidiary companies were to be absorbed later.

The second half of 1921 and 1922 saw certain managements preparing for transition, with existing duplicate services scheduled for abolition, with separate offices combined and staff reduced. An Amalgamation Tribunal was established and in December 1921 approved the merger of the L&NWR and the L&YR.

On 1st January 1922, the L&YR lost its separate identity and two Divisions of the L&NWR were established, a Northern Division which became Division B (the former L&YR territory) and a Southern Division, Division A (the former L&NWR territory). At the time, two names were mooted for the new organisation, the Greater L&NWR and the New L&NWR.

On 17th March 1922, the L&NWR and the Midland circulated shareholders about their intended merger, whilst on 1st May 1922, there was the initial issue of a combined L&NWR and former L&YR timetable. On 25th October 1922, a further L&NWR and Midland circular referred to additional provisional arrangements for the five railway companies but excluding the Caledonian Railway and the NSR. This circular referred to the new Company being known as the London, Midland & Northern Railway, as well as stating that a separate formal amalgamation of the L&NWR and the NSR would not now be needed. In November 1922, there was an announcement of titles chosen by three groups of railways under the 1921 Railway Act.

can be traced back to 4th August 1914, with the outbreak of the First World War, when the Government took control of the railways under the provisions of the Regulation of Forces Act. Control was exercised by the Railway Executive Committee, comprised of the General Managers of the principal railways.

As the war progressed, thoughts started to turn towards converting the benefits of a wartime-run more efficient railway service to an improved national railway service. In November 1917, a Railway Advisory Panel was appointed by the President of the Board of Trade to advise him from time to time on questions affecting the future of the railways. Its early conclusion was *'it became manifest that, in view of the changes that had resulted from the War, especially in the economic basis of the industry, it would be impossible for the railways to revert to pre-war conditions.'*

April 1918 saw the appointment of a Select Committee *'for the purpose of considering what steps, if any, it is desirable to take to*

RIGHT: The second Special Traffic Notice issued by the LM&SR, dated January 6th to 12th 1923, for the North Staffordshire Section as the former NSR became titled. *Author's collection*

BELOW: The Invitation Card for the Conversazione and Dance, held at the Town Hall at Stoke on 26th February 1923. This was the last, and farewell, function of the NSR and was attended by more than 1,000 people. For those attending, late trains were laid on to Keele, Uttoxeter, Stone, Leek, Alsager, Macclesfield and intermediate stations. The Special Meeting of shareholders, to approve the Resolutions for the sale of the NSR to the LM&SR, was held the following day. *Manifold collection*

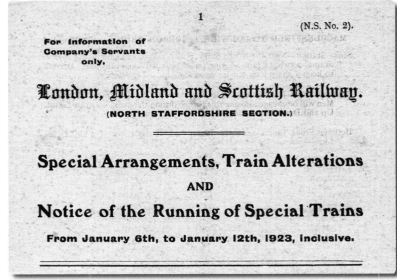

The first initiative taken to absorb the NSR into the Grouping arrangements came from the General Manager of the L&NWR, Arthur Watson, when he contacted Arthur Barnwell, the NSR General Manager, on 26th June 1922 inviting him to discussions about the amalgamation. The principal agenda item was the amount to be paid by the new Company to the NSR shareholders and Loan Stock holders, and the correspondence and comments were robust on both sides. Central to the L&NWR wish to acquire the NSR at a low price was its claim that the NSR, in 1913, had practically neither renewal funds nor reserves and that the Company had been paying higher dividends than it should have been; the NSR's proportion of reserves to capital was about half that of the combined L&NWR and L&YR. At the end of July 1922, Barnwell had stated that he was looking for a price of between £82-84 of L&NWR Ordinary Stock; in September 1922, Barnwell had dropped the price to £80-81 while the L&NWR offer was £64, a price that the NSR rejected on 24th October.

In November 1922, the L&NWR Audit Office referred scathingly to the *'supineness of the NSR in acceptance of short payments in 1913 and previous years of underpayments by the L&NWR to the NSR of the NSR share of receipts for the London traffic'* and concluded that there were underpayments that should be factored into the share price. On 26th November 1922, Barnwell indicated that he would not go below £76, whilst Watson was prepared to offer £73.10s; the price was settled at that meeting at £74. Agreement was also reached at the prices to be paid for the NSR's 3% Debenture Stock, the 3% Consolidated Preference Stock and for the Guaranteed 5% Shares that were issued in 1847 on the acquisition of the Trent & Mersey Canal.

The *Manchester Guardian* reported on 20th December 1922 on the *'Terms of the Bargain'*, though whether the NSR's Stock and Debenture Holders saw it that way is a matter of conjecture. The L&NWR had made an announcement on the previous day that a provisional agreement had been reached with the NSR, under the Railway Act 1921, leading to the amalgamation into a new group to be called the London, Midland & Scottish Railway Company, with effect from 1st January 1923.

Separate to this agreement, it was settled that the NSR would provide one Director to the new Board; this was to be Major Francis Wedgwood of Barlaston. The NSR shareholders gave approval at Ordinary and Special Meetings on 27th February 1923. Whilst this date was obviously too late for the formal/legal transfer on 1st January 1923, on a day to day operational level things moved quickly. The Weekly Special Traffic Notices were issued from the first week, in January 1923, under the banner of the LM&S

North Staffordshire Section, a description that continued to be used throughout the LM&SR era wherever it was applicable. NSR bank accounts were closed on 9th January, new creditor payment arrangements were introduced on 18th January and no local payments for salaries or wages were permitted after 26th January. On 1st April 1923, the rate of interest paid by the NSR Savings Bank was reduced from 5% to 4% *'to bring it into line'*.

In December 1922, Barnwell had negotiated arrangements to protect the employment rights of the NSR Chief Officers, Assistants and District Officers, by reason of continuing service in any capacity under the amalgamated company. At the Ordinary Meeting on 27th February, a resolution was passed authorising £10,600 to be paid out of the assets to such Directors as retire from office upon the amalgamation or for the abolition of office; this amount was to be divided between them in such proportions as they thought fit. The formal amalgamation proceeded of the North Western, Midland & West Scottish Group, now the LM&SR, with the NSR and the Caledonian Railway. The Railways Amalgamation Tribunal authorised press notices early in June 1923, with any objections to be received by 19th June 1923. The Tribunal sat on 25th June 1923, heard two objections and then approved the scheme that became effective from 1st July 1923. Thus, in a legal sense, the NSR passed into history.

The following details show the NSR's share of the newly-established London, Midland & Scottish Railway:

	NSR	LM&SR	Proportion %
Route Mileage owned	220¾	7,330	3.0
Route Mileage worked	226¾	8,309¼	2.7
Locomotives	192	10,104	1.9
Coaching Vehicles	534	26,217	2.4
Freight and Service Vehicles	6,612	326,801	2.0
Employees	6,360	258,778	2.5

The NSR area immediately became the North Staffordshire Section within the much larger structure, whilst the various LM&SR Departments underwent structural changes over the years. However, this Section remained operationally intact as an Engineering District, as a District for the control of train operations, and as a District for Passenger and Goods operations, throughout the LM&SR era.

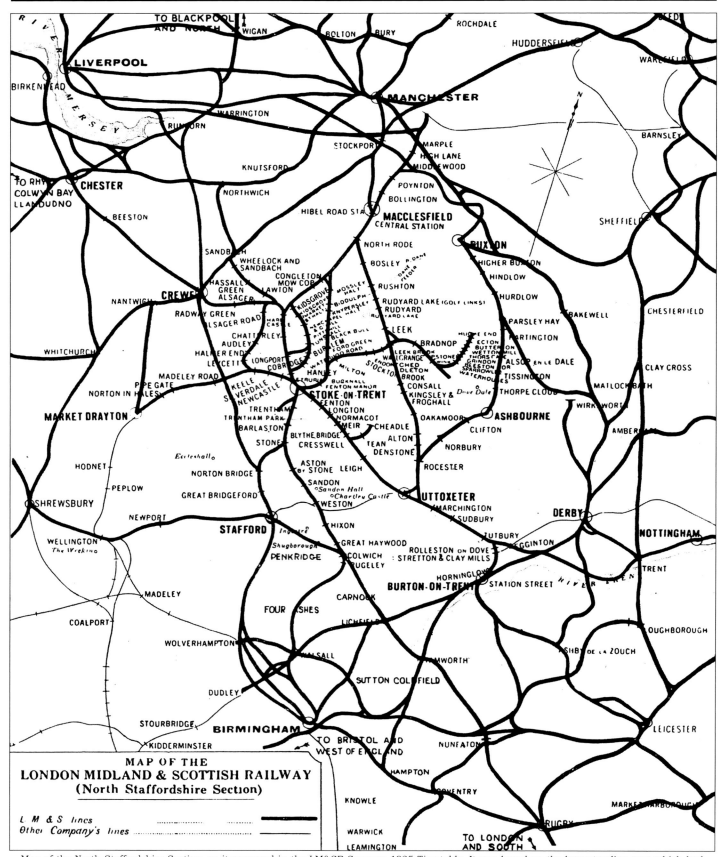

MAP OF THE
LONDON MIDLAND & SCOTTISH RAILWAY
(North Staffordshire Section)

L M & S lines .... ▬▬▬▬
Other Company's lines ....

Map of the North Staffordshire Section, as it appeared in the LM&SR Summer 1925 Timetable. It was based on the long-standing map which had appeared in NSR public timetables. *Author's collection*

2
Historical Review of the LM&SR Era
1923-1947

The LM&SR came into its inheritance during a period of transition; of economic nationalism and depressed export industries, of increased costs and a higher wage bill. In 1923, the internal combustion engine had raised the road highway from the modest role of a feeder to that of a formidable competitor for the cream of railway traffic.

The LM&SR took no time at all in tackling the problem of the groups of senior managers for each of the constituent railway companies. In the case of the NSR, Barnwell retired at the end of June 1923 with a pension of £2,000pa and a capital sum of £11,000. J.P. Wadsworth, cashier, retired in January 1924 with a pension of £550pa and Andrew Rock, electrical engineer, at the same time on £774pa, in both instances representing two thirds of salary. John Hookham, the widely-respected NSR mechanical engineer, retired on 31st December 1924 with a pension of £960pa and a capital sum of £2,000 in respect of lost fees from pupils (premium apprentices) that had averaged £570 each year for the 1919-23 period. H. Curbishley, canal engineer, retired in September 1925 on a pension of £375 and a capital sum of £1,450. C.G. Rose, engineer, was appointed district engineer for the North Staffordshire District on a protected salary of £1,800pa, a salary which was more than twice the level of the other district engineers in the newly established Western Division; Rose also received compensation of £2,000 for loss of pupils' fees.

Given that the NSR contributed barely 2% of the newly-formed LM&SR employees and given also the much larger organisational structures of the L&NWR, Midland and L&YR, it was inevitable that key positions went to those already holding senior posts at these larger railways. Probably only three former NSR employees held down positions of significant responsibility throughout the LM&SR era: George Ivatt (the NSR's assistant to the locomotive superintendent), who later became chief mechanical engineer of the LM&SR; E. Grasett (the NSR's traffic superintendent) who later became divisional superintendent of operations at Derby, and Tom Coleman (who was a draughtsman in NSR days and, latterly at the LM&SR in Derby), who held the post of chief draughtsman in charge of both Derby and Crewe locomotive drawing offices, and with an influential role in the LM&SR in designing new locomotives. The NSR area immediately became the North Staffordshire Section within much larger administrative structures and the various LM&SR departments underwent some organisational changes over the years.

Passenger traffic on the LM&SR in its early years was disappointing, with receipts dropping from £26,013,800 in 1923 to £21,763,617 for 1929. This reduction was accompanied by a 15% drop in the volume of traffic, caused by a continued economic depression and by road competition. The L&NER and the Great Western Railway also saw drops, of 19% and 10% respectively. The LM&SR sought to reduce unprofitable passenger services through the closure of stations and of branch lines, as well as to reduce operating costs through the singling of lines and the closure of engine sheds. This policy was also reflected in the sharing of station masters between two stations, and through the selective 'pooling' of services and staff with its competitors, the L&NER and the GWR, at locations such as Macclesfield and Burton under a May 1932 agreement. The network of passenger services was sharply reduced in the rural areas, though these lines remained open for the more profitable mineral and goods traffic.

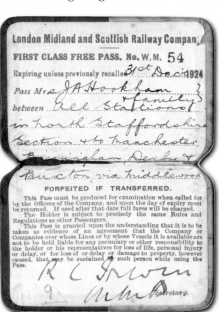

ABOVE: Arthur Barnwell was the last General Manager of the NSR, from 1919 to 1923, having previously held down various senior engineering posts at the Company for more than twenty years. He negotiated with the L&NWR the terms of the sale of the NSR to the LM&SR and was the first of its senior officers to accept redundancy terms and retire. *Manifold collection*

RIGHT: John Hookham was the highly respected locomotive superintendent of the NSR; he was retained by the LM&SR in 1923 and 1924 as mechanical engineer, retiring on 31st December 1924. This is the First Class free pass issued in 1924 for himself and his family for travel over the North Staffordshire Section and to Manchester, Birmingham, Derby, and Buxton. *Author's collection*

The LM&SR Board closed some of the unprofitable lines and services against a background of railway and bus companies seeking to secure better co-ordination between rail and road transport. A report to the LM&SR Board in 1930 cited the economies to be gained from specific closures:

Branch Line	Stations Closed	Traffic Discarded £Net	Economy £pa
Wheelock	3	138	284
Audley	4	1,677	1,307

This left the users of the passenger trains to rely on the services provide by buses. Bus competition had become an increasing threat to the railway companies, in the country areas providing a better service to customers, with more stops and a better frequency. In 1928, each of the 'Big Four' took Parliamentary powers to own and operate bus services. This led in 1929 to the LM&SR buying all the shares in Crosville Motors, a bus company serving west Cheshire and north-west Staffordshire. Similarly, in 1929, the LM&SR and the L&NER acquired a stake of just under 50% in the North Western Road Car Co. Ltd, another bus company, operating in east Cheshire, north Staffordshire and Derbyshire. This enabled the LM&SR to integrate some rail and bus provision, and close down unprofitable lines. In 1931, the LM&SR was also seeking, albeit unsuccessfully, to acquire an interest in the Potteries Electric Traction Company.

The following passenger services on the former NSR network were discontinued during the LM&SR era:
- Biddulph Valley Branch, 11th July 1927
- Wheelock Branch, 28th July 1930
- Audley Branch, 27th April 1931
- Leek & Manifold Valley Light Railway, 12th March 1934
- Waterhouses Branch, 30th September 1935

The LM&SR era also saw station closures on lines that remained open at the time, such as:
- Sideway Halt, 2nd April 1923
- Brampton Halt, 2nd April 1923
- Mossley Halt, 13th April 1925,
- Hartshill & Basford Halt, 20th September 1927
- Knutton Halt, 20th September 1927
- Madeley Road, 20th July 1931
- Waterloo Road, 4th October 1943
- Aston by Stone, 6th January 1947
- Great Haywood, 6th January 1947
- Hixon, 6th January 1947
- Weston & Ingestre, 6th January 1947

There were ninety-six NSR stations at 1st January 1923 but by 31st December 1947, these had been reduced to sixty-seven. Singling of the Audley and Market Drayton branches was completed in 1935.

There were eleven NSR engine sheds at Grouping but by the

LEFT: The sale of Weekly Workmen's tickets was an important source of passenger revenue for the NSR but was largely restricted to stations close to Stoke, Hanley and Newcastle, and those stations served by the Rail Motor service. These arrangements not only continued into the LM&SR era but were rapidly extended in 1924, through the increased availability of Weekly tickets and through the introduction of Daily tickets. Subsequently, by 1929, a large number of stations had been included and a massive expansion of the scheme for Workmen's Daily tickets had taken place. *Author's collection*

Competition from bus operators increased rapidly in the 1920s and into the 1930s. The establishment of regular bus services to country villages in north Staffordshire undermined the viability of local railway branches, hastening their decline, although the buses did provide a better local service. Here a North Western single-decker waits outside Macclesfield (Central) station circa 1935, with a service to Bollington. *Author's collection*

mid-1930s these had been reduced to four, there being no further closures during the remainder of the LM&SR era. Those closed were on the perimeter of the NSR network, often where the NSR connected with the lines of other railway companies. Closures occurred on the following dates but final demolition for many of them did not take place until the late 1930s:

- Crewe, 30th March 1923
- Derby, 30th June 1923
- Burton, 6th July 1923
- Leek Brook, 4th January 1932
- Caldon Low, 1st April 1932
- Ashbourne, 7th November 1932
- Hulme End 12th March 1934 (former L&MVLR shed)
- Market Drayton, 12th March 1934

The following table (in millions) shows LM&SR passenger traffic at selected dates between 1924 and 1937:

Year	No's (000s)	£ (000s)
1924	538,442	33,005
1929	461,283	28,723
1932	407,501	24,200
1934	432,701	24,740
1936	450,531	25,963
1937	459,547	26,994

By 1932, there had been a significant drop in the number of passengers carried of 131 million (24.3%) and the related revenue of £8 million (26.1%). It was reported to the Board in 1932, in respect of road competition, that *'there was an overwhelming case for accepting standard fares be reduced as only by the adoption of cheaper fares for the ordinary day to day travel and for the creation of new business in the shape of pleasure travel can the passenger revenue of the railway companies be improved.'*

At a special meeting of the Superintendents of the L&NER, LM&SR, and the Southern and the Metropolitan railways, a one year experiment from 1st January 1933 was agreed, whereby the existing standard fares for the ordinary single and return fares be suspended; in their place was, for example, a First Class single rate of 2d (0.8p) per mile and a Third Class single rate of 1^{1}/4d (0.5p)

TICKETS

issued between ASHBOURNE and UTTOXETER

and intermediate Stations will be

available for Return by

RAIL or ROAD

Rail Section.	Road Section.	Return Fare.
ASHBOURNE—Clifton	ASHBOURNE—Mayfield	3d.
,, —Norbury	,, —Ellastone	7d.
,, —Rocester	,, —Rocester	1/-
,, —Uttoxeter	,, —Uttoxeter	1/6
CLIFTON—Norbury	MAYFIELD—Ellastone	5d.
,, —Rocester	,, —Rocester	10d.
,, —Uttoxeter	,, —Uttoxeter	1/5
NORBURY—Rocester	DENSTONE LANE—Rocester	3d.
,, —Uttoxeter	,, ,, —Uttoxeter	10d.
ROCESTER—Uttoxeter	ROCESTER—Uttoxeter	7d.

CHILDREN under three years of age, free ; three years and under fourteen, half-fares.

CHEAP DAY RETURN TICKETS are issued by the LMS at the above fares, and are available for return on day of issue only.

Holders of Rail Return Tickets **A** between the above points may travel outward by any train and return within the period of availability by any train or by the vehicles of the Trent Motor Traction Company Ltd., without extra payment.

Holders of Bus Return Tickets between the above points, issued by the Trent Motor Traction Company Ltd., may return within the period of availability by Rail without extra payment, tickets to be exchanged at the Railway booking office.

A—Except Workmen's, Season, or tickets issued in connection with special events.

ABOVE: An extract from the summer 1935 LM&SR passenger timetable, promoting the inter-availability of rail and bus tickets between Ashbourne, Uttoxeter and intermediate stations. This particular initiative was short-lived and there was little promotion of other like schemes on the North Staffordshire Section in the 1930s. *Author's collection*

STOKE—AUDLEY BRANCH.

The Passenger Train Service at Leycett, Halmerend, Audley and Bignall End, and Alsager Road Stations has been discontinued.   The Potteries Motor Traction Company and the Crosville Motor Services Ltd., run a service of omnibuses daily (including Sundays), through the district previously served by the branch line.   For times see Local Omnibus Timetable.

Parcels traffic will continue to be dealt with at these stations, except Alsager Road, which will be covered by Alsager Station.

HARECASTLE AND WHEELOCK & SANDBACH.

The Passenger Train Service between Harecastle and Lawton, Hassall Green and Wheelock and Sandbach Stations has been discontinued.   The Potteries Motor Traction Co. run a Service of Omnibuses between Harecastle, Lawton and Sandbach Town daily (including Sundays).

The Crosville Motor Services run a Service between Sandbach Town and Wheelock daily (including Sundays), also on Thursdays only between Sandbach Town and Hassall.   For times see Local Omnibus Timetable.

Parcels traffic will continue to be dealt with at Hassall Green, but that for Lawton will be dealt with at Alsager, and for Wheelock at Sandbach.

LEEK AND WATERHOUSES.

The Passenger Train Service between Leek, Bradnop, Ipstones, Winkhill Halt, Caldon Low Halt and Waterhouses has been discontinued.

The North Western Road Car Company, the Trent Motor Traction Company and the Potteries Motor Traction Company run Services of Omnibuses through the district previously served by the Branch Line.   For times see Local Omnibus Timetable.

Parcels traffic will continue to be dealt with at all stations with the exception of Caldon Low Halt.

RIGHT: The summer 1937 passenger timetable for the North Staffordshire Section contained information on several line closures, such as the Audley, Sandbach and Waterhouses branches. *Author's collection*

A number of promotional booklets were issued to encourage rail travel to leisure destinations in North Staffordshire, south Cheshire and Derbyshire.

RIGHT: *Picturesque Staffordshire* was published by the LM&SR in 1925 and was almost identical to the very successful booklet published by the NSR in 1908. The front cover design, other than the LM&SR logo, was identical, whilst a small amount of the content was updated.

Picturesque Staffordshire
and Surrounding Districts.

AMBLES on the
LLS and in the
LLEYS.

THE GUIDE FOR ALL HIKERS
RURAL RAMBLES 1/-

INCORPORATING

50 COUNTRY WALKS
A HANDY GUIDE to the BEAUTY SPOTS OF
LANCASHIRE : DERBYSHIRE : YORKSHIRE
CHESHIRE and NORTH STAFFORDSHIRE

Published by the EVENING CHR

ALLIED NEWSPAPERS LIMITED, Printers,

LEFT: *Rural Rambles,* published in the early 1930s by the *Manchester Evening Chronicle*.

BELOW: *Walking Tours Manchester and District* was published in the early 1930s by the LM&SR.
All author's collection

ABOVE & BELOW: Two delightful photographs taken at Ashbourne Carnival in the summer of 1933, as part of the LM&SR's promotional activity for Summer Excursion tickets at 1d per mile. The advertising slogan used was 'Penny a mile, any train, any day, anywhere'. *Dr Jack Hollick*

Walking Tours
MANCHESTER
AND
DISTRICT.
LONDON MIDLAND & SCOTTISH RAILWAY

THE GREAT CUP-TIE at Maine-road, Manchester, where 25,000 Stoke City supporters saw a thrilling duel. Other vivid pictures of the match, also taken by "Sentinel" staff photographers, appear on

LEFT: The largest football crowd ever to watch a match in England outside London was the 84,569 at Maine Road, Manchester, on 3rd March 1934, when Stoke City played Manchester City in a 6th round cup-tie. Sixteen excursion trains left the Potteries for Longsight and one for Manchester (Mayfield), each consisting of ten bogie carriages; it was estimated that between 16,000 and 17,000 fans travelled by train that day to the match. Seven locomotives from Stoke shed were used, as well as engines from Crewe, Preston, Springs Branch (Wigan) and Bushbury. Evidence that the support for Stoke City was widespread is reflected in the fact that return trains went to Cresswell, Uttoxeter, Crewe/Stafford and Stone, as well as to the Potteries' towns. *Hanley Archives*

BELOW: Half-day Excursions Notice for train services in August, September and October 1933, for Stoke City home football matches. Concessionary return fares were available from more than fifty stations, from as far afield as Macclesfield, Market Drayton, Stafford and Crewe. *Author's collection*

per mile, reductions of 20% and 16²/₃% respectively. These were all intended to provide an incentive to the general public to travel by train and, even though bus travel would still be cheaper, this would be offset by greater travel comfort and a quicker journey. There were no alterations for Privilege, Season and Workmen's tickets. That there was a public appetite for discounted rail fares had been demonstrated by a national pilot scheme introduced in the summer of 1932, between Uttoxeter, Stoke and Congleton, and intermediate stations, which resulted in increases on that route in passengers carried of 37% and in revenue of 16%.

The results of the fares experiments were highly successful; the Summer tickets at 1d (0.4p) per mile resulted in a tremendous increase in the North Staffordshire Section. In 1934, this District ran ninety-three evening excursions and each train had an average load of 424 people. For 1935, the LM&SR and other railway companies provided additional facilities with the Summer ticket being altered to a Monthly ticket and with availability extended from three days to one month; tourist fares were reduced by 26% for First Class and 18% for Third Class. The impetus that flowed from these initiatives led to the following percentage improvements for 1936 over 1935:

Route	Journeys %	Receipts %
Stoke-Blackpool	+16.6	+19.2
Stoke-London	+8.0	+8.2
Congleton-Manchester	+13.5	+12.5
Macclesfield-Blackpool	+21.4	+15.2
Manchester-Stoke	+24.2	+16.2
Stoke-Wolverhampton	+24.6	+16.9
Burton-Derby	+5.2	+0.1
Crewe-Stoke	+13.9	-0.8

There is considerable information on the volume of freight traffic on the network in NSR days but there is little data on the volume of activity on the continuing North Staffordshire Section in the LM&SR era. The NSR prospered on the movement of mineral traffic, as it served collieries, iron works, steel works, chemical factories, the pottery industry and gas works. The period from 1923 down to the start of the Second World War in 1939 was a time of mixed fortunes for industry in North Staffordshire. The North Staffordshire coalfield saw the rundown and closure of some of the older and smaller collieries, some seventeen in total, such as Talk o' th' Hill, Jamage Main, Parkhall, Rookery and Burley. These losses were offset by the expansion of newer sinkings a few years before Grouping, such as Parkhouse Colliery at Chesterton and Holditch Colliery at Apedale, as well as Hem Heath at Trentham in 1924. Four ironworks were closed between 1928 and 1930, at Norton, Black Bull, Great Fenton and Apedale, though considerable new investment in the LM&SR

FOOTBALL AT STOKE

STOKE CITY v. CHELSEA—August 26th
STOKE CITY v. PORTSMOUTH—September 9th
STOKE CITY v. DERBY COUNTY—September 23rd
STOKE CITY v. WOLVERHAMPTON W.—Sept. 30th
STOKE CITY v. ASTON VILLA—October 14th
Kick-off 3.15 p.m.

HALF-DAY EXCURSIONS
By L M S to
STOKE-ON-TRENT
SATURDAYS
Aug. 26th, Sept. 9th, 23rd, 30th & Oct. 14th, 1933

FROM	Times of Departure	RETURN FARES (Third Class)	FROM	Times of Departure	RETURN FARES (Third Class)
	p.m.	s. d.		p.m.	s. d.
Alsager ...	2.15	1 0	Milton ...	2.18	0 6
Aston-by-Stone	1.34	1 0	Mow Cop ...	2.0	1 0
Barlaston	2.37	0 8	Newcastle ...	2.27	0 3
Blythe Bridge...	2.10, 2.30, 2.36	0 6	,, (L'pool Rd. Halt)	2.25	0 4½
Bucknall	2.22	0 3	Newchapel & G. ...	1.53, 2.5	0 7
Burslem	1.55, 2.1, 2.14	0 3	Normacot ...	2.15, 2.37	0 4
Cheadle	2.15	1 0	North Rode ...	1.44	1 6
Cheddleton ...	1.33	0 3	Norton Bridge ...	2.25	1 3
Cobridge	1.58, 2.3, 2.17	0 3	Norton-in-Hales ...	1.56	1 3
Congleton ...	1.35, 1.53	1 3	Oakamoor ...	1.19	2 0
Cresswell	2.5, 2.25	0 8	Pipe Gate ...	2.2	1 3
Crewe ...	2.5	1 3	Pitts Hill ...	1.55, 2.7	0 6
Endon ...	2.11	0 8	Rocester ...	2.5	2 0
Etruria ...	2.6, 2.26, 2.43	0 2	Rudyard Lake ...	1.15	1 3
Fenton ...	2.21	0 1½	Rushton ...	1.19	1 6
Great Bridgeford	2.20	1 3	Sandon ...	1.28	1 3
Hanley...	2.2, 2.8, 2.22	0 2	Silverdale ...	2.18	0 7
Harecastle	2.23	0 8	,, (Grown St. Halt)	2.20	0 6
Keele ...	2.14	0 8	Stafford ...	2.15	1 6
Kidsgrove	1.45, 2.6	0 6	Stockton Brook ...	2.13	0 7
Kingsley & F.	1.24	1 6	Stone ...	2.32	1 0
Leek ...	2.0	1 0	Tean ...	2.22	1 0
Leigh ...	1.20	1 3	Trentham ...	2.41	0 5
Longport	2.31	0 3	Tunstall ...	1.52, 1.58, 2.10	0 4
Longton	2.18, 2.40	0 3	Uttoxeter ...	2.19	1 6
Macclesfield (H.R.)	1.35	1 6	Wall Grange ...	2.6	0 10
Market Drayton	1.50	1 6	Weston & I. ...	1.25	1 3
Meir ...	2.13, 2.34	0 5			

CHILDREN under three years of age, free; three years and under fourteen, half-fares.

Passengers holding day or half-day excursion tickets by special trains are not allowed to take any luggage except small handbags, luncheon baskets, or other small articles intended for the passenger's use during the day. On the return journey only, passengers may take with them, free of charge, at Owner's Risk, goods for their own use not exceeding 60 lbs.

CONDITIONS OF ISSUE OF EXCURSION AND OTHER REDUCED FARE TICKETS.
Excursion tickets and tickets issued at fares less than the ordinary fares are issued subject to Notices and Conditions shown in the Company's Current Time Tables.

For suitable return services see overleaf.

Bemrose & Sons Ltd., Derby and London.

Parkhouse Colliery on 26th May 1917, showing the cutting of the first sod for the sinking of a new shaft, No. 3. This shaft later became the winding shaft and the colliery rapidly expanded its output and its workforce throughout the LM&SR era. Crackley Colliery can be seen on the skyline, in the background. *Metcalfe collection*

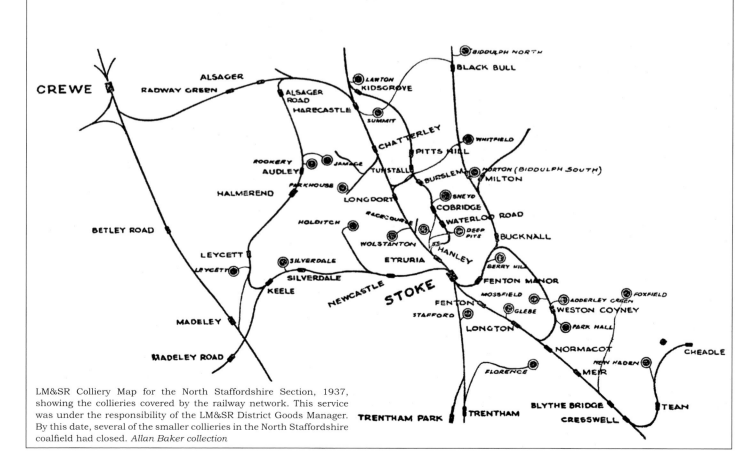

LM&SR Colliery Map for the North Staffordshire Section, 1937, showing the collieries covered by the railway network. This service was under the responsibility of the LM&SR District Goods Manager. By this date, several of the smaller collieries in the North Staffordshire coalfield had closed. *Allan Baker collection*

ABOVE: Substantial amounts of coal went from the North Staffordshire coalfield to Liverpool and Birkenhead docks. Private owner wagons dominate this picture of Birkenhead, with two Sneyd wagons near the front and several Foxfield wagons in the centre. *Manifold collection*

RIGHT: An aerial view of the Top Quarries at Caldon Low taken in the early 1970s. These quarries were opened in the late 1770s, with the opening of the Caldon Canal, and became exhausted and worked out by the late 1920s, finally closing in 1930. Note the large number of narrow gauge tramroads that ran from the quarry face to a spine tramroad, which went to the marshalling area adjacent to the winding drum, from where loaded wagons then descended to Froghall Wharf. *Derbyshire Stone*

The decline in milk traffic by rail in the 1930s is reflected in this mid-decade picture of a Wilts United Dairies Ltd flat bed lorry from their Uttoxeter depot, collecting milk in churns from a farm a little way out of the town. These churns in earlier years would have been taken by farmers to their local railway station for onward delivery by rail. *Cheddleton Railway Archives*

era continued to be made at Shelton Works and at Birchenwood.

For the LM&SR as a whole there was mixed experience on the movement of freight, as the following table shows:

Year	Tons moved (000s)	Value £ (000s)
1923	163,077	45,306
1929	149,833	43,816
1932	116,854	33,733
1937	139,098	39,573

The movement of milk by train was on a downward trend, as follows:

Year	Gallons (000s)
1928	75,758
1935	67,604
1936	62,271

During the LM&SR era, but mainly after the late 1920s, there was a reduction in the number of milk trains that ran in north Staffordshire and in the number of stations served by such trains.

The Locomotive, Carriage & Wagon Works at Stoke, whose origins dated back to 1849, employed nearly 760 people at Grouping but it was almost immediately sidelined, with no new locomotives, or coaching and wagon stock, being built there. Instead, it carried out repairs and painted stock in the new LM&SR livery. Along with several of the workshops of the smaller railways in particular, it was part of a wide ranging LM&SR review early on in its existence, which ultimately led to its closure in the summer of 1927, along with other such facilities elsewhere.

The limestone quarries at Caldon Low, which the NSR held under a 999-year lease, felt the buffeting of the Depression. With the exhaustion of the Dunkirk and Nick quarries by 1930, the LM&SR subsequently entered into a sub-lease with John Hadfield & Sons Ltd (the forerunner of Derbyshire Stone Ltd) in

WILLS'S CIGARETTES
No. 12
RAILWAY ENGINES.
A SERIES OF 50.

L. M. & S. Railway.
NORTH STAFFORDSHIRE SECTION.
Engine No. 23—0-6-0 Four-cylinder Tank.

A very interesting locomotive and unique in being the first instance of a British tank engine to have four cylinders. In the design all the modern appliances have been included, and the engine is well adapted to hauling heavy trains having frequent stops, and requiring rapid acceleration. A novel feature is the disposition of the inside and outside cranks. This engine has been working local trains around Stoke district. Built at Stoke, the weight in working order is 56½ tons.

W. D. & H. O. WILLS
BRISTOL & LONDON.
ISSUED BY THE IMPERIAL TOBACCO Co
(OF GREAT BRITAIN & IRELAND) LTD

WILLS'S CIGARETTES.

L. M. & S. R. NORTH STAFFORDSHIRE SECTION.

A set of fifty cigarette cards on railway engines was issued by W.D. & H.O. Wills in 1923-4 and no doubt contributed greatly to the craze for collecting the varied and numerous sets. This card was one of a number which recognised the birth of the LM&SR and the locomotives which had been transferred to it. It depicts one of the experimental NSR 4-cylinder 'D' Class engines. Note the reference to the North Staffordshire Section and the NSR livery. *Roland Machin collection*

1934, who promptly invested in new plant and equipment.

The LM&SR had inherited five hotels and pubs, as well as the Cliffe Park Estate at Rudyard. The Churnet Valley Hotel was sold in 1938. The Hotel Rudyard was sold in auction in August 1927 for £6,350, along with adjacent land holdings, whose ownership had dated back to 1797 and the building of Rudyard Reservoir by the T&M Canal. The nearby Cliffe Park Estate and Hall, acquired by the NSR in 1904 for leisure development purposes, remained in LM&SR ownership throughout their era, with the lease of the hall to the Youth Hostel Association eventually covering the period from 1933 to 1969. The Yew Tree Inn, at Caldon, was sold at July 1947 for £3,000 to Ind Coope & Allsopp, whilst the Bulls Head Inn, Hanley, continued to be leased to Worthington & Co. throughout the LM&SR era.

The LM&SR had to cope with increasing competition from the haulage companies for the movement of goods and parcels, and it sought to exploit new commercial opportunities. It was assisted by successive pieces of legislation, the LM&SR (Road Transport) Act of 1928, the Road & Rail Traffic Act of 1933 and the Road Traffic Act of 1934. There was significant investment in lorries and later mechanical horses, and also in containers as it diversified into new markets such as country and farm traffic. A national scheme, Country Lorry Services for Farm and Village, was introduced in 1928. In the case of north Staffordshire, a Town Cartage scheme was also established in the Stoke area from 1932. This was reinforced by significant investment in new marshalling yards in the early and mid-1930s, at Stoke and Cockshute respectively, and in goods handling facilities in the late 1930s, at Longport.

Co-operation between the 'Big Four' was evidenced by the establishment of the Railway Air Services in 1934, to carry passengers by air to a small number of destinations in the United Kingdom and the Isle of Man. This impacted locally, with the use of Meir Aerodrome (for Stoke) as a request stop on the London to Glasgow and the Liverpool to Cheltenham routes. The operating airline was taken over on 1st February 1947 by British European Airways Corporation Ltd.

The LM&SR's preparations for war start being reported in its Board Minutes of January 1939, with reference to the funding and costs of Air Raid Precautions, and to the Government's allocation of £1,359,700 to the LM&SR for control centres, signal boxes, emergency stores and twelve 35-ton steam breakdown cranes. Although war was declared on 3rd September 1939, thorough preparations for its likelihood had begun in 1937. Its impact on the north Staffordshire area was felt in several ways but principally in the production and distribution of munitions, and equally the running of Workmen's trains around the clock to and from different parts of the NSR network. Munitions factories were opened at Millway (Radway Green), Dovefields (between Marchington and Sudbury), Cold Meece/Swynnerton (between Stone and Norton Bridge), and Bromshall, near Uttoxeter. As a result, round the clock shift working required, for example, Workmen's trains to run three times a day to and from Cold Meece, with separate trains to and from Blythe Bridge, Longton, and Silverdale. Also, numerous factories in the north Staffordshire area were given over to the war effort; at the former NSR Locomotive, Carriage & Wagon Works, in the old locomotive section, by this time occupied by John Hyde & Son Ltd, munitions were manufactured, whilst a large part of the adjacent former Carriage & Wagon section was leased to Rolls Royce for the manufacture of parts for aero engines.

Regulation 69 of Defence Regulations was issued in pursuance of the Emergency Powers (Defence) Act 1939 and Royal Assent was given on 24th August 1939. On 1st September, the Government assumed control of the railways and of the gigantic task of evacuating large numbers of the population from the cities; the Minister of Transport appointed a Railway Executive Committee as agents for the purpose of giving directions. On that date, the Ministry of Transport requisitioned the use of all private owners' wagons, except for certain vehicles designed for specific traffic. Evacuation began on Friday 1st September and was spread over three days; no fewer than 80,000 people left Manchester and a large number of special trains were laid on. When war was declared on 3rd September, only nine trains were left to despatch evacuees and, in all, 72,000 people were evacuated including 23,000 adults. Children started arriving in north Staffordshire on the 1st, with several districts selected as

reception areas – Newcastle (4,000), Stone (4,500), Stafford (8,000), Congleton (2,000), Cheadle (6,000), Alsager (750), Market Drayton (1,000), Leek (2,000), Macclesfield (12,000), Bollington (800) and Crewe (6,000). Trains also ran to Cresswell and Uttoxeter. In respect of passenger services, business trains ran more or less as usual during the evacuation but all Half Day and Evening excursions bookings by special trains were immediately cancelled. The LM&SR Board held discussions after the outbreak leading to announcements on special arrangements; for example, for marshalling and traffic yards, camouflage, anti-gas measures and signalling at motive power depots. A Redundant Assets & Salvage Committee was established in January 1940 and the local campaign included collecting facilities established at Longton Goods, the North Stafford Hotel, Stoke motive power depot, Leek Goods, Macclesfield Goods and Rocester Goods. The LM&SR provided Co-ordinating Officers for the 1941 Fire Regulations and the North West Region Committee included G.H. Nutter, the District Goods & Passenger Manager for the Stoke District.

A report in March 1940, dealing with the North Staffordshire Section, commented that train services were almost at peace-time level but that there were more goods trains; local work was done by Stanier 2-6-2Ts and 2-6-4Ts, taking goods and passenger services indiscriminately. The increase in heavier freight work was reflected in the increased allocation to Stoke of former L&NWR locomotives, six 0-8-0s arriving in December 1939 and January 1940, along with two 0-6-0 'Cauliflowers' and three 0-6-0T shunting locomotives. In August 1944, it was reported that Stoke local passenger traffic was worked by 2-6-4Ts and also much of the goods traffic.

There also occurred the withdrawal of Cheap Day fares from 5th October 1942 and the disappearance, *'for the duration'*, of the last

ABOVE: The front cover of the timetable for LM&SR Passenger services issued on the outbreak of the Second World War in September 1939. *Author's collection*

RIGHT: A typical war-time scene, at Derby, with passengers looking at the notices for the Emergency Passenger Services introduced in September 1939. The posters are, from the left: the Main Line to St. Pancras; next Derby and Sheffield, Leeds, Heysham and Carlisle and Branches; then Main Line, Derby and Manchester, and Southern, Central, and Eastern Districts; penultimately, Derby-Bristol ... and Branches. The final poster is too small and out of focus to be identifiable. *Author's collection*

ABOVE: Special fire fighting engines and trains were stationed at key points on the railway system, ready to be deployed wherever they were needed. This photograph, taken on 28th October 1941, shows firemen from LMS Fire Brigade Derby carrying out a drill. One type of fire-fighting train had six locomotive tenders holding 15,000 gallons of water and several 20hp motors. This photograph had to be submitted to the wartime censor, before it could be released for publication. *Author's collection*

RIGHT: A Second World War poster inviting women to work in the nation's factories. There were several munitions factories in the north Staffordshire and south Cheshire areas, all of whom were served by numerous Workmen's trains from the Potteries' towns and, to a lesser extent, from Macclesfield and Congleton. In addition, there were numerous factories in the same areas where some or all of the output was devoted to the war effort. *Imperial War Museum*

WOMEN OF BRITAIN
COME INTO
THE FACTORIES
ASK AT ANY EMPLOYMENT EXCHANGE FOR ADVICE AND FULL DETAILS

of the many reduced rates introduced over a long period of years. Only four passenger fares remained – Ordinary Single, Monthly Return, Bulk Travel and Workmen's tickets.

By June 1943, the Railway Companies Association, representing the main line railway companies, was turning its mind to post-war policy; the thrust of this was to oppose public ownership, to seek to run the railways more efficiently and economically, and to achieve greater co-operation. More detailed work was carried out on the planning and progress of new work, and there were many schemes, including some in north Staffordshire (such as the rebuilding of Stoke shed) that had been deferred or delayed on the outbreak of war. In January 1944, the LM&SR Board considered a paper on post war development, with a price tag of £48 million, such was the enormous cost to repair a war-damaged railway system. In anticipation of the end of the war, the LM&SR reorganised Train & Traffic Control arrangements, with the appointment of four Divisional Superintendents of Operations responsible for fourteen District Operating Managers in place of forty-two District Controllers. The Stoke Control area, comprising the North Staffordshire District, was one of ten in the newly-created Western Division, with an area almost identical to the boundaries of the old NSR.

The war ended in Europe on 8th May 1945 and in the Far East on 14th August 1945. War-time events of significance in north Staffordshire were the bombing of Hanley station on 26th June 1940 (a fact that went unreported in the local press because of wartime censorship) and the massive explosion at the ammunition depot at Fauld, near Tutbury, on 27th November 1944, which killed seventy people and left a 1,000 foot diameter crater.

The newly elected Labour Government announced on 19th November 1945 its intention to '*introduce measures designed to bring transport services, essential to the well being of the nation, under public ownership and control ... In regard to inland transport, powers will be taken to bring under national ownership the railways, canals, and long-distance haulage services.*' The threat to the railway companies of nationalisation surfaced in 1936 and a pamphlet on *Railways and the State, The Problems of Nationalisation* was published by the British Railways Stockholders Union; this was countered by a publication by the Labour Research Association in 1938, entitled *Justice for the Railwaymen? Can the Companies afford it?* This skirmishing was halted by the onset of war but the Railway Companies Association, in a report on the main line railway companies' post-war policy, affirmed that the policy was to oppose public ownership and to seek to serve the community more efficiently and economically, and to develop greater co-operation. The Ministry of War Transport, established in May 1941, was dissolved in April 1946 and all its functions transferred to the Ministry of Transport. A Transport Bill was introduced in November 1946 to set up a publicly-owned system of inland transport (not air) and of port facilities; the LM&SR Board not only opposed the intended legislation but instructed Officers at headquarters and down the line to seek to influence Chambers of Commerce, Rotary Clubs, and other local bodies and individuals. Royal Assent to the legislation was given on 6th August 1947, to the establishment of the British Transport Commission and various executives, including the Railway Executive and the Docks

PRICE TWOPENCE

LMS
TRAIN SERVICES

MANCHESTER (London Road)
Macclesfield, CREWE
STOKE-ON-TRENT
Uttoxeter, Leek
STAFFORD
Wolverhampton and Birmingham
Crewe and Chester
Crewe and Shrewsbury
Stafford and Shrewsbury
including
VARIOUS THROUGH CONNECTIONS

JUNE 16th, 1947, TO OCTOBER 5th, 1947, INCLUSIVE

& Inland Waterways Executive.

On 1st April 1948, railway and canal undertakings were taken over, including main line railways and their joint committees, and all privately owned railway wagons were requisitioned by the Ministry of Transport. After 1st January 1948, no privately owned wagons could be used on the railways. British Railways acquired many former 'Knotty' employees, a railway network in the old NSR area that was still largely intact after twenty-four years of LM&SR ownership and much NSR architecture, some of which is still intact sixty years on. However, parts of the integrated railway company that had been 'the Knotty' had been hived off (the T&M Canal system and the quarries), or closed (the workshops, many branch lines for passenger services, one third of its stations and many small engine sheds) or disposed off (most of its hotels). The story of all this will be contained in this and the two companion volumes to follow.

Top: The campaign for Nationalisation of the railways was launched in 1936. Here we see a protest meeting in Stoke demanding state control of all railways, mines and banks. *Author's collection*

Middle: The front cover of the LM&SR summer 1947 passenger timetable, the penultimate one to be issued prior to Nationalisation on 1st January 1948. It covers parts of Cheshire, Staffordshire and the West Midlands. The last timetable to be published for the North Staffordshire Section was the 1939 edition. Note the LMS roundel logo. *Author's collection*

Right: At Macclesfield Hibel Road shed in the spring of 1948, Fowler 2-6-4T No. 2319 has been freshly painted in British Railways plain black livery but retains its LM&SR number and the initial 'M', indicating that the locomotive was allocated to the LM&SR Midland Division. *The late Ron Dyer collection*

ABOVE: Manchester (London Road) on 27th July 1926, with former NSR 'G' Class 4-4-0 No. 171 on an Up working to Stafford or Birmingham. The locomotive is wearing its first LM&SR number, 598, seen here being carried on a 'Claughton' tender. The engine was one of a class of four built at Stoke Works in June and July 1910, for express working between Derby and Llandudno in the summer months. This particular locomotive was the last of its class to be withdrawn, in May 1933. After the Grouping, all of the class received the LM&SR fully lined out crimson lake passenger livery, with 18 inch tender numerals and the company emblem on the cab sides. *Neville Fields collection*

3
MAIN LINE NORTH

The NSR main line, running from Macclesfield (Hibel Road) through Stoke to Colwich, with a branch to Norton Bridge, was by far the most important line that the NSR ever built. It provided the spine of the NSR network, which many of the branch lines fed into or spun off from, as well as connecting with the national railway system at Crewe, Norton Bridge and Colwich (for Rugby and London). Because the L&NWR and the NSR had reciprocal running powers, there were shared services such as the Macclesfield to Manchester passenger workings, and the Manchester to Stafford, Birmingham and London (Euston) workings. Additionally, the L&NWR used its Stockport (Heaton Norris) link to provide freight access to east Lancashire and to the West Riding of Yorkshire. The main line was 38½ miles long and, apart from a 1 in 102 climb from Hibel Road to Macclesfield Moss, was on a long descent all the way to Colwich Junction (with the L&NWR), apart from short sections which rose to clear the Trent & Mersey Canal at several locations. Returning, it was a steady climb from Colwich to Macclesfield.

The main line is here covered in two parts, the section from Macclesfield to Stoke as 'Main Line North' and that from Stoke to Colwich and Norton Bridge as 'Main Line South'. The sections had different characteristics but they did provide a through route to Stafford, Rugby and London both for passenger and goods traffic.

The line was an important spine, with branches off it at North Rode for the Churnet Valley line to Uttoxeter; at Congleton for the Biddulph Valley line; at Harecastle where it is joined by the lines from Crewe and Sandbach; at Chatterley for the Talke and Chesterton branches; at Etruria by the Loop Line from Hanley and other Pottery towns; at Newcastle Junction where the line joins it from Market Drayton; at Stoke Junction for the Biddulph Valley, Leek and Derby lines; at Trentham for the Trentham Park line; and at Stone for the line to Norton Bridge, where it joined the L&NWR main line north to Crewe and south to Stafford, Rugby and London. There were two tracks throughout, other than a section between Bradwell and Longport, and between Grange Junction (just north of Etruria) and Stoke station. Plans were considered in 1945 to widen the line between Longport and Grange Junction, and to build a new station at Longport, but these were not proceeded with.

The industries served by the Main Line North were both numerous and diverse. At the risk of oversimplification, there was silk at Macclesfield, silk and milk at Congleton, lime at Astbury, coal at Harecastle, iron and coal at Chatterley, pottery, chemicals, engineering and tile manufacture at Longport, gas production, collieries, iron and steel at Etruria, and at Stoke the pottery industry. Wagon repairing was carried out at Harecastle and Etruria. What reinforced the industrial and commercial base of the Chatterley Valley from Harecastle to Stoke was the existence of the T&M Canal, because this waterway had determined industrial settlement from the late 18th century onwards. It had enabled major industrial undertakings, such as the Goldendale Ironworks and the Shelton Iron Steel & Coal complex, to be located adjacent to the T&M (from the 1840s) and a few years later to the railway. With the demise of iron manufacture at Ravensdale and at Shelton, there grew up a new industry on site, namely of slag reduction, with Tarbitumac (1920-1940) processing slag from Goldendale, Ravensdale and the Chatterley ironworks.

At Grouping, the NSR had eleven shunting engines at six different locations on the Main Line North between Macclesfield and Stoke, carrying out trip working to a large number of works and collieries. At Macclesfield, there was one locomotive on north trips, one from Chatterley (working the Talke and Chatterley lines), three from Longport, two from Etruria and two from Stoke North. Comparable details from September 1938 were two from Macclesfield, six from Alsager and twenty-nine from Stoke shed. Main Line North was well-served by marshalling and yard facilities and, in 1929, these facilities had a wagon capacity of:

Macclesfield	141
Congleton	65
Harecastle	329
Chatterley	359
Longport	489
Etruria	76
Cliffe Vale	64
Cockshute	418
Stoke	719

PREVIOUS PAGE BOTTOM: Former 'KT' Class 4-4-0 No. 38, now renumbered 5414 and in LM&SR livery, is seen entering Manchester (London Road) hauling ex-L&NWR stock and passing underneath the elevated gantry of the L&NWR signal box, with a working from the south, possibly Birmingham or Stafford. This was the only locomotive in the class and was built at Stoke Works in 1912 for working the holiday expresses between Derby/Burton and Llandudno. It was renumbered 599 in 1923 and carried 5414 for only a few months before being withdrawn from service in August 1928. It is seen here in plain black livery. *Dudley Whitworth*

RIGHT: Former NSR 'New L' Class 0-6-2T No. 72, now as LM&SR No. 2262, at Manchester (London Road) station at the head of a Stoke passenger working in July 1928. This locomotive was sold in January 1937 to Lancashire Associated Collieries Ltd, who subsequently renamed it *Sir Robert*. *Frank Dean*

LEFT: Former 'New L' Class 0-6-2T No. 22, one of a batch of six locomotives of its class built at Stoke Works in 1921 and 1922; indeed, the first batch of six built at the works since the end of World War 1 in November 1918. It is seen here at Manchester (London Road) with the elevated L&NWR signal box on the right. The locomotive has been renumbered 2264, which was carried out with NSR transfer numerals, and has yet to be lined out. The 'New L' Class worked on the Manchester-Macclesfield-Stoke service in the early years following Grouping, before being replaced by 'K' Class 4-4-2Ts and 'M' Class 0-4-4Ts, then later by Fowler and Stanier 2-6-4Ts. *Author's collection*

BELOW: On 1st June 1936, Fowler-designed 'Patriot' Class 4-6-0 No. 5537 *Private E. Sykes VC* leaves Manchester (London Road) at the head of a rake of LM&SR carriages on the 12.05pm express for London (Euston). This crack express on the LM&SR system was given the name 'The Lancastrian' in the summer of 1927. *Pollard collection, courtesy Neville Fields*

The schemes to enlarge Stoke station and to reduce the movement of goods traffic on the goods lines going north, introduced by the NSR in its final years, were not carried forward by the LM&SR.

During the LM&SR era, there were significant enlargements to the facilities at Stoke Yard in 1929-32 costing £69,102 and to the remodelling and expansion (to a capacity of 500 wagons) of Cockshute Sidings in 1933-5 amounting to £11,218. The most significant new investment was the expansion of goods and handling facilities at Longport in 1937-40 amounting to £82,038; this included additional capacity for ninety-seven wagons, the reconstruction of the goods shed with accommodation for fifty-two

cartage vehicles, the provision of yard siding accommodation for a further 140 wagons, and the purchase of two 6-ton mechanical horse tractors and seven trailers, and twenty-nine 3-ton mechanical horse tractors and eighty-one trailers.

In respect of freight services at Grouping, there were extensive NSR local goods workings within the NSR network. Longer distance workings were divided between the NSR and the L&NWR. The NSR ran express goods between Manchester and Nuneaton, and Longport and Burton, and a through goods between Manchester and Burton; return workings included a Stretton Junction (Burton) to Manchester express goods, Norton Bridge to Alsager goods, and a Stoke to Manchester express goods. The L&NWR used the NSR main line to run a Manchester to Camden perishable goods, Burnley to Camden through goods, Hillhouse to Camden perishable goods, Heaton Norris to Bushbury through goods, and two from Copley Hill to Stafford and Harecastle; there was a Newcastle to Birmingham and a Market Drayton working.

In 1930, there were quite significant changes. Up workings consisted of Manchester to London, two Hillhouse to London and one Manchester to Burton. Down workings were more numerous and consisted of Hillhouse to Sudbury Junction, Northampton to Manchester, Stretton Junction to Manchester, Camden to Leeds, Camden to Burnley, Camden to Manchester, Nuneaton to Adswood and Willesden to Adswood.

In the summer of 1939, there were eleven Up goods workings, a Manchester to London, a Mirfield to Aston, a Hillhouse to Sudbury, a Heaton Norris to Bushbury and a Longsight to Burton, a Copley Hill to Macclesfield, Manchester to London, Longsight to Burton, Moston to London, Manchester to Sudbury and Hillhouse to London. October 1945 saw a very significant reduction, to only Heaton Norris to Nuneaton, Manchester to Camden, Moston to Sudbury Junction, Manchester to Nuneaton and Hillhouse to Camden.

Milk traffic was important to the NSR but it featured less on the main line than in other parts of its network, such as the Derby and Churnet Valley lines. Milk traffic tended to go northwards (from Harecastle and Macclesfield) to Manchester (Mayfield) station. At Grouping, there was very little milk traffic over the main line North. There was a working from Wheelock, on the Sandbach Branch, via Harecastle to Manchester (Mayfield); this service continued until 1930 but was withdrawn by 1934. At Grouping, there was a collection of milk from the Congleton Dairy Co. at Congleton, which was worked forward to Burton daily. A milk service from Congleton to Leeds started in 1932 and lasted well into BR days but the number of milk trains reduced considerably from the early 1930s, as milk was increasingly collected from farms by tankers and local dairies, and by the Milk Marketing Board from 1933.

At Grouping, there were no cattle trains on the Main Line North but Harecastle was the location for such traffic to be attached and detached. In 1930, the Garston to Grange Junction and the Crewe to Chaddesden freight workings were timetabled to detach cattle at Harecastle. In addition, the Macclesfield through freight was booked daily to collect cattle at Congleton and this was still timetabled in 1939. By 1945, there was but one cattle working timetabled, at North Rode.

The Town Cartage scheme was introduced in 1932 and for this part of the network used depots at Longport, to serve Wolstanton and Porthill, and at Stoke, to serve Fenton, Shelton, Trent Vale, Penkhull and Hartshill. By 1939, there had been no changes in the arrangements from Longport but several townships on the Main

Line South were now served by Stoke depot. LM&SR Country Lorry Services delivered to and collected from such villages as Buglawton, Astbury, Timbersbrook, Church Lawton and Butt Lane.

Turning now to passenger traffic, stations were opened at Cheshire villages like North Rode and Mow Cop, and also in the larger towns such as Macclesfield and Congleton, as well as in the valley of the Trent from Harecastle to Stoke. Stations were opened at Chatterley (for Tunstall), Longport (for Burslem) and Etruria (for Hanley) but these lost some of their importance with the opening of the Loop Line throughout in 1873-5. These stations were not among the most important passenger stations on the NSR network, though Longport subsequently became a centre for goods and parcels traffic. All these stations remained open throughout the LM&SR era, though fewer and fewer trains called at Chatterley, which eventually closed in 1949.

Passenger traffic on the main line under the NSR consisted of three elements – long distance expresses from Manchester to London and to Birmingham, and from Manchester to Stafford; short distance services from Manchester to Macclesfield and from Macclesfield to Stoke; and short distance services from Stoke to Stafford and to Birmingham. In 1905, numerous halts had been opened, which were used by the single coach rail motor and, whilst this service had all but ceased by 1923, some halts remained open for a short period afterwards.

The most well known of the NSR passenger services was the 12.05pm express from Manchester (London Road) to London (Euston), the only one of the four Manchester to London express trains from London Road that was an NSR service. The overall journey time in October 1922 had been four hours and the LM&SR continued this service. In 1927, the LM&SR introduced names to certain trains on their fastest, or crack routes; the 12.05pm train became 'The Lancastrian' and a return working, via Stoke, at 4.10pm from Euston, was named 'The Mancunian'. The following table gives the overall journey times, with improvements reflecting the introduction by the LM&SR from 1932 onwards of its acceleration policy, whilst the

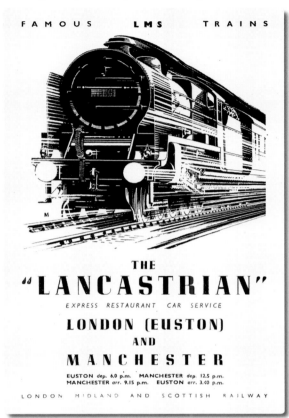

FAMOUS LMS TRAINS

THE "LANCASTRIAN"

EXPRESS RESTAURANT CAR SERVICE

LONDON (EUSTON)
AND
MANCHESTER

EUSTON dep. 6.0 p.m.   MANCHESTER dep. 12.5 p.m.
MANCHESTER arr. 9.15 p.m.   EUSTON arr. 3.40 p.m.

LONDON MIDLAND AND SCOTTISH RAILWAY

An LM&SR advertisement from the *Railway Magazine*, December 1938, for 'The Lancastrian', the premier express service between London (Euston) and Manchester (London Road). It was one of several services to which names were given, to raise the profile of the LM&SR and of the service itself. The Up service from Manchester to London departed daily at 12.05pm and was the continuation of the pre-Grouping 'Luncheon Car Express' which went via Macclesfield and Stoke, and then ran non-stop to Willesden, arriving at Euston at 4.05pm; the 1938 service arrived at Euston at 3.40pm. This particular service was dropped during WW2, with the October 1947 timetable showing the 11.55am arriving at Euston at 4.35pm. The return working of 'The Lancastrian' was a faster journey and was routed via Crewe, stopping only to set down passengers at Wilmslow. In October 1947, the 'Restaurant Car Express' departed Euston at 6pm, arriving at London Road at 10pm, calling at Crewe, Wilmslow and Stockport. The artist's impression is of a 'Royal Scot' 4-6-0, Fowler-designed and introduced from 1937. *Railway Magazine*

worsening journey times were caused by the Second World War and its immediate aftermath:

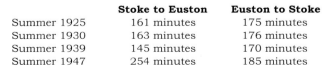

	Stoke to Euston	Euston to Stoke
Summer 1925	161 minutes	175 minutes
Summer 1930	163 minutes	176 minutes
Summer 1939	145 minutes	170 minutes
Summer 1947	254 minutes	185 minutes

The use of an NSR locomotive to work the section to Stoke was dropped shortly into the LM&SR era, to be replaced by locomotives shedded at Longsight. Initially, these were 4-4-0 'Compounds',

ABOVE: Longsight L&NWR shed for many years housed NSR engines. Seen here inside the shed is former 'New L' Class 0-6-2T No. 48, renumbered 2273 by the LM&SR; the engine was built early in 1923, one of the last batch of locomotives built at Stoke Works. This locomotive was allocated to Longsight shed in the spring of 1935, around the same time as former 'New M' Class 0-4-4T No. 1434.

LEFT: In September 1926, LM&SR No. 2326, formerly 'E' Class 0-6-0 No. 108, sits outside the shed. The locomotive was built by Vulcan Foundry in 1872 and eventually withdrawn from service in November 1930. *Both W. Potter*

then later by 4-6-0 'Claughtons', with 4-6-0 'Jubilees' starting to be used from the mid 1930s. Names of train services were withdrawn during the course of the war and had not been re-introduced by the time of Nationalisation.

There was very little change in the frequency of express trains throughout the LM&SR era; four daily in 1930, four daily in 1939 and an extra train on Saturdays; five daily in 1947. In 1930, apart from the expresses, there were also four Manchester (London Road) to Stafford workings. In 1939, the pattern of services had switched, with Manchester to Stoke, one Manchester (London Road) to Birmingham (New Street) Restaurant Car Express and one Manchester (London Road) to Stafford working. In the summer of 1939, there was a Saturdays only return working of 'The Comet', which went from London (Euston), via Stoke, to Manchester (London Road). In 1947, there was a complex provision of services, Manchester (London Road) to Stafford (2), Macclesfield to Stafford (2), Manchester (London Road) to Stoke (5) and Manchester (London Road) to Macclesfield (3).

One of the earliest passenger innovations of the new LM&SR was the introduction of the 'Eastern Counties Express' through service in the summer of 1923 from Liverpool (Lime Street) and Manchester (London Road) to Cromer, Lowestoft, and Yarmouth, via Stoke and Nottingham. This train ran in two portions, one from Liverpool (with Restaurant Car) and the other from Manchester, joining up at Stoke before going forward; similar arrangements applied for the return journey, dividing at Stoke. During the winter, the trains ran to Nottingham and not beyond. The 'Eastern Counties Express' underwent various changes in the pattern of service down

to the outbreak of war, when it was discontinued. From 1927, the Manchester portion went via Leek and joined up with the Liverpool portion at Uttoxeter. The Up working from Manchester was the 10.50am for the whole of the period from 1923 to 1939.

From 1922 to 1929 there were significant improvements in the availability of Workmen's Weekly and Daily tickets. At Grouping, availability was restricted to an area largely in a radius of five miles around Stoke but the following six years saw a considerable growth of the scheme for Workmen, as the following table for the issue of Weekly tickets shows for the 'Main Line North' stations:

Originating stations	No. of Destinations		
	Oct. 1922	Summer 1924	Mar. 1929
Macclesfield (Hibel Road)	–	1	12
Macclesfield (Central)	–	3	5
North Rode	–	1	1
Congleton	1	5	14
Mow Cop	4	7	9
Harecastle	2	10	11
Chatterley	–	2	6
Longport	4	9	10
Etruria	8	13	17
Stoke	5	30	35

At Grouping, Workmen's Daily tickets were available at a limited number (19) of stations between Blythe Bridge and Harecastle, and on the Loop Line. By 1929, such tickets were available

RIGHT: Former 'K' Class 4-4-2T No. 13 at Stockport circa 1931, hauling ex-L&NWR stock. Numbered 2184 and with the plate of the shed code (40) visible on the smokebox, this engine worked on the lines to Stoke and also to Wilmslow. There were seven members of the class, built in November/December 1911 and in July 1912. All were stabled at Longsight in April 1932 but four of them were transferred to Stockport Edgeley (16S) in March 1933. The 'K' Class were withdrawn from service between December 1933 and May 1935, No. 2184, the last survivor, being scrapped after only twenty-three years service. It is seen here in its final LM&SR livery. *Author's collection*

BELOW: Stockport (Edgeley) station in the early 1930s, looking south with Edgeley Tunnel in the background. No. 2184 features again, standing in the Up bay platform between platforms 1 and 2, engaged on carriage shunting duties, a task carried out by other 'K' Class locomotives during their stay at Stockport. Edgeley was an L&NWR station and the signalling is of an L&NWR design, the gantry having two home signal arms; the driver has the right of way. The carriage is an L&NWR brake Third, No. 22270. *Metropolitan Borough of Stockport Library Service*

BELOW: On 22nd May 1933, former 'New L' Class 0-6-2T No. 48, renumbered 2273 in 1923, powers a rake of L&NWR matching carriages between Adlington and Prestbury, on a Manchester (London Road) to Stoke or Stafford working. This locomotive was in the last batch of engines to be built at Stoke Works and was actually completed in the LM&SR era but before the NSR was absorbed into the new company on 1st July 1923. The works number, 194, was the last to be issued at Stoke. The locomotive was withdrawn from service in February 1937, after a working life of just fourteen years. *National Railway Museum*

from no fewer than sixty-eight stations. Workmen's Daily tickets (as well as the Weekly tickets) were introduced from Macclesfield (Hibel Road) to Bramhall, Cheadle Hulme, Stockport and Manchester (London Road) on the former L&NWR line to Manchester.

Excursion services were advertised and promoted to Manchester every year. In 1930, Third Class Weekly Season tickets were available to and from Stoke, whilst in 1931, Cheap Pleasure tickets were available to and from Stoke for over sixty destinations. In 1932, Cheap Daily tickets were available to Manchester and this continued until 1939, when the scheme was extended to enable stations north of Stoke to offer Cheap Daily tickets to Stafford, Wolverhampton, Dudley Port and Birmingham. In 1939, Workmen's fares were offered between Stoke and Macclesfield and intermediate stations, and also between Stoke and Stafford and intermediate stations; perhaps this latter promotion was to attract workers engaged in the construction work and in anticipation of the opening of Wedgwood's Garden Factory

at Barlaston in 1940. During the war, there was an Unadvertised Workmen's service which went from Macclesfield (Central) to Harecastle, to connect with a similar service going from the Potteries to the munitions factory at Radway Green (and obviously the return workings); this comprised two trains each way on Sundays, and one Up and two Down on weekdays.

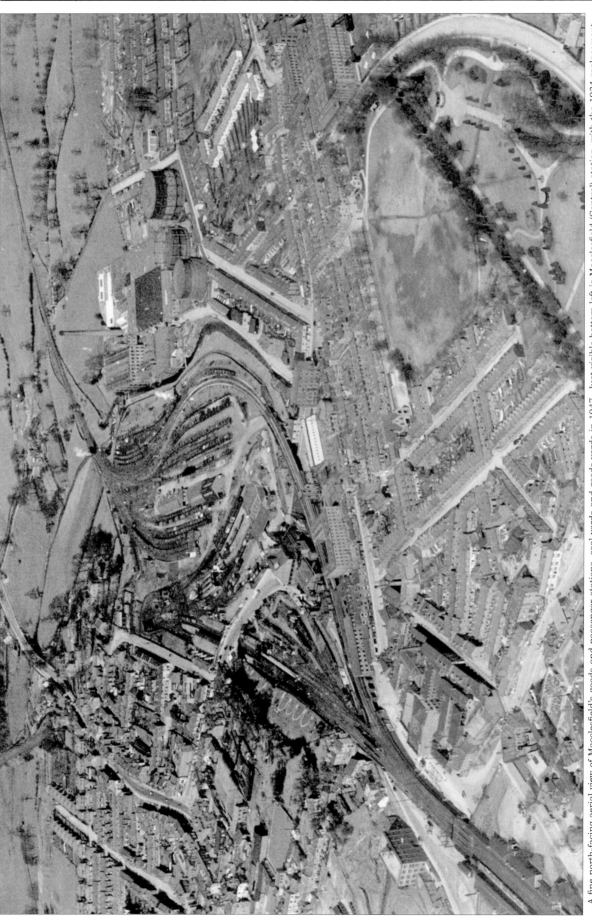

A fine north-facing aerial view of Macclesfield's goods and passenger stations, coal yards and goods yards in 1947. Just visible bottom left is Macclesfield (Central) station, with the 1934 replacement signal box and gantry. One line goes straight on past the former NSR coal yard, which at this time numbered eight coal merchants as tenants. Note the overhead coal conveyor, installed in 1937, to carry coal from the yard and over the road to the Macclesfield Corporation Gas Works, situated between the yard and the running line of the Macclesfield, Bollington & Marple Railway (MB&MR – jointly owned at Grouping by the NSR and the Great Central Railway). Presumably, the gas produced was piped to the three holders seen to the right of the picture, which were completely divorced from the rest of the works. Passing under the road just to the north of the gas works, the line reaches Hibel Road station. The goods office, flat-roofed engine shed, and the carriage and goods sidings leading to the former L&NWR/NSR three-lane goods shed can all be seen. At the side of the Up line stands the Saxby & Farmer-designed signal box. Beyond the yard tunnel, where the Hazel Grove to Macclesfield trunk road crosses the line, was the site of Beech Bridge, the Manchester & Birmingham Railway station, which lasted from 1845 to 1849 (top left). The line starting centre left at Marple Junction signal box (a box abolished in 1934 in the LM&SR resignalling scheme) is the MB&MR, initially straddling the River Bollin on a viaduct. It then sweeps round in an 'S' shape, leaving the (now) LM&SR yard on the left, and the coal yards and sidings of the 'GC', as they were known. To the right of the line are the exchange sidings, in the course of being shunted, and Lower Heys Silk Mill. The line to Bollington sweeps round to the right and a light engine can just be seen to the left of Macclesfield Goods Junction signal box. *Author's collection*

An Etruria to Manchester excursion passing Prestbury station and signal box, looking south towards Macclesfield on 5th June 1933. Fowler '4F' 0-6-0 No. 4505 was one of twenty engines of this class allocated new to Stoke (North Staffordshire Section) in 1927 and was additionally one of thirty members of the class completed by North British locomotive in that year. *Neville Fields collection*

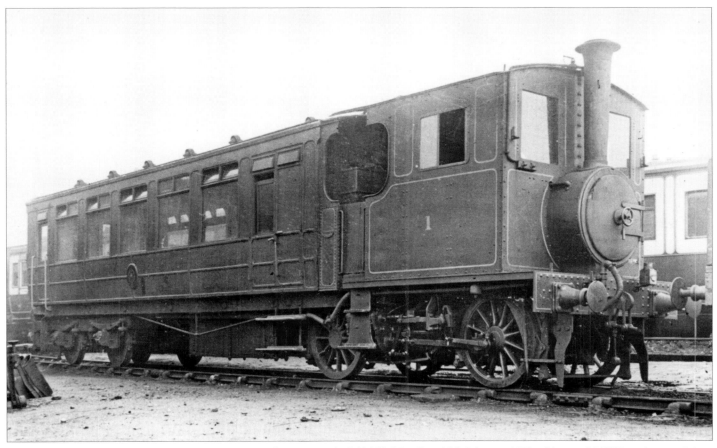

NSR Steam Rail Motor No. 1 seen here in the carriage sidings at Macclesfield (Hibel Road) on 25th February 1923, with some L&NWR carriage stock in the background. This rail motor was one of three of its type, costing £2,000 each and purchased from Beyer, Peacock & Co. in 1905, in order to meet the growing competition of the time from electric tramways. In addition to forty Third Class seats and six seats in a Smoking compartment, there was a very small compartment for the guard and for light luggage. The rail motor was capable of reaching 30mph and had rapid acceleration. In 1922, a 'Motor Rail Service' had been introduced on the Churnet Valley line to augment the existing service; this locomotive was mainly used between North Rode and Kingsley & Froghall, as well as to Stoke on the Leek Market days of Wednesday and Saturday. There was only one working each day south of Kingsley & Froghall and this went as far as Rocester. There was also a limited rail motor service from Macclesfield (Hibel Road) to Stoke via Leek, stopping at all stations; the booked time from Rushton to Stoke was 52 minutes. All three rail motors retained their NSR livery after Grouping. The locomotives did not feature in the LM&SR numbering scheme and they were later placed in store at Crewe North stock shed, eventually being scrapped in June 1927. *Author's collection*

LEFT: Former NSR 'DX' Class 0-6-2T No. 155 also photographed on 25th February 1923. At this time, the legal formalities between the NSR and the LM&SR were being concluded and obviously there had been no change yet to the livery or numbers. This locomotive was one of a class of six built at Stoke Works between 1899 and 1902; it was renumbered 2236 in 1923 and was withdrawn from service in 1929. *A.G. Ellis collection*

CENTRE LEFT: From the late 1920s to around 1935, the 'New M' Class were the mainstay of passenger workings from Macclesfield (Hibel Road) to Uttoxeter and Stoke; they did not work north to Manchester. No. 1438, an 0-4-4T with flared bunker, is seen here at the Hibel Road carriage sidings in 1931. They were replaced at Hibel Road in the spring of 1935 by Stanier 2-6-2Ts. The building in the background is the warehouse of the MB&MR, renamed in 1930 having previously been the Great Central & North Staffordshire Railway Committee, and then managed by the L&NER & LM&SR Group Committee No. 1 until Nationalisation in 1948. *E.R. Morten*

BELOW: Former 'New F' Class 0-6-4T No. 118, renumbered 2052 in 1923, on the Hibel Road turntable on 16th August 1933. It was one of a class of six built between 1916 and 1919; normally a batch of six would be completed at Stoke Works in four/six months but difficulty in getting raw materials during the First World War meant that only limited new build took place during the war years. Until Grouping, this particular locomotive was used on the crack Manchester to London L&NWR 12.05pm express, working the train as far as Stoke, but this practice was discontinued after Grouping. The class was eventually used on local passenger working and No. 2052 was withdrawn from service after only eighteen years in October 1936. *E.R. Morten*

Macclesfield (Hibel Road) Shed

The NSR shed at Hibel Road, Macclesfield, dated back to 1850; it had twin roads and a new 40 foot turntable was installed in 1864. At the time of Grouping, Macclesfield workings consisted of ordinary goods trains to Etruria, Biddulph, Chatterley, Congleton, Uttoxeter and Stoke, and an express goods train to Manchester. There were passenger workings to Uttoxeter and Manchester (London Road), as well as a rail motor service. There was also a busy goods yard (jointly owned with the L&NWR) and a coal yard to service. Although the shed was very largely used by NSR locomotives, there was some use by L&NWR engines, though the L&NWR never had any formal allocation to it. Definitive information on locomotive allocation is not available prior to Grouping but personal recollections indicate that, at the time, passenger workings to Manchester and to Uttoxeter were performed by 'B' Class 2-4-0Ts and 'L' Class 0-6-2T locomotives, with goods services being provided by 'E' Class 0-6-0 engines; yard shunting was carried out by 'D' Class 0-6-0Ts.

The official allocation to Hibel Road towards the end of the NSR era was twelve but in 1925 this had increased to fourteen, the third largest of the thirteen NSR sheds. Under the LM&SR shed numbering scheme, Stoke was allocated No. 40 in the Western Division list in 1926 and this covered all of the sheds in the North Staffordshire Section. It was not until March 1935, when a revised shed numbering scheme was introduced, that information on the precise allocation to Hibel Road and of individual locomotives became available. Hibel Road's number was 9C, a sub-shed of Longsight (9A). The March 1935 list for Macclesfield shed showed nineteen locomotives, consisting of six former NSR types (four 'New L', one 'New M', and one 'C' Class), six Fowler 2-6-4Ts, two LM&SR Fowler 0-6-0 '4F's, three former L&NWR 'G1' 0-8-0s and two Fowler

0-6-0 Class '3F' shunting engines. The NSR 'B' Class engines had been withdrawn from the passenger workings, to be replaced by a mixture of 'F', 'New L', 'K', and 'New M' Class locomotives down to 1935. LM&SR Fowler 2-6-4Ts were introduced on passenger workings in 1929 and the arrival of nine new Stanier 2-6-2Ts, coupled with the withdrawal of the remaining 'New M' and 'New L' Class locomotives from Hibel Road during 1935, resulted in the end of NSR engines working from that shed. From August 1935, it was reported that '*all 2-6-2Ts at Macclesfield work on the Manchester to Macclesfield to Stoke in turn from the 2-6-2Ts from Stoke and Stafford.*' For the goods turns, the NSR '159' and 'E' Class 0-6-0s were replaced over a period of time by Fowler '4F' 0-6-0s and by the arrival of former L&NWR 'G1' and 'G2' class engines.

The number allocated to Hibel Road was as follows:

March 1935	November 1945	December 1947
19	8	9

From 1929 to 1947, there were only seventeen locomotives which came new to Hibel Road and none after 1937. There were two '3F' 0-6-0Ts which arrived in May 1932, six Stanier 2-6-4Ts in 1936 and 1937, and nine Stanier 2-6-2Ts that arrived between 1935 and 1937. There were numerous locomotive transfers to and from Hibel Road, including one Fowler '4F' 0-6-0 in 1935, one former L&NWR 0-8-0 in 1936 and two Stanier 2-6-4Ts in 1940.

By the end of 1945, work had reduced considerably, with only eight locomotives allocated, six Fowler 2-6-4Ts and two Stanier 2-6-2Ts whose popularity and performance had diminished. In December 1947, the allocation of nine consisted entirely of Fowler 2-6-4Ts. The shed closed on 12th June 1961.

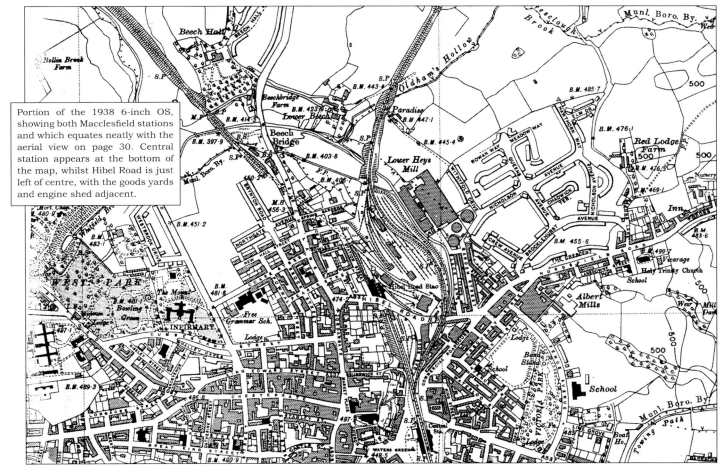

Portion of the 1938 6-inch OS, showing both Macclesfield stations and which equates neatly with the aerial view on page 30. Central station appears at the bottom of the map, whilst Hibel Road is just left of centre, with the goods yards and engine shed adjacent.

Newly arrived Stanier 2-6-2T No. 76 at Hibel Road in April 1935. No. 76 was built at Derby and allocated new to Stoke MPD in March 1935, being transferred to Macclesfield in the following month. It was the first of the class to be allocated to the Stoke District and in 1935 no fewer than twenty-four were allocated to former NSR sheds. Performance over the years was not considered to be satisfactory on the North Staffordshire Section, however, and in November 1945 the number had dropped to fourteen and by December 1947 had been further reduced to eleven. To the right is Hibel Road signal box, a McKenzie & Holland hipped roof design. In the background, LM&SR signalling has replaced that of the NSR, after the 1934 resignalling of both Hibel Road and Central, as well as the goods yard and exchange sidings, resulted in two signal boxes being abolished. The station master on the right is E.A. Weatherley, who had been in charge of Central station also from 1st March 1934 as a consequence of the 'Pooling Agreement' between the LM&SR and the L&NER to rationalize posts and activities. *Author's collection*

Hibel Road on 3rd November 1938, looking across to the former NSR engine shed. The building is awaiting re-roofing, possibly having been damaged by fire. The nearest locomotive is Stanier 2-6-2T No. 109, off Stoke shed; behind it, well-coaled, is Fowler 2-6-4T No. 2301, one of the first batch built at Derby in 1927 and transferred to the Stoke District in April 1934. Beyond the shed, on the right, are the offices of the MB&M goods warehouse and in front, with the roof showing, is the original (temporary) station of the MB&M, in use from 1869-73 and subsequently used as stables and as a garage before its demolition in 1947. In the background, on the left, is the roof of the former Manchester Sheffield & Lincolnshire Railway engine shed, built in 1873 to house the locomotives working the MB&M; it was a two-road shed, capable of housing the normal complement of six locomotives and was closed in November 1935, being demolished in 1937. In the foreground, the hoardings on the wall carry some splendid advertisements – for Black Cat cigarettes, the Drome cinema and Wrigley's spearmint chewing gum. *W.A. Camwell*

The entrance to Hibel Road station goods yard, seen here circa 1931, dropped steeply down from Hibel Road. Clearly visible against the skyline is the diamond shaped weight restriction notice, where Hibel Road bridge crosses the railway line. In the centre is the parcels receiving office, with several barrows visible. To the left is the rear of the station building, with the two platforms just glimpsed through an opening in the wall. Advertising hoardings complete this fascinating view – promoting Ewbank floor cleaners (on the left), with the *Daily Dispatch*, *News of the World* and many others on the right. From 1934, the two separate posts of goods agent at Hibel Road and Central stations were combined into one position of joint goods agent following the 'Pooling Agreement'. *National Railway Museum*

The entrance to Hibel Road station circa 1931, with a fine array of notice boards advertising excursion trips to different parts of the country, including one for Chester and Rhyl. This station was demolished in the early 1960s after it had closed for passenger traffic on 7th November 1960. Directly behind the station entrance can be seen the glazed roof of the Up platform. *National Railway Museum*

LEFT: Hibel Road station looking south, with the station staff on the Down platform in 1926. Third from the left is Bernard Bowers, then Sam Ashton and in the centre (with a flat cap) is Jack Warren. On the right and out of sight was the North Stafford bay, from which Hibel Road to Manchester (London Road) passenger trains would depart. Just visible on the left is the station nameboard, to an L&NWR design. The station in pre-Grouping days was jointly owned and managed by the NSR and L&NWR. It was dark and not well located for the town and, inevitably, its location some 650 yards from Central created inefficiencies and duplication. *Author's collection*

ABOVE: An NSR Third Class ticket issued at Hibel Road on 6th April 1924. *David Geldart collection*

RIGHT: Railway Ambulance competitions were keenly fought. Here we see a victorious Macclesfield team from around 1945 proudly displaying the cup; station master Lightfoot is seated on the left and Arthur Hayward on the right, sitting on the table. *Hayward family collection*

BELOW: This Macclesfield Gas Department 8-plank wagon was built by Charles Roberts & Co. of Wakefield. These were the first wagons ordered by Macclesfield Gas Department, the order being placed on 19th September 1939, for ten wagons No's 1-10. They were ordered as 12 tonners but supplied as 13 tons capacity following Government instructions and, with the outbreak of the Second World War, was probably requisitioned immediately. *Author's collection*

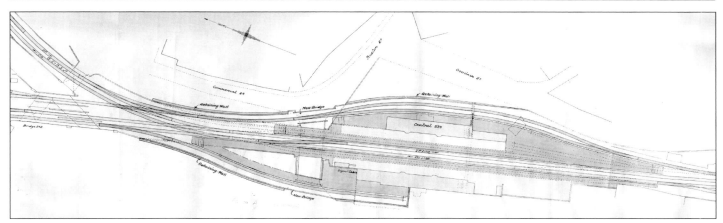

ABOVE: Plan for Macclesfield (Central) station prepared in 1933, for proposals to close Hibel Road station and concentrate passenger facilities on the one site.

The main line from Hibel Road crosses the centre of the plan; both the platform lines have been removed and a bay platform added bottom left, with the line from Bollington coming in top left to its terminus and a run round loop installed. This was part of the LM&SR's radical review of ways that it could squeeze operating costs by eliminating duplication of facilities and singling lines. This particular scheme came to nothing but the major resignalling scheme of 1934 resulted in the closure of two signal boxes. *Author's collection*

RIGHT: Central station on 21st September 1938, with Stanier 2-6-2T No. 77 on the middle road banking an express up the 1:112 gradient for the two miles to Macclesfield Moss signal box. In the background can be seen the cab of the L&NER steam railcar which provided a shuttle service between Central and Bollington eleven times a day each way. No. 77 was built at Derby in 1935 and allocated to Macclesfield shed in April 1937; by the time of Nationalisation in 1948 it had transferred to Stockport (Edgeley) shed. *E.R. Morten*

ABOVE: Central station looking towards Hibel Road in 1939, as a southbound express, framed by the gantry, powers its way through on the running line. The locomotive is 'Jubilee' Class 4-6-0 No. 5668 *Madden*, off Longsight shed, built at Crewe in 1935. Behind the tender appears to be three strengthening carriages, the first being an L&NWR Corridor Third and the second an LM&SR Stanier Brake Third. The left-hand signals protect the main line, whilst those on the right protect (left) the coal yard and (right) the line to Bollington. The NSR influence is retained on the facing wall on the right, with the wooden passenger notice to use the subway and, beneath, the cast iron trespass notice. *E.R. Morten*

Macclesfield Central station circa 1947, again looking north, with a former L&NWR 'Prince of Wales' Class 4-6-0 on a Manchester to Stafford working, hauling a four-coach set and supported by a banking engine in the rear. At this time, four of the surviving locomotives of this class were allocated to Stafford shed. Also seen on this very damp day is an L&NER carriage on the left and note, too, the elevated LM&SR Macclesfield Central signal box in partial view behind the smoke from the locomotive. *Author's collection*

Macclesfield Moss signal box, seen here circa 1954, was erected in the LM&SR era and to a standard LM&SR design. It replaced an NSR box at the same location, provided in 1905 to serve the siding and workings of the British Moss Litter Co. Ltd. Rail traffic to and from these peat workings lasted until the early 1960s. *National Railway Museum*

RIGHT: A view of North Rode station looking south on 18th June 1932, as the five coaches forming part of the Down 'Pines Express' from Bournemouth West pass by. The train is powered by large-boilered former L&NWR 'Claughton' Class 4-6-0 No. 5975 *Talisman.* The station building here was the tallest on the NSR network. *Gordon Walwyn*

BELOW: North Rode looking south again, on 19th August 1939. Ex-L&NWR 'Prince of Wales' Class 4-6-0 No. 25674 *Scott* powers through with the 2.0pm Birmingham (New Street) to Manchester (London Road) Saturdays only express. Of particular interest on the left is an extremely rare glimpse of the brickworks here, part of the Sneyd empire, with four chimneys and three kilns just visible from the lineside. *Gordon Walwyn*

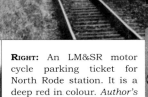

RIGHT: An LM&SR motor cycle parking ticket for North Rode station. It is a deep red in colour. *Author's collection*

L.M.& S.R. FOR CONDITIONS SEE BACK
Valid on day of issue only
PARKING TICKET FOR
MOTOR CYCLE
AT
NORTH RODE
Registration No.
Fee ·/3
N 042
0420

BELOW: North Rode station on 9th April 1932, this time looking north, with Fowler 2-6-4T No. 2346 at the head of the 12.20pm Manchester (London Road) Restaurant Car Express (ex-L&NWR carriage just visible) to Birmingham (New Street), timed to arrive at 2.58pm. Note the diamond-patterned brickwork, an architectural feature of the original contractor. Although North Rode station has long been demolished, this design feature can still be seen elsewhere on the network, for example at Longport and Stoke stations. No. 2346, built at Derby, had been allocated to Stoke shed in June 1929 and, along with others of the class, was regularly working trains between Stoke and Manchester. *E.R. Morten*

ABOVE: North Rode Junction on 9th April 1932, a view looking south and showing North Rode Junction signal box, a McKenzie & Holland design, in the right background. Veering off to the left is the Churnet Valley line to Uttoxeter. Former 'New C' Class 0-6-4T No. 5, renumbered 2047 in 1923, is at the head of a standard three-coach set of L&NWR carriages used on the Macclesfield to Uttoxeter working. There were six of this class of locomotive, built in 1914/15 and powerful performers but, by this date, reduced to working easy local passenger workings, as seen here. This particular locomotive was the first of the class to be withdrawn from service, in March 1934, and all were withdrawn by November 1937. The bulk of Congleton Cloud, which here forms the border between Cheshire and Staffordshire, dominates the skyline. *E.R. Morten*

LEFT: An NSR ground disc by the Up Churnet siding at North Rode, a remarkable survivor pictured here on 31st May 1957. *Manifold collection*

BELOW: North Rode Junction looking due south along the main line.

ABOVE: Congleton station looking south on 25th May 1927. The waiting shelters on both platforms were of an NSR design to be found also on the line from Alsager through to Egginton. The footbridge was also to a standard NSR design but even at this date, barely four years after the Grouping, L&NWR signalling had been introduced, as evidenced by the upper quadrant signal. Just visible is the hip roof of Congleton signal box, which also protected the level crossing. To the right and out of sight, is the two-road goods warehouse (which still survives) and the siding which served the Congleton Dairy of the CWS. The importance of milk to the local economy was also reflected in the siding put in behind the Up platform for the Nestle's Anglo Swiss Condensed Milk Company. This work was completed in November 1930; by 1937 the company was known as Nestle Milk Products Ltd. *A.G. Ellis collection*

ABOVE: Stanier 2-6-2T No. 106 shunting at Congleton circa 1938. This locomotive was built at Derby in 1935 and allocated to Stoke shed in October 1935. The private owner wagon belongs to Stephenson Clarke, a large London coal factor and supplier. *Author's collection*

INSET TOP: An LM&SR Third Class Period Return ticket for a trip from Congleton to Douglas, on the Isle of Man. The journey was via Liverpool and included Steerage Class passage on one of the IoM Steam Packet Co's steamers. Pulling on the tab revealed an advert. *Author's collection*

RIGHT: Former 'New M' Class 0-4-4T No. 54, now with LM&SR No. 1439, working wrong line on a local passenger train at Congleton on 15th December 1930. This class was used extensively on local passenger work on the North Staffordshire Section, though No. 54 was withdrawn from use in 1931 after only eleven years' service. Note the LM&SR board promoting excursions and, just discernible, the diamond pattern brickwork on the station buildings. *Manifold collection*

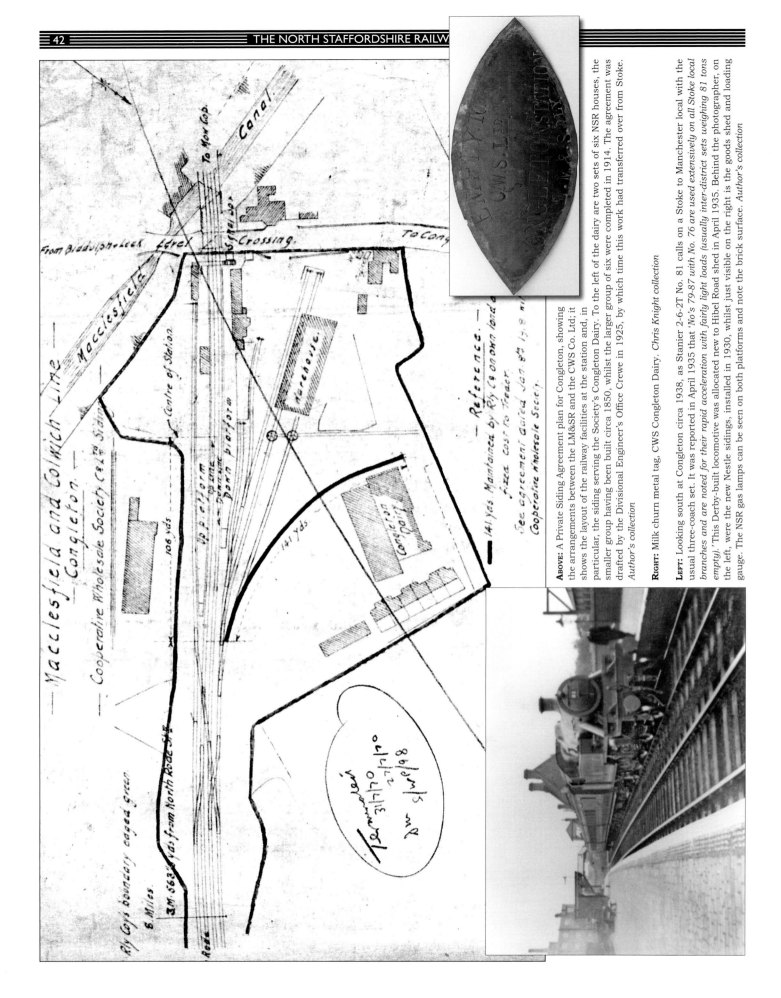

— — — Macclesfield and Colwich Line — — —
— — — Congleton. — — —
— — — Cooperative Wholesale Society (Col.Tol Siding — — —

Reference.

141 Yds Maintained by Rly Co on own land at
fixed cost to Trader.

See agreement dated Jan.8th 19.8 with
Cooperative Wholesale Society.

Above: A Private Siding Agreement plan for Congleton, showing the arrangements between the LM&SR and the CWS Co. Ltd; it shows the layout of the railway facilities at the station and, in particular, the siding serving the Society's Congleton Dairy. To the left of the dairy are two sets of six NSR houses, the smaller group having been built circa 1850, whilst the larger group of six were completed in 1914. The agreement was drafted by the Divisional Engineer's Office Crewe in 1925, by which time this work had transferred over from Stoke. *Author's collection*

Right: Milk churn metal tag, CWS Congleton Dairy. *Chris Knight collection*

Left: Looking south at Congleton circa 1938, as Stanier 2-6-2T No. 81 calls on a Stoke to Manchester local with the usual three-coach set. It was reported in April 1935 that 'No's 79-87 with No. 76 are used extensively on all Stoke local branches and are noted for their rapid acceleration with fairly light loads (usually inter-district sets weighing 81 tons empty).' This Derby-built locomotive was allocated new to Hibel Road shed in April 1935. Behind the photographer, on the left, were the new Nestle sidings, installed in 1930, whilst just visible on the right is the goods shed and loading gauge. The NSR gas lamps can be seen on both platforms and note the brick surface. *Author's collection*

This circa 1925 postcard view shows the station master's house at Congleton, on the left, with The Cloud, at the foot of the Pennines, in the background. The house was built on a small strip of land situated behind the Macclesfield Canal, on the right, and the main line, just visible at the left of the picture. By one of those ironies of British railway history, the Macclesfield Canal was actually owned by the L&NER. Having rejected a proposal for the canal to be taken over by the NSR in 1845, an agreement had been reached with the Sheffield, Ashton-under-Lyne & Manchester Railway instead, which subsequently became part of the GCR and in turn the L&NER at Grouping. *Author's collection*

The Cloud, Congleton.

LEFT: Handbill for the Congleton and Biddulph holidays on 21st August 1935, promoting a half-day excursion to Blackpool North. Of particular interest is that the arrangements provide for the train to call at Ford Green and Biddulph stations, even though the Biddulph Valley line had closed for passenger traffic in July 1927. *Robert Keys collection*

RIGHT: LM&SR handbill of April 1939 advertising a half day trip to Bournville starting from Harecastle. *Cheddleton Railway Archives*

RIGHT: Maryhill Colliery at Kidsgrove, seen here looking north circa 1930 and owned by Harecastle Collieries Ltd, was known to be in existence by 1905. The colliery was on a hill and coal was brought down to the screens by a short tramway. In 1923, there were 152 miners employed here. In January 1930, a large inrush of water trapped and drowned three men; the colliery closed but the footrails* below ground remained open. In 1932, there were still 108 miners employed below ground and 39 above, with an annual output of 50,000 tons. Following the closure of the last of the three footrails, operations ceased in January 1939. In this view, the winding engine house is on the left, behind the chimney and boilers. The headgear and the downcast shaft are to the right, with the pump house on the far right, whilst the purpose of the buildings behind is unclear – they may be farm buildings. In the foreground is a narrow gauge tramway, with a 3-plank coal tub and a small flat wagon with support stakes. *Bill Jack*

* A footrail was an adit, driven in on an incline, or from the side of a hill, the coal face thus being directly accessible by foot from the surface.

RIGHT: The 0-4-0ST *Maryhill*, seen here sometime in the mid 1930s awaiting its next turn of duty, was delivered new to the colliery from Peckett & Sons Ltd of Bristol (Works No. 1606) in 1923. Following closure of the colliery, it was sold at auction in February 1939, being bought by locomotive dealers Sheppard & Son of Bridgend and was subsequently sold on to Williams & Son Ltd for use at Dagenham Dock. Maryhill Colliery was connected to the main line just north of Harecastle station. *H.W. Robinson*

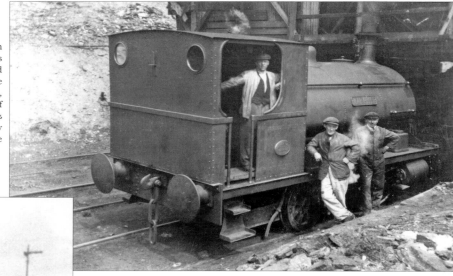

LEFT: Harecastle looking north in the late 1920s, with an unidentified 'B' Class locomotive passing over the Trent & Mersey Canal. Harecastle Junction signal box and Harecastle station are behind the engine. *Author's collection*

BELOW: This Tarmac 5-plank, side door wagon No. K3953 was assigned to the company's Kidsgrove operations and was from an order for 100 wagons built by Hurst, Nelson in 1925. The livery was black body with white lettering; the italics on the door read '*Repairs Advise Wagon Repairs, Ltd. Stoke-on-Trent*' and at bottom right '*Return Empty to Tarmac (Kidsgrove) Ltd, Bathpool Sidings, Harecastle, NSR*'. *Historical Model Railway Society*

A panoramic view of Chatterley in 1925, looking south. On the far left is the Goldendale Works of Tarbitumac Ltd, a subsidiary of Brookes Ltd of Halifax, several of whose private owner wagons can be seen; operations had commenced in 1920, hence the apparent newness of the works. Rail access was gained from the Up side of the NSR main line, just south of Chatterley station, via the Goldendale Ironworks line and a bridge over the Trent & Mersey (the second and higher of the bridges in the picture). Beyond Tarbitumac is Goldendale Ironworks, with its towering slag tips. In the centre is the canal, with the roof of the T&M warehouse just visible on the left. In the foreground is the trackbed of the recently lifted gated siding which served the early 19th century plateway from the old pits at Goldenhill – Bradfield Colliery and Goldenhill Colliery. In 1923, this latter colliery employed 32 people, reducing to 18 in 1927; its output went via Newchapel & Goldenhill station on the Loop Line. In the right distance is a spoil tip, behind which is just visible Peake's Tilery Colliery. Beyond the gate, in the distance, is Chatterley Junction signal box with, on the right, a set of tall repeater signals it controlled. *Manifold collection*

LEFT & BOTTOM LEFT: The 0-4-0ST *Tarbitumac* at Goldendale Ironworks in the early 1930s. This locomotive arrived new from Peckett & Sons Ltd (Works No. 1681) in 1925 and stayed until the works closed in 1940, after which it was sold to the Shap Granite Co. Ltd. *H.W. Robinson*

BELOW: This standard 12-ton wagon was built for the company by Charles Roberts & Co. of Wakefield, in 1925. It was equipped with side doors only and most wagons built for this traffic also had steel floors – the tare weight is suggestive of this wagon being so fitted. The italic lettering at bottom right reads '*Empty to Tarbitumac Ltd., Private Siding, Goldendale, Chatterley LM&SR*'. *Wakefield collection*

A view north through Chatterley station in 1947, which is looking worn and desolate, and with only a short period to go to full closure, on 27th September 1948. Originally built to serve the town of Tunstall on the opening of the main line in 1848, and prior to the opening to Tunstall in 1874 of the Loop Line, it subsequently attracted very little passenger traffic. It was surprising that the station did not close in the LM&SR era and, in the summer of 1947, only two passenger trains a day called, with an extra one on Sundays. Note the unusual stone building on the left, similar in architectural style to the structure of the 1823 Harecastle Tunnel, which is just 20 yards or so to the left. *Author's collection*

The Talke and Chesterton Branches

The Talke Branch owed its origins to the need to serve the mines at Talk o' th' Hill. Initially, the Sneyd's Railway Act of 1861 and the 1864 Act gave the NSR powers to lease most of the line that it eventually purchased in 1904. The line was 1 mile 1,210 yards long, passing through countryside and climbing on a ruling gradient of between 1 in 36 and 1 in 39. In 1872, the original company was reconstituted as the North Staffordshire Coal & Iron Co. Ltd, owning also tileries and a small colliery at High Carr. In

the late 1890s, a battery of seventy regenerative Simon Carves by-product coke ovens was erected. In 1920, John Summers & Sons Ltd acquired the colliery and carbon works, in order to enable its fellow subsidiary, the Shelton Iron, Steel & Coal Co. Ltd, to make economic use of its iron making capacity, through a plentiful supply of good quality coking coal within a reasonable distance. The colliery closed on 25th March 1928, when the recommended heavy expenditure to modernise it was deemed unjustifiable, owing to the

Talk o' th' Hill Colliery in the mid-1920s, when prospects for the mine must have been good – note the new engine house and other buildings nearing completion on the left. The view is looking west with the small settlement of Foxholes in the background. The coke ovens were located behind the photographer. The two sets of headgear can be seen far left and in the centre of the picture, and on the right are the wagon and locomotive repair shops. A couple of trains of loaded wagons are being assembled in the centre. In 1923, there were 710 working underground and 251 above ground, a level of employment that remained largely unchanged until the complex closed in 1928. *Manifold collection*

limited remaining reserves of coal for future working. Dismantling soon followed, with Tarbitumac being contracted to remove the slag. In order to replace lost output, Summers acquired a nearby replacement pit, Holditch Colliery, from Brymbo Steel in January 1930. The branch also served a tilery siding at High Carr, belonging to roofing tile makers J.F. & E. Rowley and the line was cut back to here in 1931; Rowley's siding ceased to be used in 1954. The LM&SR Country Lorry Services delivered to the villages of Talke and Talke Pits from the town cartage depot at Harecastle.

At Grouping, there were four trips daily between Chatterley Junction and the colliery and one to the tilery, all worked by the Chatterley No. 1 shunter, one of two based there. In 1930, following the colliery's closure, there was one trip daily between Chatterley and Talke, with the return working calling at High Carr and serving the Chesterton Branch. In 1938, the branch was served by a 2-6-2T on trip working off Alsager shed, calling at High

Carr once a day. In 1946, trip working allowed for one train daily to and from the Metallic Tile Co. at Chesterton when needed. In 1929, Chatterley had a siding capacity of 120 wagons, for the main line and the Talke and Chesterton branches.

The Chesterton Branch, built under powers contained in the NSR 1864 New Works Act, served the coal and ironstone mines at Chesterton. It branched off the Talke Branch, with a terminus 1 mile 1,606 yards from Chatterley Junction, and was reached by a steep climb at 1 in 47 and 1 in 50, before a 1 in 255 approach to Chesterton, where sidings were laid out on the level to form the goods yard. Despite its short length, the branch and spurs served Parkhouse Colliery, whose coal and ironstone mining in different proportions underpinned the financial viability of the branch, as well as the various other industries, whilst also carrying general merchandise to and from Chesterton goods yard.

The branch served several brick and tile works, private sidings

RIGHT: Parkhouse Colliery circa 1930, looking south. On the left is No. 3 shaft, sunk in 1917, which later became the main winding shaft and was 500 yards deep. To the right are the original coal shafts, sunk in the 1870s. The mine was first sunk for ironstone in the 1850s. After several changes of ownership, in 1913 it became part of the Robert Heath empire, from which it was sold on when in receivership in 1929. This led to Parkhouse Collieries Ltd being formed. Employment was 437 in 1923, 600 in 1927 when output was 180,000 tons, and in 1947, the year of Nationalisation of the coal industry, there were 700 employees and output was 196,294 tons. Ironstone production had ceased in 1924. *Bill Jack*

LEFT: A Parkhouse Collieries Ltd private owner wagon, No. 1167. This was an 8-plank 12-ton wagon, one of a batch of fifty built by Edward Eastwood of Chesterfield between August and November 1936. It was fitted with side and end doors. The livery was red with white lettering, shaded black. *Allan Baker collection*

RIGHT: This Peckett 0-4-0ST, seen shunting at Parkhouse Colliery in the mid-1930s, arrived here at an unknown date, having previously worked in the steel industry at Sheffield and Rotherham. Works No. 973 of 1904, it was one of three Pecketts to work at the colliery and went on to become part of the NCB West Midlands Division fleet, before being finally withdrawn from service in May 1964. It has previously been stated elsewhere that behind the engine are examples of the patent all-steel wagons built by the Butterley Company, probably on loan or on hire to the colliery. However, they were of a standard design and the two seen here are clearly of different heights. Further, there are no records of Butterley wagons being supplied to Parkhouse Collieries. *H.W. Robinson*

giving access to the following: Rufus Brick & Tile Co., Metallic Tile Co., United Tile Manufacturers, North Staffordshire Brick & Tile Co. and the Rose Vale Brick & Tile Co. During the LM&SR era, new sidings were installed at the Rufus Brick & Tile Co. in 1928, when it was referred to as Proctor Bros' Siding, and Golden Vale Tileries in 1936. Forge Pit (owned by the Midland Coal, Coke & Iron Co.) closed in December 1926, whilst the Chesterton Chemical Co. (owned by Midland Tar Distillers) closed in the mid-1930s. At Grouping, there were two services daily between Chatterley and

Chesterton, worked by the Chatterley shunter. In 1930, with the expansion of Parkhouse Colliery, there were three trains daily each way between Chatterley and Chesterton. In 1938, the branch was served by Trip 80, off Alsager shed, along with the Talke Branch, calling at Chesterton twice daily and the Rufus Brick & Tile Co. (Procter's Siding) at Hem Heath once; the motive power used was a Fowler 0-6-0T. In 1946, there were three trains daily each way between Chatterley Junction and Hem Heath. The LM&SR Town Cartage scheme also served Chesterton.

ABOVE: These two pictures show the Parkhouse Colliery sidings and the Metallic Tile Co. in the mid-1930s. This first view is looking south-east across the valley of the Trent, with Hanley beyond, and is full of interest. Chimneys and kilns dominate the scene, whilst in the centre, stacks of completed production await despatch. Just visible between the two Parkhouse wagons is one belonging to Stanley Couzens, coal merchant of Stone. *Author's collection*

LEFT: This view is looking south towards Newcastle, with the A34 trunk road on the centre right climbing up towards Bradwell. Note how the three colliery sidings come flush up against the road, immediately beyond which the branch line passed underneath it. The Metallic Tile Co's works features top left and there is a spoil tip immediately behind. Top right can be seen the chimney of the Chesterton Chemical Company. *Author's collection*

RIGHT: Bradwell Wood Tileries, seen here on 27th June 1953 in a view looking southwards, was typical of the many small tileries in the Chatterley Valley and the climb up to Chesterton. Note the surviving NSR shunt signal with large 'S' affixed to the signal arm, which protected the trailing connection between the Down Slow line and the sidings of the Staffordshire Chemical Company; these are visible between the two chimneys in the centre of the picture. Part of the works of Staffordshire Chemicals can be seen left background. *Manifold collection*

The Staffordshire Chemical Company Ltd at Longport had chemical plants on both sides of the Main Line, and dated back to the 1880s. They were established to process the by-products of coke manufacture at Talk o' th' Hill Colliery and subsequently from other local large iron, steel and coal owning companies. The transfer by a series of pipes of tar, creosote and other liquors between the two plants was covered by a 1902 easement with the NSR and this easement was continued through the LM&SR era. The Company was reconstituted during the First World War – usually a sign of financial problems – and changed its name to the Staffordshire Chemical Co. (1917) Ltd. The name was changed again to Staffordshire Chemicals Ltd in 1957.

ABOVE: Staffordshire Chemicals acquired this Peckett 0-4-0ST from new, Works No. 978 delivered in 1904, which they numbered 1. It is seen here against the background of the plant on the west side of the main line and Bradwell Wood Tileries; a portion of Bradwell Wood can just be glimpsed in the left background. No. 1 was scrapped circa 1962. *Manifold collection*

BELOW LEFT: Staffordshire Chemicals No. 2 was an 0-4-0 box tank built by William Bagnall in 1892 (Works No. 1392), which arrived at the plant from Talk o' th' Hill Colliery in 1918. It was withdrawn from service in the middle of 1952 and scrapped in May 1953, having been superceded by No. 3, an 0-4-0 diesel which had arrived new from John Fowler of Leeds in 1951. *H.W. Robinson*

BELOW RIGHT: One of three 14-ton, all-steel rail tanks built by Charles Roberts in September 1937. By this time Staffordshire Chemicals produced no tar of its own but distilled 12,734 tons brought in from elsewhere. The livery details are unknown. *Historical Model Railway Society*

Longport Junction signal box, seen here in the early 1950s in a view looking south to Longport station, was built to a standard LM&SR design, and was a replacement for the original NSR box. It was probably built as part of the major expansion of the Longport goods facilities which were approved by the LM&SR at a cost of £82,038 in 1937. LM&SR signals are clearly visible and a surviving NSR water column can be seen. In the centre background is the bronze foundry of Birkett, Billington & Newton. Previously, until around 1923, it had been the engineering works of William Boulton Ltd, manufacturers of machinery for the pottery and tilery industries. *R.J. Essery*

Longport station, looking north in the early 1930s, with the hipped roofed McKenzie & Holland signal box situated alongside the level crossing gates. The station building on the right has the diamond shape brickwork that could be seen at North Rode and Congleton stations and note, too, the decorative stone gables. In the background can be seen the outline of the original Longport Junction signal box. The advertising hoarding on the right carries advertisements for Mitchell & Butler's beers and for Symington's coffee, whilst the mixture of L&NWR signals in the foreground and NSR signals in the background completes the picture. *National Railway Museum*

RIGHT: Longport station in the early 1930s, a view taken from Station Road and looking west towards the level crossing gates. The buildings were designed in what is known as a Jacobean style. On the left is an LM&SR express parcels van. *National Railway Museum*

BELOW: An LM&SR Third Class Bulk Travel ticket for journeys from Longport to Liverpool (Lime Street). *Author's collection*

L. M. & S.R.
FOR CONDITIONS SEE BACK
BULK TRAVEL
LONGPORT TO
LIVERPOOL (LIME STREET)
VIA CREWE
THIRD CLASS 2644(S) (BT)
LIME ST.
167

RIGHT: A Longport luggage label from 1933. *Author's collection*

E.R.O. 21556/95
2/33
L. M. S. R.
LONGPORT

Another early 1930s view, looking north to Longport station. In the foreground left are freshly planted seedlings on an allotment, which has encroached on to railway land; a common occurrence and probably belonging to a railwayman. Behind is the White Hall Pottery Works, manufacturers of general fittings. Note the long siding on the right with two horse boxes, one of which is at the parcels loading dock, whilst the Down signals in front of the level crossing gates now have the shorter LM&SR arms. On the left, in the background, is the roof of the works owned by William Boulton Ltd. Dominating the skyline on the right is the gas holder of Burslem Gas Works, municipally owned and which had opened by 1851; it was rail connected and conveniently located adjacent to the main line and near the T&M Canal. The gas works passed to the new County Borough of Stoke in 1910 and was closed circa 1939. *National Railway Museum*

RIGHT: A view to the south of Longport on 4th August 1930, as the 2.50pm London to Macclesfield express thunders past, powered by former L&NWR 'Claughton' Class 4-6-0 No. 5980. On the left are the slag tips of Shelton Works and in the foreground is a platelayers' hut. Note the two NSR home signals, between which in the background can just be seen the spire of Hartshill Church. The Wolstanton Colliery headshunt is on the right; it had previously been a loop but had recently been cut back (eventually to Grange Junction), with the signal controlling exit from it still in situ. *Gordon Walwyn*

ABOVE: Wolstanton Colliery in 1948, a view taken from Wolstanton churchyard looking east. Two shafts were sunk between 1916 and 1919, originally for ironstone but later for coal as well. In 1923, there were 275 workers underground and 75 above ground. In 1939, with 950 workers underground and 275 above ground, coal output was 280,000 tons and ironstone 150,000 tons. Towards the end of the LM&SR era, in 1945, there were 600 workers underground and 215 above. By this date the mine was owned by North Staffordshire Land & Minerals Ltd, whose fifteen undertakings accounted for 90% of the total output of the North Staffordshire district. Foxfield and Florence were the only collieries not part of this group. On the skyline, from left to right, are the dirt tips of five other pits – Chatterley-Whitfield, Sneyd (two tips), Norton (in the distance between the two Sneyd pits), Hanley Deep and Racecourse. *E.J.D. Warrilow, Keele University Library*

RIGHT: A wagon for Wolstanton Colliery, supplied in January 1933 by the Gloucester Railway Carriage & Wagon Co. Ltd. This wagon had an interesting history, as indicated by the array of plates on the solebar. It was originally built in 1917 by Hall, Lewis & Co. of Cardiff and registered by the GWR. It was one of four secondhand wagons hired to Birmingham and Stoke-on-Trent coal merchants Geo. Hale & Co., for three years in 1933, who had it lettered for Wolstanton 'Cardox' coals. Fifty more were hired in 1936, whilst Hale also bought four new wagons from GRC&W Co. in the same year. It appears most were lettered for Wolstanton but Hale had previously had connections with Sneyd and Madeley Wood collieries. *Gloucestershire Archives*

LEFT: On 9th July 1932, former 'New L' Class 0-6-2T No. 26, built in 1921 and now renumbered 2266, poses against an industrial backdrop at Etruria Junction. The engine was withdrawn from service as early as 1936. Behind, from left to right, are the Shelton slag tips, the blast furnaces charging hoists and gantries, the steel melting shop, and the rolling mills. Note the Wedgwood sign, promoting the nearby famous pottery works of Josiah Wedgwood.

BELOW: An unidentified Fowler '4F' 0-6-0 4F at the head of a nine-coach Manchester (London Road) to Birmingham (New Street) bank holiday special with ex-L&NWR and LM&SR carriages, at the same location in August 1937. The Down yard, serving Shelton Works, can be seen on the left in the distance, whilst just in front of the locomotive the Loop Line curves away to pass alongside the works and over the T&M Canal. *Both E.R. Morten*

Back to 9th July 1932 for this view of 'The Lancastrian', the Up 12.05pm Restaurant Car Express from Manchester (London Road) to London (Euston) approaching Etruria Junction, at the head of a mix of ex-L&NWR and LM&SR carriages. This particular train had through carriages from Colne, Burnley, Blackburn, Bolton and Manchester (Victoria), and it was booked to arrive at Stoke at 1.09pm, then working non-stop to Euston, arriving at 3.55 pm. Haulage power on this occasion is provided by former L&NWR large-boilered, Bowen-Cooke 'Claughton' Class 4-6-0 No. 5975 *Talisman*. The backdrop is the slag bank from the decades of operations of the Shelton Iron, Steel & Coal Co. and, just above the first carriage, can be seen the patriotic advertisement for Shelton. *E.R. Morten*

Etruria station looking north on 30th April 1933, with Fowler 2-6-2T No. 15550, numbered 51 in 1934, working a local passenger train to Stoke. This class of locomotive (seventy in all) was built at Derby between 1930 and 1932; only a few came over to the North Staffordshire Section in 1930 and 1933, and did not prove to be popular. Two of the class, including this particular locomotive, worked out of Macclesfield shed from 1944 for a couple of years or so. The main station buildings are in the background, passenger traffic being served by the island platforms. Note the station nameboard, a fine example of NSR design and, unusually, mounted on two distinctive poles. Just to the right of No. 15550's bunker is the large rotating 'B' signal, used to regulate Loop Line and mineral trains being propelled into Etruria Yard. *H.C. Casserley*

INSET: This NSR Third Class ticket, Etruria to Carlisle, was issued on 17th April 1934, eleven years after Grouping. *David Geldart collection*

RIGHT: An aerial view of Wengers Works, Etruria, looking north-west and taken from a company advertising card of the mid-1930s, with the main line running from top left to centre right. The station booking office, located on the Hanley to Newcastle road, can be seen top left, whilst the elevated viewpoint clearly shows the shape of the island platform, in the form of a narrow 'V', in the centre. Wengers was a sizeable ceramic, colour and chemical manufactory, and different workshop areas can be seen, with the works entrance on Grange Street at the bottom centre. This factory dated back to 1898/99, with the first private siding agreement with the NSR signed on 28th June 1899. *Author's collection*

LEFT: Pictured blowing off steam whilst paused to the north of Stoke, against a typical Potteries backdrop of chimneys and bottle ovens, is Beyer-Garratt 2-6-0+0-6-2 No. 7969, which was fitted with a rotating bunker. The photograph dates from around 1945. *John Birchenough*

RIGHT: Cliffe Vale signal box, a view looking west in the spring of 1946. This LM&SR-designed box replaced an earlier NSR cabin at the same location. To the left of the box is the bridge carrying the Newcastle Road over the main line, behind which can be seen the three former NSR carriage sheds and, beyond, the additional sidings of 1932. In the background can be seen part of the Market Drayton line climbing the 1 in 102 gradient from Newcastle Junction to Hartshill, in the front of which is the south end of the works of Johnson Fireclay. In the centre are loaded coal wagons destined for the gas works, with construction work relating to its expansion in progress in the foreground. *E.J.D. Warrilow, Keele University collection*

Looking north-west in 1946 from the top of Etruria Gas Works, with the station in the background. Top left, above the gas holder, is the southern end of Wengers Works, whilst on the far left of the picture is Twyford's new sanitary ware factory, which was not rail-connected. In front of this was the slightly curved siding used by the famous Barnum & Bailey circus, for winter storage of the special circus train of American-type vans built by W.R. Renshaw & Co. Ltd. On the very far left is a section of the Phoenix Works, formerly occupied by Renshaws, wagon builders, but, since 1931, jointly housing the Central Wagon Co. Ltd and Johnson Fireclays Co. Ltd. *E.J.D. Warrilow, Keele University collection*

RIGHT: Cliffe Vale carriage sheds in the summer of 1924, with former NSR 'G' Class 4-4-0 No. 171, now LM&SR No. 598, waiting to leave to collect a non-stop working from Stoke to the Wembley Exhibition. This locomotive was especially adapted to pick up water from the troughs *en route* but it is still awaiting its new LM&SR livery. *Manifold collection*

BELOW: Shelton Wharf circa 1933 looking south on the west side of the Trent & Mersey Canal. On the far left can be seen Winton Pottery, with LM&SR and NSR signals dominating the skyline. Running across the picture from left to right is the wooden fencing on the east side of the canal. A varied collection of private owner wagons can be seen in the foreground, starting with two ROP tank wagons, owned by Russian Oil Producers Ltd, a London-based distribution agency for the Russian oil industry. To their right, in order, are coal wagons belonging to West Cannock Colliery Co. Ltd, E. Steele, Florence Coal & Iron Co. Ltd (with a white 'F' painted on the end of the wagon) and the Shelton Iron, Steel & Coal Co. Ltd. Also centre right are an interesting group of motor lorries, into some of which coal is being offloaded; they will have accessed the wharf from Vernon Road. In the background is Minton Hollins Pottery. *National Railway Museum*

Shelton Wharf, again circa 1933 and looking south but with the main line in the foreground. Behind the gantries and barely visible in the distance are the new Stoke North and North Yard signal boxes. Note the wooden retaining fence bounding the busy Wharf area and, despite the major resignalling, the two NSR starter signals. The bottle ovens belong to Minton Hollins, encaustic tile manufacturers, where an additional siding had been installed in 1926. Amongst the private owners are wagons belonging to Madeley Collieries, Littleton Collieries, Chatterley–Whitfield Colliery and E. Steele, coal merchant of Stoke-on-Trent. The T&M can just be glimpsed as it passes under the main line, with Cockshott Lock behind the photographer. *National Railway Museum*

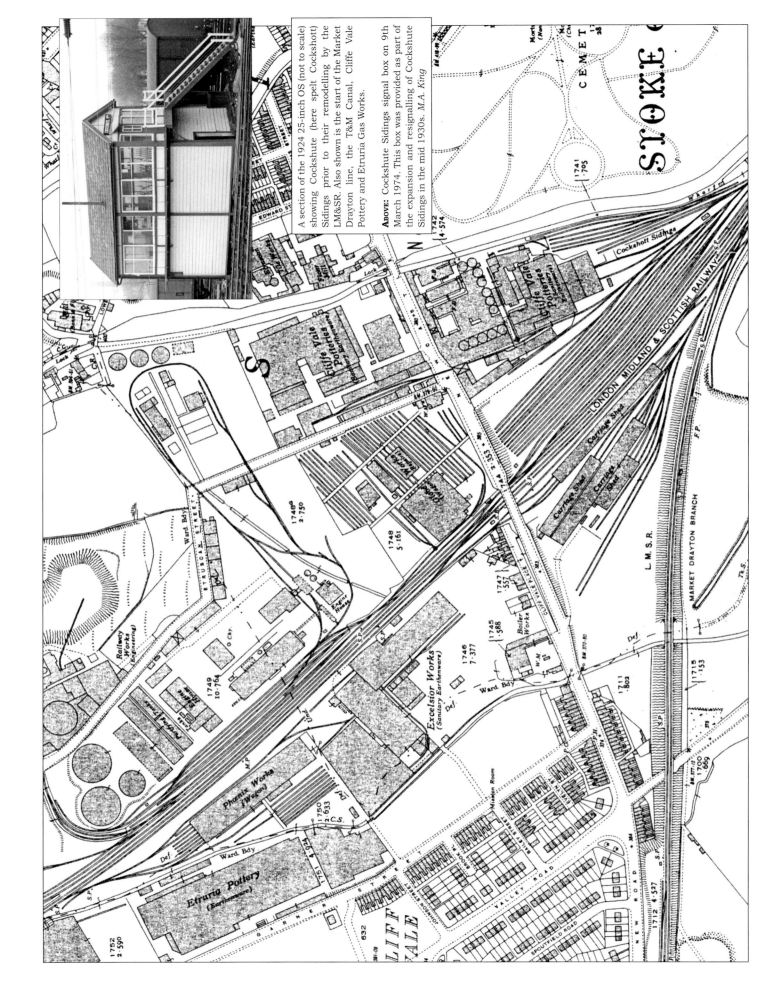

A section of the 1924 25-inch OS (not to scale) showing Cockshute (here spelt Cockshott) Sidings prior to their remodelling by the LM&SR. Also shown is the start of the Market Drayton line, the T&M Canal, Cliffe Vale Pottery and Etruria Gas Works.

ABOVE: Cockshute Sidings signal box on 9th March 1974. This box was provided as part of the expansion and resignalling of Cockshute Sidings in the mid 1930s. *M.A. King*

LEFT: Stoke Yard in the early 1960s, showing the two LM&SR signal boxes, Stoke North Yard on the left and Stoke North on the right, installed by September 1931 as part of the remodelling and expansion of Stoke Yard. *National Railway Museum*

BELOW: LM&SR 'Jubilee' Class 4-6-0 No. 5741 *Leinster* approaches Stoke Road Bridge at the head of the 9.52am Manchester (London Road) to London Euston express on 3rd August 1945, with not an NSR signal left in sight. On the far left are the enlarged sidings of the 1930/32 scheme. The line running in from the left and behind Newcastle Junction signal box served Foster's timber yard (in Vernon Road) and Minton Hollins Pottery; the Minton Hollins siding was installed new at a cost of £970 in 1926 and was covered by a Private Siding Agreement dated 8th January 1926. Climbing up and away to the left is the line to Market Drayton. Visible behind the gantries in the centre of the picture are the carriage sheds and immediately to the right of the express train is a 2-6-4T on a local freight. To the right are the remodelled Cockshute Sidings, with Newcastle Road in the background, whilst the LM&SR-built Cockshute Sidings signal box is just visible between the two poles carrying lights. These sidings were remodelled and extended between 1933 and 1935 at a cost of £11,218. This provided an increase in siding capacity from 394 to 500 wagons and an increase in siding roads from 32 to 54. At the same time, the repair of crippled wagons was transferred to the old L&NWR yard, and shunting and marshalling activities was transferred from Pratt's Sidings to Cockshute. Twyford's Cliffe Vale Pottery is in the background and a water tank is partially in view on the right. Bottom right is the T&M towpath as it approaches Cockshott Lock. *John Birchenough*

LEFT: The original Stoke North signal box just features on the right of this view, taken on 5th May 1928, as former L&NWR 4-6-2T No. 6951 prepares to back on to its train. The four-road carriage shed in the background was demolished during the extensive remodelling programme carried out here during the early 1930s. Behind it can be distinguished the tops of the bottle ovens of Winton Pottery. A 'B' Class locomotive can also be made out just behind the tank engine. *Gordon Walwyn*

RIGHT: Stoke North signal box was one of the busiest cabins on the NSR network. Pictured here on 21st September 1929, it was replaced by two new LM&SR signal boxes in 1931, as part of the major expansion and resignalling scheme carried out in this area. Standing in front of the box is former NSR 'A' Class 2-4-2T No. 52, built as a 2-4-0 at Stoke Works in 1879 and rebuilt in 1898. It was one of a class of eight engines built between 1878 and 1881, and is seen here with its LM&SR number 1454. The engine had only a little longer left in service than the signal box, being withdrawn in August 1932. Note the NSR water column on the right. *Leslie Good*

Stoke goods marshalling yards, looking south from the new Stoke North signal box circa 1932. This whole area had been subject to a major remodelling programme approved in 1929/30 and completed in February 1932 at a cost of £69,102. The work involved the levelling of ground at the south end of the station between the railway, the warehouse and the canal, the construction of several single storey warehouses and a new stable block, the provision of new sidings for mineral traffic and permanent way stores, and the construction of a new boundary fence at Shelton Wharf. On the left is the Newcastle bay at Stoke station, in front of which is a former 'New F' or 'New C' Class locomotive and LM&SR quadrant signals. In the background can be seen the tall chimney of the former Locomotive, Carriage & Wagon works, which had been leased to Robert Hyde & Son Ltd, foundry engineers, since 1927. Centre left are two running lines, in NSR days between Stoke North Cabin and Stoke South Outlet but now replaced by two new LM&SR signal boxes, Stoke North and Stoke North Yard. In the centre background is the outline of the goods warehouse, whilst the sidings consisted of 14 lines beyond which runs the T&M. The private owner on the far right carries the distinctive white lettering of the Madeley Coal & Iron Co. Ltd. *National Railway Museum*

An atmospheric panoramic study just to the north of Stoke station on 1st August 1937, with a Manchester (London Road) to Birmingham (New Street) bank holiday excursion, hauled by Stanier 4-6-0 No. 5354, just arriving. The NSR-built Stoke signal box and carriage shed have been demolished and there is now an unobstructed view of Winton Pottery to the right. On the left is an unidentified Stanier 2-6-4T, Stoke North Yard (LM&SR) signal box can be seen in the background and pausing with its train on the right is a Stanier 2-6-2T. *Gordon Walwyn*

ABOVE: An LM&SR HM Forces ticket, Stoke to Grimsby Docks, via Macclesfield and Manchester (London Road). *Author's collection*

RIGHT: Coming in to Stoke station from the north on 25th March 1931 is the powerful former L&NWR 4-6-0 rebuilt 'Claughton' No. 5946 *Duke of Connaught*, at the head of a Manchester (London Road) to London (Euston) working. A fine array of NSR signals are on the left and Stoke North signal box is visible above the former L&Y Dynamometer car. *Manifold collection*

RIGHT: Former NSR '100' Class 0-6-0 No. 100, built in 1896 at Stoke Works, strikes a nice pose in the same location on the same day. Renumbered in 1923 as 2347, the locomotive is seen here with its March 1928 LM&SR number 8669. There were ten locomotives of this class, built between 1896 and 1907, never in batches of more than two. All of them were withdrawn by September 1931, so No. 8669 had only a short while left in service when this picture was taken. *Manifold collection*

LEFT: Looking north-west from Stoke station towards Shelton Wharf on 15th April 1933, with Stoke North and Stoke North Yard signal boxes in the background, and a combination of NSR (near) and LM&SR (background) signals. Former L&NWR 4-4-0 Bowen-Cooke 'George V' Class No. 5347 *Elkhound* is taking water, whilst on a Stafford to Manchester (London Road) working. *Gordon Walwyn*

BELOW: Looking northwards from the Down platform again, on 5th November 1932, with former L&NWR 'Precursor' Class 4-4-0 No. 5248 *Amphion* on a Coventry to Manchester excursion. *Gordon Walwyn*

BELOW: Stoke station Down platform looking north in the mid 1920s. Ex-Midland Compound No. 1053 is about to depart for Manchester with an express from London. Derby-built in 1924 and one of the first ten built after Grouping, No. 5248 was the first of its class to be seen in Stoke. *G.J.R. Gossling*

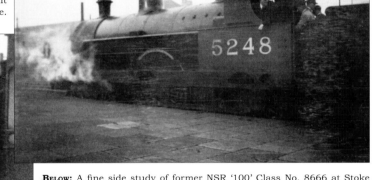

BELOW: A fine side study of former NSR '100' Class No. 8666 at Stoke shortly before its withdrawal in 1929. This locomotive began life as NSR No. 78, was numbered 2344 in 1923 and renumbered 8666 in March 1928. The surviving members of this ex-NSR class were quickly withdrawn following the arrival of the Fowler '4F's at Stoke from 1927 onwards. *Gordon Coltas*

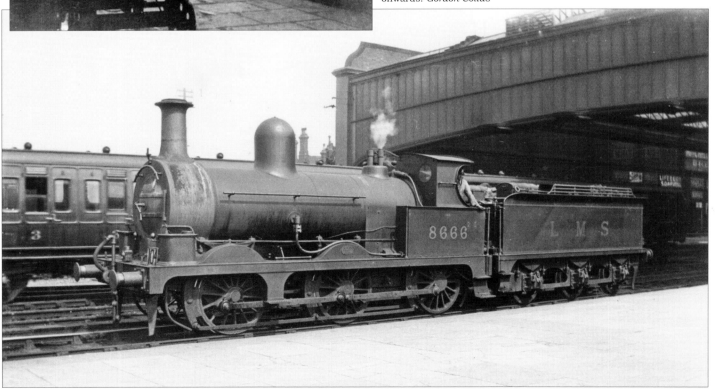

L.N.E.R.
LUGGAGE.
M 9801
From
To **STOKE**

G.W.R.

STOKE-ON-TRENT

ABOVE: Former 'New L' Class 0-6-2T No. 156, renumbered as 2248, rumbles through Stoke station on the middle lane with a northbound train of empty bolster wagons, probably bound for Shelton Steelworks, on 6th July 1931. This locomotive was built in 1908 and withdrawn from service in June 1937. Note on the far left the former NSR houses in Winton Square that, by this time, were increasingly being let to non-railway organisations as superior office accommodation. In 1938, the LM&SR disposed of 7½ acres of land, previously used by the NSR and then by the LM&SR, to the City of Stoke-on-Trent Council for £11,900. This was for use by the North Staffordshire Technical College, to enable it to expand behind the North Stafford Hotel. Other land on Station Road was sold in 1937 to the North Staffordshire Chamber of Commerce. *Manifold collection*

INSET ABOVE & LEFT: Examples of L&NER and GWR Stoke-on-Trent luggage labels. *Author's collection*

ABOVE: The Down (northbound) *Mancunian* Restaurant Car Express, with ex-L&NWR 'Claughton' 4-6-0 No. 6018 *Private Wood VC* in charge, at Stoke on 10th August 1929. This train had departed Euston at 4.10pm, arriving Stoke at 7.06pm and was eventually due in to Manchester (London Road) at 8.07pm. *Gordon Walwyn*

LEFT: A similar viewpoint, although from the end of the platform, with former L&NWR Bowen-Cooke 'George V' Class 4-4-0 No. 5363 *Harrier,* off Chester shed, at the head of a Nottingham to North Wales holiday express on 19th August 1933. Note the reporting number, 683, has been chalked on the smokebox door. On the far left is an ex-L&NWR 50ft full brake. *Gordon Walwyn*

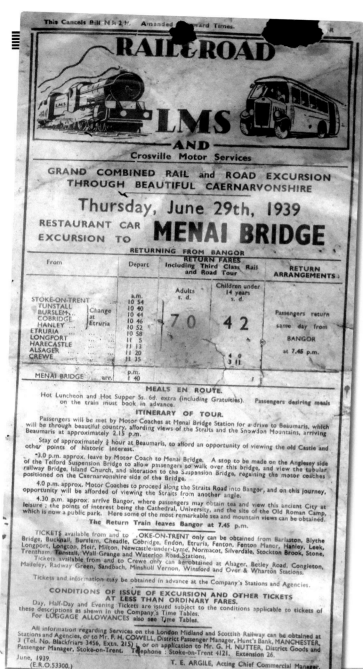

ABOVE: Former 'L' Class 0-6-2T No. 2242 on the middle road at Stoke circa 1934. This locomotive was one of a batch of six built by Vulcan Foundry in November and December 1903 for the NSR. It was withdrawn from service in August 1936, other classmates going between 1933 and 1936. Note the sun streaming through the glazed windows. Numerous improvements in the fabric of the station were carried out during the 1930s; in 1932 the girder work for the roof was strengthened at a cost of £2,188, in November 1935 renewal and further strengthening of the passenger train roof on safety grounds was approved at a cost of £18,253, and in 1936 a central heating system was installed for £1,700. *Author's collection*

LEFT: An LM&SR/Crosville Motor Services joint handbill for a Restaurant Car Excursion to Menai Bridge in June 1939. *Cheddleton Railway Archives*

ABOVE & LEFT: Two views of Fowler 'Royal Scot' Class 4-6-0 No. 6141, on the occasion of the ceremony naming it as *The North Staffordshire Regiment* at Stoke station on 13th June 1936. This locomotive was built at the North British locomotive works in 1927 and named *Caledonian* in 1928. The nameplates were changed when a locomotive overhaul was completed during the period ending 20th April 1936. *Claude Moreton*

BELOW: NSR First Class ticket for Burslem issued at Stoke on 30th April 1933. *David Geldart collection*

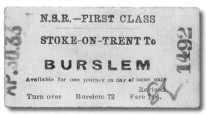

4
MAIN LINE SOUTH

The part of the main line that is south of Stoke was, at the time of Grouping, of lesser economic importance than the section from Macclesfield to Stoke. The population of the Potteries had spread eastwards towards Longton, Fenton and such suburbs as Normacot and Meir, and there was a more broader base of industry, with a heavy concentration of collieries and potteries. First along the line was the California Works of Kerr, Stuart & Co. Ltd, around 1,700 yards south of Stoke station. Then came the large industrial complex that was the Stafford Coal, Coke & Iron Co. Ltd, at Sideway, which dated back to 1875, whilst just over one mile further on could be found the Florence Coal & Iron Co. Ltd, near Trentham. Stafford Colliery expanded in 1924-6 with the sinking of Hem Heath Colliery, also near Trentham. Beyond there, at Grouping, the communities were mostly agricultural, apart from Stone, which had an industrial base of brewing, shoes and pottery.

The main line had two branches off it, one the last section of passenger railway to be opened by the NSR (in 1910), from Trentham Junction to Trentham Park, the second being the line from Stone to Norton Bridge (three miles 1,242 yards long), where it connected with the L&NWR line running northwards from Stafford to Crewe, and southwards to Colwich and ultimately to London. The line south from Stone continued to pass through open countryside, with small country stations such as Sandon, Weston & Ingestre, Hixon and Great Heywood, before reaching Colwich where the NSR had its own engine shed; however, this was closed many years before Grouping. The line to Colwich was on a falling gradient and, with its easy running, was used by Stoke Works for running in locomotives straight out of 'Shops'.

The LM&SR era did see some very significant changes in the industrial base served by the line. In addition to the sinking of Hem Heath Colliery, the Michelin Tyre Company established a major plant just south of Stoke Junction in 1928, whilst Josiah Wedgwood moved an important part of their manufacturing operations from cramped and inefficient surroundings at Etruria to a major greenfield site at Barlaston, leading to a 'Garden Factory' being built there and a railway halt being opened on 1st January 1940. The construction of the first of two power stations

The exterior of Stoke station circa 1924-5, decorated in celebration probably of one of several Royal Visits that took place around this time. Electric lights illuminate the station, motor taxis await custom and the one notice board visible bears the full title 'London Midland and Scottish Railway'. Through the door can just be seen the iron shutter gates barring access to the platforms. *E.J.D. Warrilow, Keele University collection*

A floral welcome arch and streamers of bunting decorate the frontage of the station in this view looking north and also taken circa 1925. Two LM&SR noticeboards are visible on the left, one promoting trips to Stockport and Manchester. *E.J.D. Warrilow, Keele University collection*

at Meaford commenced in 1945 and, subsequently, they consumed a substantial amount of coal that came by rail. In 1929, there was capacity for 393 wagons at Sideway, 288 at Trentham, 243 at Stone and 50 at Colwich, with exchange sidings.

The through goods and passenger traffic, mainly from Manchester, has been covered in the section on 'Main Line North'; this section will deal with traffic originating from the Stoke area and going south, and the return workings. At Grouping, the freight traffic south of Stoke consisted of two Stoke to Bushbury L&NWR trains, with NSR services consisting of one Stoke to Colwich, one Trentham to Bushbury (mineral train), and one Norton Bridge to Alsager goods working. There was also a Sandbach to Stone, as well as a Stone to Pratt's Sidings, working. Throughout the LM&SR era, there was a substantial increase in traffic originating from Stoke southwards and to Stoke from the south. In the summer of 1930, longer distance workings were Stoke to Bushbury (twice daily), the crack evening freight from Stoke to Camden, mineral trains from Trentham and a Stoke to Rugby; trip workings served the Michelin factory and Trentham Park. Down workings included a Bushbury and a Nuneaton to Stoke Yard. By 1939, this had reduced to Stoke to Bushbury (twice daily) and the evening Stoke to Camden. By 1945 however, there had been a substantial increase in the volume of traffic, with six workings to Bushbury from the Stoke area, a Sideway to Rugby and a Sideway to Sudbury Junction, plus trip workings including Wedgwood and the Barlaston Power sidings at Meaford Power Station.

In September 1938, there were eleven trips in respect of the 'Main Line South'. Two each were worked out of Macclesfield and Alsager sheds, the remaining seven being from Stoke shed. Of

these, only one was a pick-up freight, calling at nearly all stations to Rugeley, via Colwich, but including construction materials for Wedgwood's 'garden factory' at Barlaston. All of the other trips went to the collieries served by Sideway and by Trentham Sidings; one trip included Trentham Park. Compared with the level of activity of trip workings north of Stoke, however, the amount was small.

At Grouping, an evening cattle train still ran from Stone to Stoke every alternate Tuesday, for what was described as the 'Big Auction'. Another cattle train ran on alternate Mondays and Tuesdays between Norton Bridge and Stoke, with a passenger train for Stafford calling at Norton Bridge to set passengers down on alternate Tuesdays. However, these dedicated cattle trains no longer featured in timetables by 1930.

In 1923, no milk trains appeared in the NSR timetables for milk collection on the 'Main Line South'. By 1928, milk was being collected by rail daily from Stone, Aston-by-Stone, Sandon, Weston, Hixon and Colwich but, by 1934, these arrangements had disappeared from the timetables.

The LM&SR Town Cartage scheme had no depots south of Stoke serving the 'Main Line South' but Trent Vale and Penkhull (from 1932), Trentham (from 1935) and Barlaston (from 1939) were all served from Stoke depot. The LM&SR Country Lorry Services delivered to and collected from villages such as Hilderstone, Milwich, Gayton, Salt and Shirleywich.

At Grouping, in addition to the L&NWR services from Manchester (London Road) to London (Euston), to Stafford and to Birmingham (New Street), which all worked via NSR metals, the L&NWR also ran passenger services from Stoke to Walsall, Stone to Stafford, and Stoke to Stafford and Birmingham. In 1930, this had changed

RIGHT: Station Road, Stoke, looking north in the mid 1920s, with the Post Office building foreground left and the entrance to the station behind. In the left foreground is a Post Office motor van, whilst behind, to the left is an LM&SR parcels lorry and to the right is a horse-drawn parcels van. Behind the wall on the right was the (ex-NSR) Engineer's Department Works and beyond was the former NSR rifle range. *Author's collection*

BELOW: Stoke station frontage on 28th July 1953, still bearing the hallmarks of both the LM&SR and NSR eras. *Author's collection*

to two Stoke to London expresses and one non-express, as well as four Stoke to Stafford locals; the former L&NWR workings had been dropped from the timetables. In 1939, there were six Stoke to Stafford locals with two extra trains on Saturdays. By the summer of 1947, there was a reduced Stoke to Stafford service, an increased Stoke to Birmingham service, just one train daily to Euston and one Stoke to Stone Saturdays only.

The one station closure in the LM&SR era on the 'Main Line South' was the halt at Sideway; this occurred on 2nd April 1923, before the legal formalities had been concluded for the LM&SR to purchase the NSR and it was the continuation of an NSR policy of closing down halts. These small platforms had been built at several locations in 1905, as part of the introduction of the rail motor service of Third Class Workmen's trains. By 1923, only one train called there daily, though four other trains were timetabled to call there on request.

The Second World War led to separate developments which

generated railway traffic, as a result of the national wartime requirement to build munitions factories. This led to the need to transport workers to the sites, initially to construct them and then subsequently to work there. New Ordnance factories were built in North Staffordshire at Swynnerton (between Stone and Norton Bridge) and in South Staffordshire at Ford Houses (just under four miles north of Wolverhampton). Unadvertised Workmen's rail services took workers from the Potteries to help build them. Two such trains to Norton Bridge came from the Potteries for the construction phase; one was from Silverdale, picking up at Newcastle and Stoke, and one from Burslem, picking up at Hanley, both setting down at the newly-built Badnall Wharf platform, adjacent to the Crewe to Stafford ex-L&NWR line. This service continued to Badnall Wharf after the factory became operational from mid-1940 and until the new Cold Meece station platforms could receive workmen in August 1941. It was not timetabled after May 1942, having been replaced by an intensive service from the Potteries to Cold Meece. There were, by October 1941, three trains from the Potteries (Unadvertised Workmen's trains) coming from Silverdale, Blythe Bridge and Longton, for each of the three shifts for seven days a week and, from April 1942, this increased to four; from September 1942, trains originated from Silverdale, Newchapel & Goldenhill, Blythe Bridge and Longton. This frequency continued until May 1946, when it was reduced to three trains a day for one shift, including Saturdays. With very minor variations, the three-train daily service continued until 1958. No material or movement of munitions came in via the former NSR Norton Bridge line; instead, everything was worked via Badnall Wharf and off the former L&NWR line.

There was also the construction phase of the Royal Ordnance Factory Featherstone at Ford Houses. Its station opened on 5th August 1941, with construction of the factory starting after Swynnerton was largely complete. There was one Unadvertised

LEFT: Former Midland Railway Johnson 4-2-2 No. 311 at Stoke circa 1930. Note the large 7ft driving wheel. This locomotive was built in 1877 and withdrawn from service in October 1934. Behind the tender is probably a former Midland Railway van, used to convey stores and supplies to stations in the area. The building immediately beyond the locomotive housed the Post Office. *Manifold collection*

BELOW: Three views taken at Stoke station Up platform on 19th August 1933.
TOP: Fowler 3-cylinder Compound 4-4-0 No. 936, off Derby shed, at the head of a North Wales-Nottingham holiday express.
MIDDLE: Former L&NWR 'Claughton' No. 6015 *Private E. Sykes VC*, off Longsight shed, at the head of the Up 'Lancastrian' Restaurant Car Express.
BOTTOM: Fowler 2-6-2T No. 15551, renumbered 52 in 1934, on a Congleton to Stafford working. *All Gordon Walwyn*

Workmen's train daily from Silverdale. ROF Featherstone started production in May 1942, drawing its workforce locally, with none of them coming by special trains. There were no trains timetabled to run after October 1942, whilst Featherstone is thought to have closed in 1945.

In order to retain its skilled workforce, Wedgwood worked with the LM&SR to establish a new halt, close to the new factory. This was the only passenger station which appeared in the passenger timetables that was opened by the LM&SR on the North Staffordshire Section. Much of the workforce came in by train but the only Unadvertised Workmen's train was the late afternoon return working to Stoke, the remainder travelling by normal service trains.

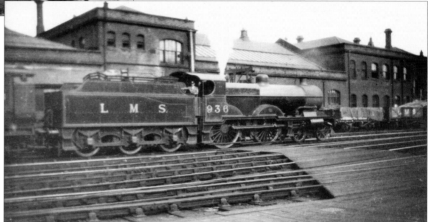

This part of the NSR network was poorly served by the availability of Workmen's tickets at the time of Grouping. The tickets were linked historically to the Rail Motor service which connected the Newcastle area, and its halts in particular, to Sideway Halt and Trentham. For example, although they were barely to last into Grouping, Workmen's Weekly tickets were available to Sideway Halt from six stations. In 1924, their availability from originating stations was increased by the inclusion of Trentham and Barlaston, and of Stafford on the former L&NWR network. By 1929, there had been further improvements through the addition of Aston-by-Stone to the list of originating stations and also through the very widespread introduction of Workmen's Daily tickets. As a result of these arrangements, Weston, Norton Bridge and Armitage were now included.

The year 1930 saw the introduction, for one year only, of Third Class Weekly Season tickets between Stoke and the stations on the Main Line South, in either direction, down to Colwich, Norton Bridge and Stafford. The following year, Cheap tickets were brought in on Thursdays and Saturdays to Birmingham, from the Main Line North, from the Loop Line, Trentham, Barlaston and Stone; this promotion lasted through until the outbreak of the Second World War. The significant expansion of promotional fares occurred in 1939 when (i) Cheap Daily Returns were introduced between Stoke and Stafford and intermediate stations, (ii) Workmen's fares with similar arrangements and (iii) four additional trains daily were put on the Birmingham service, calling at Stafford, Wolverhampton, and Dudley Port, with a further two trains on Thursdays and Saturdays. However, these new promotions did not last into the war years.

RIGHT: Looking south from Stoke station on 11th June 1932, with the Down 'Mancunian' powered by a double-header of former L&NWR locomotives, Whale 'Precedent' or 'Jumbo' Class 2-4-0 No. 5011 *Director* and Bowen-Cooke 'Prince of Wales' Class 4-6-0 No. 5615 *Oliver Goldsmith*. The 'Jumbo' had been attached at Rugby and would detach here at Stoke, from where it would then work the Pipe Gate milk train empties, returning in due course to Rugby having collected milk at Market Drayton and Pipe Gate. On the left is Fowler 2-6-4T No. 2352, in front of the Post Office building. *Gordon Walwyn*

Two photographs showing former NSR locomotives shunting in Stoke Yard in the mid-1920s, with the rear of Stoke station forming a backdrop.

LEFT: Former 'KS' Class 0-6-0 No. 75, now carrying LM&SR No. 1603, was sold out of service in 1933 to Nunnery Colliery, Sheffield. It had been bought new from the nearby Kerr, Stuart & Co. works in 1919, one of a class of two acquired from that source.

BELOW: Former 'E' Class 0-6-0 No. 110 is seen here wearing its LM&SR guise as No. 8655. Built at Vulcan Foundry in 1872, the engine was withdrawn from service in December 1929. *Both author's collection*

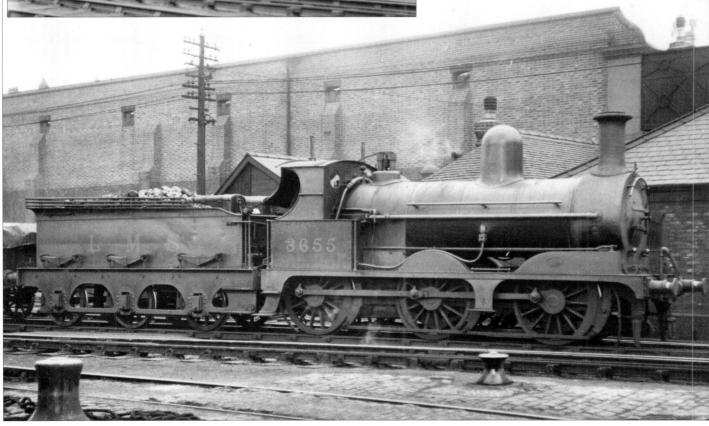

LEFT: Seen immediately south of Stoke station on 3rd January 1947 is former Johnson Midland 0-6-0 No. 22916, working a local freight in a snowy setting. Three members of this class were allocated to Stoke shed in December 1946 and January 1947, and this particular locomotive, which had enjoyed an earlier spell at Stoke in 1938, was to be withdrawn from service shortly after this picture was taken, in January 1947. The six warehouse buildings in the background were part of the 1929/30 major expansion of warehouses and sidings that cost £69,102. The building on the far left was the goods office. *Brunel University Transport collection*

ABOVE: Stoke goods circa 1933, looking north, with the rails typically sunk into the cobbles, allowing road vehicles easy access to all parts of the yard. The warehouse part seen on the left is new, whilst that in the centre had been rebuilt. Dominating the picture in the background is the original NSR warehouse, whilst the hut just visible on the right belongs to Chas. Booth of Sheffield, building contractors for the new warehouse buildings and, incidentally, for the renovation of the North Stafford Hotel. The sign on the brick wall reads 'Engines Strictly Prohibited'. Numerous capstans are visible around the yard, used for shunting with ropes. The wagons, left to right are an LM&SR 12-ton ventilated van, an ex-L&NWR 10-ton 4-plank open wagon, an ex-GER 10-ton van, an ex-MR 10-ton 3-plank dropsided wagon and an unidentified open with sheeted load. *National Railway Museum*

INSET RIGHT: Thousands of pounds worth of machinery and merchandise were destroyed in a disastrous early morning fire at Stoke goods warehouse on 11th June 1937, with the large four-storey former NSR brick warehouse being gutted and damage estimated at £28,000. The fire was spectacular and the flames from the 50 foot high building created a glow that could be seen for miles. The view on the left was taken from the west bank of the T&M Canal. In addition to the local fire crews used to fight the conflagration, the red 'fire train' was brought in from Crewe, manned by nine members of the LM&SR Fire Brigade at that town. The LM&SR later decided to only partially replace the damage caused, at a cost of £12,595. *The Sentinel Newspaper Group*

LEFT: Glebe Street turntable was located on the Up side just south of Stoke station. It was a 60 foot turntable and was installed in order to avoid the necessity of large engines which needed to turn having to travel the 24 miles to Leek Brook triangle, or having to work to Crewe to turn. It cost £729 and was installed in 1938. Seen here is Stanier 2-6-2T No. 79, which was transferred to Stoke shed in October 1936. *G.N. Nowell-Gossling*

RIGHT: Glebe Street signal box is approached by an Up London Sunday excursion on 13th July 1930, headed by former L&NWR large-boilered 'Claughton' 4-6-0 No. 5906 *Ralph Brocklebank*. On the left can be seen the recently erected steelwork for the new goods warehouse, behind which is South Outlet signal box. To the left of the locomotive's buffer beam are a workshop, lamp stores and water tank, whilst in the background is the sub-station which, from 1893 to 1933, supplied Stoke station with electricity. *Gordon Walwyn*

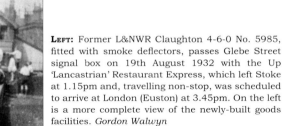

LEFT: Former L&NWR Claughton 4-6-0 No. 5985, fitted with smoke deflectors, passes Glebe Street signal box on 19th August 1932 with the Up 'Lancastrian' Restaurant Express, which left Stoke at 1.15pm and, travelling non-stop, was scheduled to arrive at London (Euston) at 3.45pm. On the left is a more complete view of the newly-built goods facilities. *Gordon Walwyn*

RIGHT: Here, former L&NWR George 'V' Class No. 5379 *Woodcock*, off Stoke shed, is seen with an Up Sunday excursion for London Euston on 12th June 1932. On the left is the goods office and, behind, the new goods warehouse again. *Gordon Walwyn*

This elevated view of the southern approach to Stoke was taken in September 1939, from the top of the coaling tower adjacent to the engine shed and looking north, with the station barely visible in the background. A 2-6-4T can be seen alongside a train of loaded coal wagons in the foreground. The lines cross City Road and the houses on the left-hand side of the road comprise twenty railway cottages, erected in 1849 for the NSR's first employees, including those engaged at the Stoke Locomotive, Carriage & Wagon Works; these houses were finally demolished in 1985 to make way for road widening. The buildings bottom right accommodate the stonemasons' workshops. To the right of the Worthington sign is an advertisement for the North Stafford Hotel, for which the LM&SR resumed direct management in January 1933. The electricity pylon blighting the scene was part of a grid system erected in 1936-7 and to its left can be seen the tall Up gantry signals for the Biddulph Valley, Derby and main lines. *A.E. Ellis collection*

Stoke Junction in 1929, showing the original and replacement Stoke Junction signal boxes. In the summer of 1926, the LM&SR approved, at an estimated cost of £9,140, a major scheme consisting of the replacement of the original box, the elimination of wrong lane working and extra shunting, and an expansion of signalling capacity by means of a larger new box. The top view shows the rear of both signal boxes, the new one on the left, with the original and much smaller McKenzie & Holland box undergoing demolition on the right. The second view, below, shows the front of the replacement much larger box, built to an L&NWR design. It was one of several boxes to L&NWR designs that were erected in the North Staffordshire Section between 1923 and 1930. The box was located on the Up line to Derby, facing the main line and the roundhouse. *Both Manifold collection*

LEFT: An Up goods train of Shelton wagons, with the signals on the gantry in the middle distance (which had replaced the original NSR gantry) set for the Derby line. The locomotive is former 'D' Class 0-6-0T No. 37, here as LM&SR No. 1554. On the right is Fowler 0-6-0T No. 16742, which was renumbered 7659 in 1934; this locomotive was transferred to the War Department during WW2. It was one of a class of 415 built between 1924 and 1931, an important element in the policy of standardisation of locomotive building by the LM&SR. In the North Staffordshire Section, they largely replaced the 'D' Class engines and could be found working Rushton to Stoke passenger services in 1927. Others were allocated new to Alsager shed in 1929 and to Macclesfield in 1932. *W.H. Whitworth*

RIGHT: The L&NWR Royal Train of six coaches being worked empty through Stoke Junction to the Biddulph Valley 0n 5th June 1932. From there they were taken to Congleton Upper Junction, before returning to Trentham Sidings, where former L&NWR 'George' Class No. 5404 *Colwyn Bay* was waiting to work the train back to London Euston (see page 80). LM&SR No. 2050 was former 'New F' Class 0-6-4T No. 116. There were eight locomotives in the class, built between 1916 and 1919, construction being held up by the wartime lack of materials. No. 2050 was withdrawn from service in February 1935. *L. Henstock*

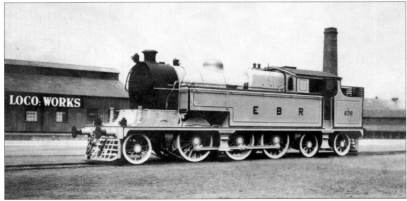

Kerr, Stuart's California Works was situated on the Down side of the main line, around 1,700 yards south of Stoke station, and occupied 31 acres. KS was established in 1881 originally as James Kerr & Company, assuming the name of Kerr, Stuart Ltd in Glasgow in 1883. In 1893, the Company acquired the business of Hartley, Arnoux & Fanning, of California Works, Stoke, an important sub-contractor, enabling KS to become a locomotive builder in its own right. Kerr, Stuart went into liquidation in 1930 and the works was sold to George Cohen & Sons & Co. Ltd in the same year. Cohen sold part of the works to the Berrisford Engineering Co. Ltd and, after this company's liquidation in 1932, the site was owned by Brookfield Foundry & Engineering. From 1935, California Works was owned by Wagon Repairs. Brookfield leased part of the works to the Admiralty throughout the Second World War (and subsequently to 1959). The two pictures presented here were taken in 1925 when California Works was operating at full capacity and employing 1,300 people, nearly twice the number employed at the NSR/LM&SR Locomotive Works nearby.

ABOVE LEFT: This 2-8-4 locomotive for the East Bengal Railway was one of six ordered and all were delivered in April and May 1925. It was built for 5ft 6ins gauge and the photograph was taken outside the erecting shop. *Manifold collection*

LEFT: Newly-built Fowler '4F' 0-6-0 on parade in works grey livery. This class represented the LM&SR initiative to introduce a range of new locomotives in the immediate post-Grouping era and to begin replacing the large number and types of freight engines that the LM&SR had inherited from its constituent companies. This particular locomotive was in a batch of 25 built by KS in 1925 and the Company subsequently built a further batch of 25 for the LM&SR in 1926-7. *Hanley Archives*

The foremen and departmental chiefs of Kerr Stuart & Co., Ltd., with a completed L.M.S engine, built under their supervision. Taken on date of delivery in December, 1925.

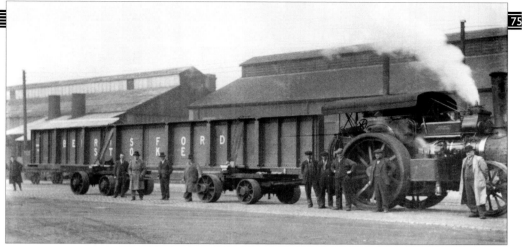

Right: California Works circa 1935, with a Fowler road locomotive ready to haul a newly fabricated large steel bridge girder. Its destination is unfortunately not recorded. As the lettering on the girder indicates, by this date, part of the California Works site had been acquired by Berrisford Engineering. *Author's collection*

Above: An aerial view of the Stafford Coal & Iron Co's site at Great Fenton, dating from around 1930 and looking north-east. The two tall buildings, centre left alongside the chimney, are the winding houses for the overhead crank winding engines of the Homer and Sutherland pit shafts. Their height was necessitated by the design of the winding engines and, at this time, these were the main coal winding shafts at the pit, Pender, Bourne and Kemball pit shafts being off the picture to the top right. To the right of the pit shafts can be seen the blast furnaces and stoves, with the tall building housing the beam blowing engine below them and the wagon repair shop in the foreground. Centre right can be seen the chemical works associated with the blast furnaces and top left is the coal washer. Note in particular the large mileage (9 miles in total) of railway sidings, along with the number of wagons and railway activity generally. The associated marl hole and brick works are off the picture to the right. The blast furnaces were producing around 80,000 tons of pig iron in 1924 but closed in 1931. Coal output was 532,277 tons in 1932, 597,701 in 1940 and 422,383 tons in 1946. *Author's collection*

Right: Peckett 0-4-0ST *Sapper*, supplied new in 1892 and one of many industrial locomotives used in the Stafford Coal & Iron complex. This picture probably dates from the early 1930s and *Sapper* was transferred to Bignal Hill Colliery circa 1944. *Manifold collection*

The Michelin Tyre Company

The Michelin Tyre Company was a subsidiary of the French Compagnie Générale des Établissements Michelin and its first British operations were established in London in 1905. In France, Michelin provided tyres for Citroen and Renault, and when both these companies opened factories in West London in 1926 and 1927 respectively, Michelin decided to open a works in Great Britain in order to avoid import tariffs on tyres from France. Stoke was chosen in December 1925, amidst fierce competition, as the site for its first manufacturing activities. The location chosen was an 80-acre site of waste land fairly close to Stoke-on-Trent city centre. In July 1926, work commenced on constructing a rail link (the Link Line) between the LM&SR main line at Sideway and its new works on the west side of Campbell Road. Three miles of track were laid, half within the works and half outside. Interestingly, the track within the works was imported from France. The route outside crossed both the Trent & Mersey Canal and the River Trent, and there was a level crossing and signal box at Campbell Road. The

line was initially used to convey materials for construction work. The period of construction lasted for approximately 100 weeks and, when the works opened, at a cost of £500,000, it consisted of three major production buildings and five support workshops, totalling 500,000 square feet. The cost of provision of siding accommodation amounted to £8,885, with £7,149 of this being borne by Stoke Corporation. For the LM&SR, the establishment of the Michelin Tyre Company was very lucrative business, generating no less than £75,750 in freight traffic receipts between 1928 and 1932. The arrival of MTC generated substantial new employment opportunities and some of the workforce who had been made redundant at the NSR/LM&SR Locomotive Works in the spring of 1927 found alternative employment there. Manufacturing commenced in November 1927, with the initial workforce approaching 1,500, a figure which had risen to over 2,000 by 1929. Initially, production consisted of bicycle, car and motor cycle tyres, and this required some 900 tons of coal and 130,000 gallons of canal water (which was recycled) per

An aerial view of circa 1929 of the site (later expanded in the 1950s and 60s) which contained the original Michelin factory and support facilities. The site is bounded on the left by a boundary wall beyond which, for several hundred yards, is the bed of the former Newcastle-under-Lyme Canal; Michelin purchased a long strip of land from the LM&SR on which this boundary wall was erected. The site is bounded on the right first by a wall and then by Campbell Road. Just off the picture, bottom right, is where the Link Line passed over it, protected by a level crossing. Top left of the picture is the warehouse building, then comes the main cycle and inner tube section, and then the Head Office of Michelin in this country, where it had moved from Fulham in 1927. Next comes the wooden cooling tower and gas holder, as the factory was self-sufficient in both electricity and gas. In front of this can be seen the large building housing the curing department, the main car and truck tyre making department, the fabrication department and then the main rubber processing department. In the centre of the picture is the boiler house, behind which is the Banbury rubber mixing department. Bottom left are the engineering workshops, whilst bottom right the wire drawing departments are under construction. Land beyond the bottom of the picture (to the south), together with land acquired that was owned by the former Trent Vale Tileries, was developed in the 1960s and 1970s, to accommodate a new warehouse, a new fabrication department, the internal transfer of the retread activities to cope with increased demand, and a new training centre. At its peak after the war, approximately 10,000 workers were employed on the site. *Michelin Tyres PLC*

annum. In 1936, one week's holiday with pay was introduced for the workforce, one of the first employers in the country to do so.

With the outbreak of the Second World War, the works lost a lot of its first recruits and women were allowed to work on night shift, whilst production took place on a 24-hour day, seven days a week basis.Employment averaged 1,800 during the war and 12-hour shifts were common place. After the civilian market for tyres was suspended in October 1940, the works geared production to an all-out war effort, making tyres for military vehicles after the loss of 63,000 vehicles at Dunkirk. Later, assembly began from 'Knock Down' kits, initially of American Federal Tank Tranporter units and, later, of Canadian military pattern lorries. In addition, four new departments were established, whose remit was to design and produce special types and sizes of tyres for the enormous range of military vehicles. The works also turned out tank transporter trailers, radio location trailers, and many machine parts for tanks and other armoured vehicles. Another wartime achievement was the design and production of a tyre specially to the order of the Ministry of Supply, for use on amphibious landing craft. Michelin used a variety of storage facilities, including part of the Carriage & Wagon Section of the former NSR Works for the storage of tyres awaiting repairs.

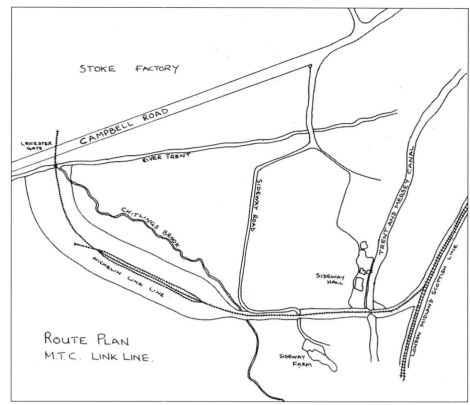

ROUTE PLAN
M.T.C. LINK LINE.

ABOVE: The route of the Michelin Link Line. Note the passing loops. Stoke-on-Trent Corporation required an Act of Parliament in 1926 for the construction of the railway works and the building of the level crossing. This Act was fiercely opposed by Michelin's great rival, Dunlop.

All Michelin Tyres PLC

ABOVE LEFT: This 0-4-0 petrol-electric mechanical shunter, carrying the Michelin Tyre Co. name on its cab side, left, arrived new in 1927, built at a cost of £2,026 by Locotracteurs Gaston Moyse of La Corneuve, Seine, France. It was powered by a 4-cylinder Panhard & Levasseur petrol engine, which in turn drove a Thomson-Houston electric generator that provided the direct current to operate two electric motors connected to the axles. It was rebuilt around 1936 as a diesel electric and was scrapped on site circa 1949-50.
LEFT: A view of Sideway in 1926-7 looking north, showing where the Link Line left the Down main line. Note the new bridge over the railway and the sidings at Sideway of the Stafford Coal & Iron Co. Ltd.
ABOVE RIGHT: The shunter working over Campbell Road level crossing, with the signal box on the left.
RIGHT: The line under construction at the point it entered the works, later named Leicester Gate.

MICHELIN TYRES
are made at
STOKE-ON-TRENT
and sent
ALL OVER THE WORLD

ABOVE: The Michelin Man, known as *Bibendum*, was the international brand of Michelin Tyres and was first used in promotional work in 1898. This particular advertisement appeared in 1957 and reflected the international nature of the Michelin business at Stoke-on-Trent.

ABOVE RIGHT: During WW2, the activities of the Michelin Tyre Company at Stoke were devoted to the war effort. This was reflected in the design and production of tyres suitable for equipment used in the war and in the assembly of armaments. This Federal Tank Transporter, one of 4,765 that arrived at Stoke from the United States as part of the wartime lend-lease arrangements, came in CKD (Completely Knocked Down) kit form.

RIGHT: A circa 1948 view of newly built Fowler diesel mechanical 0-4-0 locomotive *Bibendum* on shunting duties on the Michelin internal railway system. It survived at Stoke until 1962, when rail services to the works ceased, and it was then sold to T.W. Ward. At various times when the Michelin locomotives were undergoing repairs, engines were hired from the LM&SR and later BR; these included an L&YR 'Pug'. *All Michelin Tyres PLC*

LEFT: PO wagon of the North Staffordshire Slag & Tarmacadam Co. Ltd, built by the Central Wagon Co. of Wigan. The writing on the side includes '*Empty to Sideway Siding Trentham, NS Ry. (LM&S)*'. The slag company was partially owned by Tarmac and was wound up in February 1932. *Historical Model Railway Society collection*

RIGHT: Sideway signal box, seen here on 19th March 1960, was another of the L&NWR-style cabins that was erected on the former NSR network in the first few years of the LM&SR era. It was provided in 1927-8 for the line serving Michelin's new works. It was situated on the site of a former NSR signal box almost equidistant from Stoke Junction and Trentham Junction boxes. Behind, the two houses are of a late NSR design and were built in 1900 at this somewhat remote location. Directly facing the box was the site of Sideway Halt, which was served until 1919 by rail motors running between Leycett and Stone. The service to this halt continued even after the rail motors were withdrawn, although several of the other halts were closed. Sideway Halt finally closed on 2nd April 1923, by which time only one Up train was booked to stop there daily, whilst four Up and Down trains would call on request. It was located 1 mile 1,144 yards south of Stoke station. Railway sidings on the main line were subsequently installed for the MTC in 1934, at a cost of £8,885, which was shared by Michelin, the LM&SR and the City Council. *National Railway Museum*

ABOVE: Florence Colliery in 1951. Sinking operations began in 1874 and the colliery was originally owned by the Duke of Sutherland, after whose eldest daughter it was named. By 1916, three shafts had been sunk here and, from 1911 onwards, its parent company was the Shelton Iron, Steel & Coal Co. Ltd. The colliery was served by a private railway from the main line at Trentham, which was approximately 2½ miles long. In 1924, 2,087 miners were employed here but, following the coal strike of 1926, the number had dropped to 1,211 by 1933, picking up again after the war to 1,390 in 1947. Output was 389,350 tons in 1947. Between 1950 and 1964, the pit was modernised extensively and it finally closed in 1990. *Metcalfe collection*

RIGHT: Wagons belonging to the Florence Coal & Iron Co. Ltd, a picture probably taken at the time of the 1924 or 1926 coal strikes. This appears to be a view of workmen loading slack into the wagons. *Author's collection*

BELOW RIGHT: Builders' portrait of a Florence wagon, one of a batch of 100 built by Charles Roberts in 1934. They were 12-ton mineral wagons fitted with side and end doors, and carrying the symbol of the Staffordshire Knot. The instructions bottom left read 'EMPTY TO TRENTHAM STATION L.M.S. N.S. SECT.' and bottom right 'FOR REPAIRS FLORENCE COLLIERY'. The livery was slate grey, with white lettering shaded black. *Historical Model Railway Society collection*

BELOW: Pictured at Florence on 14th June 1932, 0-6-0ST *No. 1* was built by Black, Hawthorn & Co. Ltd in 1890 and came new to the colliery. For a time, the engine also carried the name *Major*. It saw fifty years of service here before being retired and was dismantled in 1942. *R.S. Pratt collection, Allan Baker*

On 5th June 1925, former L&NWR 'George V' Class 4-4-0 No. 5404 *Colwyn Bay* is seen beautifully turned out awaiting its return journey hauling the Royal Train. It was scheduled to leave Trentham at 4.30pm and to arrive at Windsor at 7.50pm. The purpose of the Royal Visit was to lay the foundation stone at the North Staffordshire Royal Infirmary, but, during the visit, His Majesty also conferred City status on the County Borough of Stoke-on-Trent. Just visible behind the locomotive is the headgear of the new (1924) Hem Heath Colliery and the recently built chimney carrying the initials of the Stafford Coal & Iron Co. Ltd. *Author's collection*

LEFT: Trentham station on the same day, with preparations underway to make the station attractive for the few minutes that King George V and Queen Mary would spend there at the end of their 4-hour visit to the Potteries. There are nine men busy tacking down carpet or felt, whilst another is arranging the pots and the foreman in his trilby hat is busying himself. Of particular interest is the gas lamp and the noticeboard advising passengers how to cross over the line to the Junction station for Trentham Park. A policeman keeps a watchful eye. *H.W. Robinson*

Seen approaching Trentham station from the north about 1930 is Fowler '4F' 4-4-0 No. 1134 (off Rugby shed and built at Horwich in 1926) at the head of a Manchester (London Road) to London (Euston) express. Trentham Junction signal box is on the left and the line going off to the left beyond the two NSR ground discs is the Trentham Park Branch, at this time closed for scheduled passenger traffic. The PO wagons on the right are a Crewe Co-operative Society 5-plank, along with 5-plank and 6-plank wagons belonging to Miller & Lilley, Devon-based coal factors. Behind the wagons can be seen the landscape scarred by the Hem Heath Colliery workings. *Author's collection*

BELOW: Looking north at Trentham in 1929, a fine view partially showing the station buildings, with their elegant pantile roofing. These buildings were specially designed in 1851 for the prominent local landowner, the Duke of Sutherland. His extensive industrial interests also included a colliery at Brora, in the family's native county of Sutherland in Scotland. Fowler '4F' 0-6-0 No. 4311 heads an Up goods train behind which can be seen the extensive marshalling yards for Florence Colliery. No. 4311 was one of twenty engines of this class that were allocated to Stoke in 1927-8, replacing the 'New L' Class locomotives on mineral and freight workings over the next eight years. Visible in the centre background are the Sutherland and Homer shafts of the Stafford Coal & Iron Co's extensive colliery and iron works site at Great Fenton (seen on page 75), whilst further to the right are the Kemball, Pender and Bourne shafts, all part of the same complex. Note on the Up platform on the right, the LM&SR noticeboard, in contrast to the attractive NSR gas lamp and bench, with the shaded lettering TRENTHAM painted on the seat back. *Author's collection*

RIGHT: Wagon label, Florence Coal & Iron Co. Ltd, 1935. *Chris Knight collection*

FROM THE
Florence Coal & Iron Co. Ltd.
TRENTHAM STATION, LMS (N.S.)

Quality _____ Date _____

TO _____ Stone

Via _____ S. Rly.
T. C.

Owner &
No. of Wagon }
Consignee _____ Weight _____

The Trentham Park Branch

The origins of the Trentham Park Branch lay with the gift of the Trentham Park Estate by the Duke of Sutherland to the newly created (in 1910) County Borough of Stoke-on-Trent. Trentham Hall was quickly demolished and the estate itself was opened to the public. The line was one mile 14 chains from Trentham Junction to Trentham Park station and was opened as a single track branch on 1st April 1910. The final NSR service comprised seven trains daily, which in summer was increased up to ten on Thursdays and eleven on Saturdays, and with Sunday trains. Pruning of this service began soon into the LM&SR era; three trains were cut out in 1924, whilst the 1925 winter timetable saw the branch service reduced to three in each direction. By 1927, the line was open Thursdays

and Saturdays only and, in September of that year, it was closed except for excursion traffic, which was mainly from the Potteries at public holidays. However, the branch was reopened in 1935, with excursions run during Stoke Wakes Week, and in 1939 there were five trains each way on Sundays, with a through carriage to Tunstall. During the war, evacuated Ministry offices were housed in buildings in the Park and a daily goods trip over the branch brought in supplies; this was discontinued circa 1947-8. Excursion traffic continued throughout the war and the branch also accommodated ambulance trains during this period. It was also occasionally used as a night berth for the Royal Train. The terminus was renamed Trentham Gardens on 7th October 1946.

ABOVE: Trentham Junction station in 1958, looking west. This was the final design of NSR station, and the buildings here and at Trentham Park were the last stations to be built by the NSR, in 1910. The Trentham Gardens Branch was opened to take advantage of the NSR rail motors. *Author's collection*

LEFT: Trentham Park station in the mid 1930s, looking east towards Trentham Junction station and with a train approaching. This station was the last to be built by the NSR and had a single island platform with run round loops on both sides. The station and the branch closed to regular services from September 1927 to June 1935, the 1927 service being Thursdays, Saturdays and Sundays only. From 1935 to the outbreak of WW2, the service ran from June to September with five journeys scheduled in each direction. Note the NSR design station nameboard on the left. *Gordon Walwyn*

BELOW: LM&SR tickets: Trentham Park to Trentham and a child's ticket for Trentham Park to Tunstall. *Both Author's collection*

RIGHT: Excursion Notice for August 1935 for Trentham Park and Trentham Gardens. This was the year that the branch opened for holiday traffic for five days during Wakes Week. On Tuesday and Thursday, there were fifteen trains each way including two from Silverdale. In an attempt to attract visitors to the gardens from wider afield, Cheap Day Return fares were offered from thirty-one stations; these included Crewe, Leek, Congleton, Newcastle and Meir but excluded any stations south of Trentham on the main line. There were cheap single fares from Trentham Park to Stoke and to the Loop Line stations. *Robert Keys collection*

BELOW: The bridge over the A34 at Trentham circa 1941, a view looking east with demolition in progress. This large steel girder bridge was located a hundred yards or so west of Trentham Park station. It was part of an imaginative scheme, promoted by the NSR in 1914, as the Trentham, Silverdale & Newcastle-under-Lyme Light Railway, just over 5¾ miles in length and running partially along the route of the former Newcastle-under-Lyme Canal, to link Trentham with the Pool Dam Branch at Newcastle. The intention behind the scheme was to route mineral traffic away from Stoke, and thereby ease congestion on the main line and through Stoke station. The line was not constructed, apart from this bridge, which was a local landmark for nearly thirty years. Construction of the Light Railway was held up because of the First World War and neither the NSR, nor later the LM&SR, wished to take advantage of the powers to be build the line subsequently; the scheme was formally abandoned in 1922. Demolition of the bridge at this time was no doubt a result of the wartime drive for scrap metal. Note that, despite the war, the LM&SR billboard promotes cheap trips from Stoke to Blackpool. *E.J.D. Warrilow, Keele University collection*

PLEASE RETAIN THIS PROGRAM

N. 69/R

LMS

STOKE WAKES HOLIDAYS, 1935

Sunday, Monday, Tuesday, Wednesday, Thursday & Friday

August 4th, 5th, 6th, 7th, 8th & 9th

CHEAP EXCURSION TICKETS

TO

TRENTHAM, BARLASTON STONE and STAFFORD

AND ON

Monday, Tuesday, Wednesday, Thursday & Friday

August 5th, 6th, 7th, 8th & 9th

TO

ASTON-BY-STONE, SANDON, WESTON HIXON, GREAT HAYWOOD & COLWICH

For particulars of Fares and Train Services, please see pages 2, 3 and 4.

STOKE WAKES HOLIDAY CONTRACT TICKETS will also be available for travel by any of the Services shewn herein.

CONDITIONS OF ISSUE OF EXCURSION AND OTHER TICKETS AT LESS THAN ORDINARY FARES.
These Tickets are issued subject to the Notices and Conditions shewn in the Company's Current Time Tables.
For LUGGAGE ALLOWANCES also see Time Tables.

9,000 125 P.   Bemrose & Sons Ltd., Derby and London.

Wedgwood

The Josiah Wedgwood Pottery Works was established at Etruria in 1769, alongside the route of the then shortly to be constructed Trent & Mersey Canal. By the mid-1930s, there were increasing production problems at this site, caused by land subsidence and by the poor environment close to Shelton Works. This situation was compounded by Shelton's wish to undertake further mining at deeper levels, directly underneath the Wedgwood Works.

Wedgwood decided to review options for locations away from Etruria, not just for manufacturing but also for establishing a factory village along the lines of Rowntree, Cadbury, or Welwyn Garden City. Sites were visited at Knutton and at Meir but problems were encountered at both locations, where there was too little space to establish a village. After reviewing the Keele Hall Estate and the Park Hall Estate, a site at Barlaston was chosen, with the project made public and the foundation stone laid on 10th September 1938. Some 1,600 employees were carried by bus and rail for the occasion.

Some works had commenced in the summer of 1937 and a siding was laid into the site in the spring of 1938. The LM&SR paid for the signalling, earthworks and gates for the siding, at a cost of £500, with an obligation that it would own and maintain them and with Wedgwood paying an annual rental of £70pa. That sum was subject to abatement depending upon the volume of freight traffic. During the construction period, 10-12 wagons came in and out of the site daily and it was anticipated that when the factory became operational, goods traffic would not be greater and would consist of inward raw materials and fuel.

At the same time, Wedgwood negotiated with the railway company for the construction of a passenger halt for its workforce and agreement was reached in April 1938 for the LM&SR to build,

at its own cost, timber platforms, shelters, signalling and a sleeper paving at the level crossing, to provide train services, and to appoint a crossing keeper. Wedgwood, for its part, undertook to guarantee passenger receipts to and from the halt of £1,500pa, and to influence employees to travel to and from work by rail. No LM&SR staff would be required at the halt and the cost of additional train services would be £1,914. The cost of building the halt came to £2,969, which included the provision of cycle gates and a booking office. It was estimated at the time that 500 employees would travel to the factory daily by train.

The halt opened on 1st January 1940, the only new publicly-timetabled passenger station to be opened by the LM&SR on the North Staffordshire Section. The cost of the factory and ancillary facilities amounted to £250,000 and production started in the summer of 1940. In July 1939, 150 houses were planned for employees on part of the estate named Potters Green but, because of the war, this was scaled down to a nominal twenty.

Included in the Ministry of Transport Inspection Report of 18th October 1945 were the following comments: '... the workforce passed over the crossing within a few minutes ... The crossing keeper referred to constant difficulty in controlling men and boys when trains were passing ... boys were in the habit of climbing over the main gates when fast and frequent trains were passing through'. Employment at Etruria and at Barlaston dropped during the war, as employees were switched to work at munitions factories at Swynnerton and Radway Green. China continued to be produced at Etruria until 1947, production there eventually ceasing in 1951. Employees travelled to the factory on the normal service trains but returned on weekdays on the 5.25pm Unadvertised Workmen's train to Stoke.

ABOVE: An artist's impression from 1937 of the new Wedgwood factory at Barlaston. The proposed trailing siding from the Up main line can be seen in the foreground. *Wedgwood Archives*

LEFT: Looking north at Wedgwood on 4th July 1947, with Fowler 'Royal Scot' Class 4-6-0 No. 6129 *The Scottish Horse* working the 2.10pm Manchester (London Road) to London (Euston) express. The train is seen here passing Wedgwood's factory on the right, with the trailing siding dropping down on a 1 in 50 gradient in to the site. At this time there was one goods train a day each way calling here. The elegant greenhouse was no doubt contributing to the post-war recovery effort. *Gordon Walwyn*

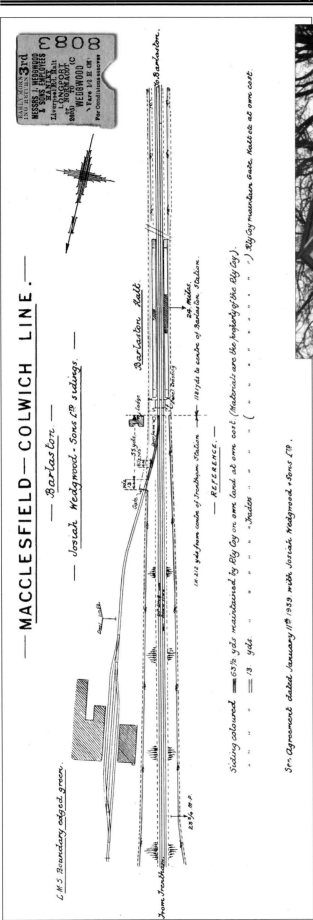

MACCLESFIELD—COLWICH LINE.

— Barlaston. —

— Josiah Wedgwood & Sons Lt.ᵈ sidings. —

L.M.S Boundary edged green.

Barlaston Halt.

24 miles.

1121 yds to centre of Barlaston Station.

— REFERENCE. —

1M 212 yds from centre of Trentham Station.

Siding coloured ▬▬▬▬ 63½ yds maintained by Rly Coy on own land at own cost. (Materials are the property of the Rly Coy.)

" " " ▬▬▬ 13. yds. " " " " " " " " "

" " " ━━━ "Trados" " " " " " " " " " "

" " " ━━ ") Rly Coy maintain Gate. Halts at own cost.

Ser. Agreement dated January 11ᵗʰ 1939. with Josiah Wedgwood & Sons Lt.ᵈ

ABOVE: Private Siding plan between the LM&SR and Josiah Wedgwood & Sons Ltd, dated 11th January 1939. The actual agreement detailed the railway arrangements, and the siding serving the boiler house and the warehouse. Note the level crossing and the lodge building occupied by the LM&SR crossing keeper. *Author's collection*

INSET: Workmen's Ticket, Wedgwood Halt, from early BR days. *Author's collection*

ABOVE: The 1940 booking office at Wedgwood Halt, which was located on the Down platform, pictured here in January 1974. *Author's collection*

LEFT: Wedgwood Halt on 25 August 1957, a view looking south with the factory behind the photographer on the left. Note the station nameboard to the traditional NSR design, even though the halt opened on 1st January 1940, nearly seventeen years after 'the Knotty's' demise. The waiting shelter on the Up line on the left is much smaller than the one facing on the Down platform, reflecting the predominant flow of workmen passengers returning to the Stoke area. Note the narrowness of the Up platform and of the Down platform in front of the shelter. It was because of the danger to waiting passengers that the Down platform was widened in 1951. A booking office is partially visible on the right and a sloping path drops down to the level crossing. The halt was 1 mile, 212 yards south of Trentham station and 1,121 yards north of Barlaston station. *Author's collection*

RIGHT: Crossing keeper's cottage between Wedgwood and Barlaston, with the single lever ground frame for working the level crossing. The lever was electrically released from Barlaston signal box. *Author's collection*

BELOW: Barlaston station looking south in the late 1950s, with ex-NSR trolley, benches, waiting shelters and signal box all visible. The former NSR goods warehouse is behind the tall LM&SR Down distant signal on the right. In the background can be seen the twin chimneys of the Meaford 'A' & 'B' power stations. *Author's collection*

INSET: LMS Ordering Ticket, Barlaston. *Author's collection*

LEFT: Meaford 'A' Power Station under construction, a general view of the site looking north on 25th October 1945, ten days after the Board of Trade railway inspection. At this time, there was a daily goods working from Trentham to Barlaston Power Sidings, and from Barlaston Power Sidings to Barlaston. Construction was carried out by G. Percy of Trentham and commenced in February 1945. On the far left is the contractor's locomotive, an 0-4-0ST built by Walker Bros of Wigan in 1881. The framework for the loading bay is in place on the left, with the steelwork for the turbine house and the boiler house on the right; a 60-ton crane is on the right in the background. There were two generating stations on this site, both commissioned by the North West Midlands Joint Electricity Authority. Meaford 'A' was opened on 27th November 1947, with construction finally completed in June 1948. It was the first post-war power station brought into use. *Clive Guthrie collection*

ABOVE: Barlaston Power Sidings signal box, a view taken in the late 1950s looking south from the carriage window of a Down passenger train. This brick-based box was to an LM&SR design and was possibly the last box erected on the North Staffordshire Section in the LM&SR era. In the background are 'A' and 'B' power stations, the 'B' station being commissioned in November 1955. There were approximately nine miles of sidings. The T&M Canal can be seen on the right, the power stations being sited on the west side of the canal. *National Railway Museum*

ABOVE. Taylor Tunnicliff & Co. Ltd's porcelain and refractory works at Stone was served by this eponymously named Bagnall 0-4-0ST, pictured on 18th August 1946. The locomotive was built in 1932 and came new to the works. The factory itself dated from 1920 and was served by sidings connected to the Down main line just north of Stone station. *Bernard Roberts, IRS collection*

LEFT: A view taken just north of Stone, with the outline of the station building visible in the background. A lengthy Down goods trundles through, with motive power being provided by former 'New F' Class 0-6-4T No. 121, renumbered 2055 by the LM&SR. This locomotive was the last of its class to be built, in 1919, and was withdrawn from service in August 1934. *Manifold collection*

LEFT: Stone station, in the mid 1920s looking towards Colwich, with former 'K' Class 4-4-2T standing with a train for Stoke at the Down Colwich line platform. Stone was a busy market town and much activity was centred round its station. Four coal merchants and a timber merchant traded from the station yard and cattle came through for auction at Stone's Smithfield market on alternate Tuesdays. The distinctive front elevation of the station is of three shaped or Dutch gables. *Manifold collection*

BELOW: Former NSR 'A' Class 2-4-2T No. 35, renumbered as No. 1455, is at the head of a short rake of LM&SR non-standard corridor stock, forming a Stoke to Stafford working at Stone on 14th March 1931. This locomotive was built at Stoke Works in 1881 as a 2-4-0T but was rebuilt as a 2-4-2T in 1898 and withdrawn from service in October 1932. The tall Down starter signal for the Colwich platforms is visible beyond the train. Note the weighing machine just to the right of the locomotive. Stone was one of a handful of NSR stations to have a W.H. Smith bookstall. *Manifold collection*

BELOW: Three wagon labels for consignments going to Stone: two are from locations on the LM&SR; from Bristol, top, routed via Birmingham and Norton Bridge, and malt from Gloucester Docks, bottom, sent via Burton. The third is a GWR label for timber from Caersws, on the old Cambrian main line between Welshpool and Machynlleth, and routed via Whitchurch and Crewe. *Author's collection*

FAR RIGHT: An LM&SR Third Class Excursion ticket, Stone to Llandudno, which included a trip on one of the North Wales Steam Ship Co's steamers, and an NSR First Class ticket issued on 21st December 1937. *Author's collection; David Geldart collection*

A view just to the south of Stone station, in the cutting on the Colwich line with Granville Terrace above, which provides a rare glimpse of the rebuilt unique 4-cylinder 0-6-0 tender locomotive, formerly NSR No. 23. Renumbered 2367 by the LM&SR in March 1924, the engine is seen here hard at work around 1925 at the head of a train including an ex-L&NWR van, an ex-Midland Railway 5-plank open wagon and an ex-L&NWR full brake van. This locomotive was built originally as a 'D' Class 0-6-0T, to an experimental design by John Hookham at Stoke Works in 1922, in order to tackle the intensive suburban services and severe gradients on the Loop Line. It was tested in the spring of 1923 but, after nearly twelve months of unsatisfactory working on local passenger trains, it was converted at Stoke Works early in 1924 to a tender engine. It was then utilised on the Stafford and Colwich goods service. It was renumbered 8689 in March 1928, before being withdrawn from service in December of that year. *Manifold collection*

ABOVE: Aston-by-Stone in the late 1920s, a view looking north towards Stone. The NSR-built signal box with its L&NWR signal is in the foreground and the NSR single storey crossing house is just visible on the right. The box closed in the 1931/34 period. This station was one of the last NSR stations to be built, being opened in February 1902 in order to meet the needs of the busy expanding market town of Stone, which was creating its own suburb. The station closed for passenger traffic on 6th January 1947, although goods traffic continued until 13th August 1962. *Author's collection*

FAR RIGHT: LM&SR Third Class single ticket, Sandon to Aston-by-Stone. *Author's collection*

L M & S Station & House, Weston, Stafford

ABOVE: Weston & Ingestre station, seen here in the 1920s looking east towards Uttoxeter, was a typical NSR country station with goods yard, timber warehouse and cattle pens. On the left is the original McKenzie & Holland signal box, which eventually closed on 6th March 1967 when electrification arrived. The level crossing, replaced by a footbridge in 1938, appears in the background and to the right are the station buildings, goods office and warehouse. The station closed to passengers on 6th January 1947 and for goods traffic on 2nd September 1963. **INSET ABOVE & LEFT:** Two LM&SR Weston & Ingestre tickets. *Both author's collection*

Shirleywich level crossing, with its ornate crossing keeper's house, in May 1953; this house was typical of the many surviving single storey houses that were built between the late 1840s and the early 1870s. It was located between Weston & Ingestre and Hixon stations, and near the L&NER (formerly Great Northern Railway) Stafford to Derby (Friargate) line. There was also a siding here. *Author's collection*

RIGHT: Two more country stations were closed by the LM&SR for passenger and goods traffic on 6th January 1947. One of them was Hixon, seen here in a view looking north on 4th November 1961, with LM&SR design level crossing and cabin, and also station houses on the right in the background. *L&GRP*

BELOW: The other was Great Haywood, photographed here in 1947 looking south towards Colwich. The original waiting shelters were long gone by this stage but the timber platforms remained. *Real Photographs*

BELOW: Colwich station in August 1935, with former 'New M' Class 0-4-4T No. 15, renumbered by the LM&SR as No. 1436, on an early morning local passenger train from Walsall to Stoke. This view is looking south. Just to the right of the locomotive are station indicator signs and also an advertising board promoting excursions to Edinburgh. Pre-Grouping, Colwich was a station jointly owned and operated by the NSR and L&NWR. *P.S. Kendrick*

RIGHT: Colwich was the most southerly outpost of the NSR, with its shared station with the L&NWR, the 1883 NSR houses (which still survive), engine shed and turntable. During 1936, a major track reorganisation occurred here, with the abolition of North Stafford Sidings signal box and alterations to the signalling and permanent way, costing in total £3,185. This track improvement was part of the LM&SR's Acceleration Policy, designed to speed up express trains to the North and Scotland. In January 1937, following a review which determined that the engine shed, pump house, turntable and permanent way were no longer required, the LM&SR Works Committee agreed that they all be removed. This is the shed on 24th September 1936, which was already in a state of gross disrepair. *W.A. Camwell*

A view south in 1937 of the site of the former NSR engine shed. In the centre is the L&NWR signal box, whilst Colwich station is just visible below the L&NWR bracket signal gantry. The station was in a Jacobean style, designed by the short-lived Trent Valley Railway. *Author's collection*

Royal Ordnance Factory 5 Cold Meece

Royal Ordnance Factory 5, Cold Meece, was part of a 1939 programme of filling factories for the Army and the RAF. The site at Swynnerton comprised 1,284 acres, and the construction cost of the factory amounted to £13.6 million. Work began on 18th October 1939 and, at the peak, 21,450 workers were engaged in the construction, which lasted for six months, with men and materials coming in via Badnall Wharf on the former Crewe to Stafford L&NWR line. The factory became operational from mid-1940, with the workforce increasing from 1,040 in November 1940 to 18,511 in June 1942.

BELOW: Swynnerton Junction signal box, seen here on 3rd April 1958, was sited at the head of a half mile double track line to Cold Meece station and ROF 5, named the Yarnfield Spur Railway. This junction is almost two miles from Stone station, with the line veering to the left to Norton Bridge and to the right to Cold Meece. The building of the line was carried out by Mowlem, because the LM&SR did not have the resources, though they did construct the signal box and laid the permanent way. The speed limits were 15mph through the junction at Swynnerton, 25mph on the line to Cold Meece and 10mph through the entry to the station. The signal box had 13 working levers and 7 spare. Note the box had a distinct backwards lean. *National Railway Museum*

ABOVE: No. 4 Platform at Cold Meece station circa 1944, shortly after the arrival of an early afternoon mid-winter Workmen's train. The passengers are predominantly women and the few men appear mostly to be elderly. The first train for workmen was on 10th August 1941, coming in on Platforms 3 and 4, and it was not until the spring of 1942 that Platforms 1 and 2 came into use. The Workmen's service to Cold Meece in the summer of 1944 was not advertised and consisted of three traffic corridors: from Silverdale and Newcastle, from Newchapel & Goldenhill and from Blythe Bridge via Stoke. This pattern was reflected on weekdays in the three-shift working at Cold Meece, the first shift leaving around 5.35am, the second around 1.35pm and the third around 8.35pm; the return workings follwed a similar pattern. On Sundays, there were two workings from Silverdale and Blythe Bridge, and three from Newchapel & Goldenhill. The trains collected the workforce from all the passenger stations en route to Stoke but, apart from one Saturday evening working, none called at the stations south of Stoke. At maximum periods during the war, up to nineteen passenger trains were moved in a short space of time but, soon after hostilities had ceased, the traffic was reduced in October 1945 to eight trains at the beginning and end of the day's shift, with six of them being dealt with in half an hour. *H.C. Casserley*

ABOVE: The approach to Cold Meece station on 2nd April 1958. The wide '6-foot' way resulted from the construction of two distinctly separate embankments and the two lines were connected by means of a hand-worked emergency crossover in the foreground. Note the Down home signal with mechanical route indicator, beyond which can be seen the scissors crossover at the station throat, with coaches standing in the north carriage siding. Cold Meece signal box is in the distance, with 35 levers. It was built by Mowlem to a standard LM&SR design, with the railway company providing the signalling requirements. The box worked four platforms, two run-round lines and two carriage sidings. It closed on 3rd August 1959. *National Railway Museum*

RIGHT: LM&SR station staff and US military personnel at Cold Meece in January 1945. *Chris Knight collection*

ABOVE: Cold Meece station on 28th February 1958, with a 'Black 5' 4-6-0 at the head of the 4.50pm train for Newchapel & Goldenhill, in the platform on the left, having received the right-away signal. The platforms were 900 feet long. The station was constructed for the Ministry of Supply and the station buildings were built in late 1941/early 1942, with the station master taking possession on 10th January 1942. Initially there was two-shift working but three-shift working had been introduced completely by July 1941, with 8,500 people being conveyed daily and workers being issued with weekly travel passes. One consequence of this extra passenger traffic on the North Staffordshire Section was that additional sidings for Workmen's trains had to be provided, at a cost of £2,150 at Newchapel & Goldenhill and for £5,485 at Cresswell, where they were available in August 1941. New goods loop lines and a new signal box at Caverswall were also required to ease the problem of traffic congestion. *National Railway Museum*

LEFT: Two examples of LM&SR Third Class Workmen's Weekly tickets to Cold Meece, from Cobridge and from Newchapel & Goldenhill. *Both Dave Bourne collection*

LEFT: Cold Meece on 3rd April 1958, with an Easter Maundy train, hauled by an unidentified Class '4F' 0-6-0 off Stoke shed, on Platform 2. This class of locomotive along with 2-6-4Ts provided the bulk of the motive power for Cold Meece workings for nearly twenty years. Peak employment at Cold Meece was in June 1942 but obviously at the end of the war there was a rapid reduction in what was required of ROF 5. In 1945, a decision was made that the factory should be retained as a permanent facility. On 6th May 1946, the train service was reduced to three trains a day in and out for the one shift (including Saturdays), plus a recreational service for people living in the hostels on the site. From 16th June 1947, the Saturday afternoon shift services were withdrawn, followed by the withdrawal on 29th November of the recreational service that had run throughout the war. Production ceased in May 1958, with many of the remaining employees being transferred to ROF Radway Green. On 3rd March 1958, the Silverdale service was withdrawn, on 17th March the Blythe Bridge service ceased and the last train to Newchapel & Goldenhill ran on 27th June. The Yarnfield Spur Railway was removed by September 1963. *National Railway Museum*

Norton Bridge Junction, with the former L&NWR line to nearby Badnall Wharf and to Crewe on the left and the former NSR line to Swynnerton Junction and Stone on the right. In the centre is the goods shed and beyond the sidings for Norton Bridge (NSR) goods depot. Norton Bridge was important for goods traffic and was one of a small number of NSR stations that had, at Grouping, both a station master and a goods agent. *Author's collection*

Norton Bridge Junction signal box, a tall and elegant box to a McKenzie & Holland design. The line to Stone from here was three miles 1,242 yards long. *Author's collection*

LEFT: Norton Bridge station looking north on 7th May 1932, with former L&NWR 'Prince of Wales' Class 4-6-0 No. 5690, off Stoke shed, on a Stoke to Stafford train. This locomotive was one of two of this class allocated to Stoke shed. Note the footbridge and also the station buildings on the island platform, on the left, which were to be destroyed by a fire in the following year. *Gordon Walwyn*

RIGHT: At Norton Bridge on 17th September 1934 is ex-L&NWR 4-6-2T No. 6993, on a Stoke to Birmingham (New Street) local train. *Gordon Walwyn*

BELOW: Norton Bridge, looking northwards again, on 27th March 1937, with former L&NWR Whale '19ins Goods' 4-6-0 No. 8850 on a lengthy mineral train from the North Staffordshire Section. The station nameboard, on the right, is in the standard LM&SR colours of black letters on a yellow background. *Gordon Walwyn*

FAR RIGHT: An NSR Third Class Privilege ticket issued on 4th August 1934, Norton Bridge to Stoke. *Author's collection*

RIGHT: The unusual frontage to Norton Bridge station from the road approach in 1952. The station entrance remained unchanged for many years, and the solitary motor car and enamelled signs add to the period feel. The entrance canopy appears something of a hydbrid design and the supports are also quite distinctive. The station building rooms on the island platform suffered damage amounting to £738 in the fire which occurred on 20th April 1933. *L&GRP*

A fine double header pictured near Great Bridgeford, between Norton Bridge and Stafford, with former 'K' Class 4-4-2T No. 8, renumbered 2180, piloting an unidentified ex-L&NWR 2-4-0. All seven members of this NSR class were withdrawn from service between 1933 and 1935. The train is largely comprised of a permanently coupled rake of Midland Railway non-corridor carriages. This location is on the four-line section of the L&NWR main line between Crewe and the south. *A.G. Ellis collection.*

ABOVE: With its regular procession of passing trains, the four-track section of the L&NWR main line near Great Bridgeford was a favoured spot for photographers, as the pictures on this page show. Here, former 'New M' Class 0-4-4T No. 15, renumbered in 1923 as 1436 and seen in early LM&SR livery, is at the head of a rake of ex-NSR 6-wheeled carriages, including four with Webb-style radial underframes copied from the L&NWR, with an ex-NSR 6-wheeled milk van bringing up the rear. *L&GRP*

ABOVE: An Up Stafford train passes, comprised of a collection of ex-L&NWR stock and hauled by an unidentified former 'New C' Class 0-6-4T. *Manifold collection*

RIGHT: Former 'E' Class 0-6-0 No. 113, wearing its LM&SR number 2331, hurries by with a Down Stafford to Stoke working. This particular locomotive was built at Vulcan Foundry in 1872 and was finally withdrawn from service in December 1928. It was part of a group of twenty-one 0-6-0 tender locomotives built between 1871 and 1877 by Stoke Works, Vulcan Foundry and Beyer, Peacock, nearly all of which were withdrawn from service between 1926 and 1934. Again the carriages are of L&NWR design. *Manifold collection*

An Up passenger train arrives at Stafford in the mid 1920s, with motive power provided by former 'H1' Class 0-6-0 No. 91, now carrying LM&SR number 2365. The train of bogie carriages includes a Brake Third with four compartments as the first vehicle. The locomotive was one of four of this class built in 1910-11 at Stoke Works and all of which were withdrawn in 1929-30. This view is looking north from Bagnall's Bridge and shows the splendid array of signals on the gantry controlling the northern approaches to Stafford. To the left are the Shrewsbury line signals, in the centre those for the main line and on the right those for the L&NER (formerly GNR) line to Uttoxeter and Derby (Friargate). *Manifold collection*

Great Bridgeford on 27th October 1932, with former 'New L' Class 0-6-2T No. 64, now carrying LM&SR No. 2255, on a Stafford to Stoke working at the head of a three-coach set of former L&NWR non-corridor bogie stock, with a five-compartment Brake Third at the leading end. This locomotive was built in November 1913 at Stoke Works and withdrawn from service in May 1936. Note the shed plate, 40, for Stoke. *Author's collection*

ABOVE: Former 'K' Class 4-4-2T No. 55 as LM&SR No. 2183 at Stafford towards the end of 1933. Built in December 1911, its working life was relatively short, being withdrawn from service in December 1933, very soon after this photograph was taken. *Manifold collection*

RIGHT: LM&SR Voucher for use on a Potteries Motor Traction omnibus from Stafford to Hanley. *Author's collection*

L. M. & S. R.
ON SURRENDER OF THIS VOUCHER TO THE
CONDUCTOR, THE HOLDER OF Single Outward half of Return half of
...............TICKET NO...............FROM
.......................to.....................
will be allowed to travel by
P. M. T. OMNIBUS from
STAFFORD To HANLEY
without charge.

BELOW: Seen to the south of Stafford station and looking isolated amongst the running lines is former 'New F' Class 0-6-4T No. 118, renumbered by the LM&SR as 2052. Built at Stoke Works in 1919, this batch of locomotives was delayed because of materials shortages during the First World War. No. 2052 was the last of the class to be withdrawn from service, in December 1936. *Manifold collection*

The two photographs on this page both show Up goods trains leaving Stafford on the Wolverhampton line in the early 1930s. Seen here working a Stoke to Bushbury goods train is former L&NWR 'Experiment' Class 4-6-0 No. 5466 *Glendower*, one of a group of six of the class that were transferred from Camden to Stoke shed early in 1929. *P.S. Kendrick*

Ex-L&YR Barton Wright 'F15' Class 0-6-0 No. 12053 is seen here south of Colwich with a freight from Wichnor Junction to Stoke in the summer of 1935. Former L&Y locomotives were allocated from time to time to Stoke shed between 1930-35. *P.S. Kendrick*

RIGHT: The location for this photograph is at milepost 125, north of Rugeley on the Trent Valley line. Here, on a slightly misty day around 1930, an unidentified former NSR 'K' Class 4-4-2T speeds past the photographer with a southbound passenger service. *P.S. Kendrick*

LEFT: LM&SR Workman's Third Class ticket, Stoke to Ford Houses. *Author's collection*

LEFT: Also seen at milepost 125 was this Stoke to Walsall passenger working, catching the evening sun one day in 1935, with former 'New M' Class 0-4-4T numbered as LM&SR 1436, at the head of a three-coach set of LM&SR coaches. Built in 1920 at Stoke Works, this was the last ex-NSR locomotive to be withdrawn, in August 1939. Along with the only other NSR survivor at the time, No. 1434, there were plans early in 1940 to bring it back into service to assist with the wartime effort but these never materialised. *P.S. Kendrick*

BELOW: Stanier 2-6-0 No. 2983, built at Crewe in 1934, is seen here in 1935 with its 5D shed code (Stoke) south of Rugeley. It is on the return working of the evening Camden Goods from Stoke, the only fast fitted freight which worked out of the Midlands city. *W. Leslie Good, courtesy Bob Essery*

5
An INTRODUCTION to the NSR CANAL SYSTEM

This section deals with a review of the Trent & Mersey Canal network, of which the T&M itself is the most important element; in a later chapter, the Newcastle-under-Lyme Canal is also covered, together with the railways in that area. The remaining canals in the network, the Caldon, the Leek, and the Uttoxeter, together with Rudyard Lake, will all be dealt with in a later volume, which will also include adjacent railway lines and the Caldon inclines and tramroads.

In the years running up to Grouping, the NSR's canal system enjoyed mixed fortunes as the following table shows:

Year	Receipts £	Expenditure £	Surplus/(Deficit) £
1913	57,264	33,205	24,059
1922	57,185	64,527	(7,342)

Note that operating costs rose sharply after the war as a result of high wage settlements.

On its canal system, the NSR had its own wharves at Shardlow, Horninglow, Fradley, Rugeley, Stone, Stoke, Etruria, Longport, Lawton, Wheelock, Middlewich and Preston Brook; the Company had ceased to be carriers in 1895. At Grouping, the principal carriers on the system were The Anderton Co. Ltd, with its own wharves at Stoke, Etruria, Hanley, Burslem and Longport, and The Mersey Weaver & Ship Canal Carrying Co. Ltd, with wharves at Stoke, Etruria and Longport. Both carriers served Liverpool, Manchester and other port destinations. Fellows, Morton & Clayton provided a carrying service from Rugeley to London, and from Shardlow to all parts, and John Wood Gandy from Horninglow to the East Midlands and to Liverpool. The Shropshire Union Railways & Canal Co. had wharves at Stoke, Burslem, Middlewich and Leek, and were carriers to Chester and Ellesmere Port. The T&M had agents at Burton, Derby, Leicester, Middlewich, Nottingham, Rugeley, Runcorn Dock and Sandbach, and at Derby, Nottingham and South Staffordshire through Fellows, Morton & Clayton Ltd.

The NSR had its own boat yards at Etruria and Stone, and maintenance yards at Fradley, Stone, Etruria and Middlewich, and at Cheddleton on the Caldon Canal. There was a Canal Engineer who had his offices at Etruria and two Inspectors, one based at Etruria and the other at Fradley. There was one dredger, that worked between Lostock and Anderton, plus three steam tugs, which worked the Barnton, Saltersford and Preston Brook tunnels.

The flow of waterways traffic between the Potteries and Runcorn was facilitated by the Anderton Boat Lift near Northwich, which connected the two competing waterways that flowed through Cheshire, the Weaver Navigation and the T&M. The traffic using the lift declined during the LM&SR era by as much as two-thirds.

One of the issues left over at the time of Grouping was what action, if any, was needed to be taken to 'modernise' England's waterway system, following the recommendation of the 1905 Royal Commission on Canals & Inland Waterways that 30-ton narrow boats should be replaced with vessels carrying 100 tons of cargo, towed in trains of three. This strategic scheme was intended to secure improved navigation to the rivers Mersey, Humber and Trent. One key component of this was the intention to improve waterway communications between the Mersey and the Midlands, using a route following the Weaver Navigation to Northwich, continuing by the T&M, and then on to Wolverhampton via the Staffordshire & Worcestershire Canal and to Birmingham via the Fazeley Canal. The scheme was to cost £2,559,541 for the canal to Birmingham and £416,225 for the branch to Wolverhampton.

Shardlow was an important 18th century canal port, with all its associated wharves and warehouses, several of which still survive. Originally a river port, Shardlow developed greatly with the arrival in 1770 of the T&M, connecting it initially with the River Trent, followed by its opening throughout in 1777. Goods were transshipped here from river craft to canal craft. Subsequent development of the village saw the establishment of other businesses and the erection of further buildings to support the carriers, boat builders, ropewalks, workshops, stores, stables, offices, workers' cottages and owners' houses. With the arrival of the Midland Railway in the 1840s, the port went into decline although commercial activity linked to the canal, despite reducing, continued throughout the LM&SR era. This view of the original warehouse and the terminus of the T&M was taken circa 1950. The main building was erected in 1780 by the T&M and originally it bore the title 'NAVIGATION FROM THE TRENT TO THE MERSEY'. As built, it also housed a clock and was known to boatmen as the 'Clock Warehouse'. Like the T&M's other warehouse at Shardlow, it straddled a canal arm. In its later years, it served as a corn mill, one of two owned at Shardlow by F.E. Stevens. The building here looks very much the worse for wear. A variety of vessels can be seen in the foreground, with a canoe on the left, in the centre what appears to be an eccentric conversion of a Midland Railway clerestory carriage into a boat and on the right a small cruiser. *Nottingham Local Studies Library*

L M S

TRENT AND MERSEY CANAL

TRENT AND MERSEY CANAL
— Incorporated 1766 —

NEWCASTLE-UNDER-LYNE CANAL
— Incorporated 1795 —

Canal open for Navigation coloured Red

Continued on Sheet N° 1.

SANDBACH

TOP O'TH'HILL LOCKS
BETCHTON HEATH
DUBTHORNE

WHEELOCK
Snarkeys B⁴ N°156
Wheelock forge B⁴ N°155
River Wheelock

Malkin's Bank Upper Locks
Malkin's Bank Lower Locks
Hibberd's Locks
WHEELOCK LOCKS
BIDNER'S LOCKS
GARDEN LOCKS
Longcroft Locks
Ellison's Locks
HASSALL GREEN UPPER LOCK
HASSALL GREEN LOWER LOCKS
HASSALL GREEN
DEAN HILL
DAISY BANK
Roughwell Hall Farm

PIERPOINTS LOWER LOCK
PIERPOINTS UPPER LOCK
CHELLSHILL AQUEDUCT N°143
Thurlwood Farm
THURLWOOD LOWER LOCKS
THURLWOOD UPPER LOCKS
Rode Neath B⁴ N°140
RODE HEATH
Walkers B⁴ N°138
SNAPE'S AQUEDUCT N°138

C H E S H I R E

LOWER LOCKS
MIDDLE LOCKS (UPPER LOCKS)
LAWTON LOCKS
HALL'S LOCK
CHURCH LOWER LOCKS
CHURCH UPPER LOCKS
HALLGREEN
LAWTON GATE
LAWTON
ALSAGER
From Crewe
ALSAGER
Church B⁴ N°135
Red Bull B⁴ N°134
Red Bull Hall
RED BULL LOCKS
TOWNFIELD LOCKS
KENT'S LOCKS
YEW TREE LOCKS
Red Bull Aqueduct N°4
Hardingswood B⁴ N°133
HARDINGWOOD LOCKS
BUTT LANE
KIDSGROVE
HARECASTLE
From Audley

To Macclesfield
MACCLESFIELD CANAL
Hall Green Lock
Hall Green B⁴ N°7
Lawton
CHESHIRE
STAFFORDSHIRE
To Biddulph

KNYPERSLEY HALL
Knyper
KNYPE
BLACK BULL
Greenway Bank
Bridge over Spillway
BRINLEY FORD
RIDGEWAY

OLD TUNNEL (DISUSED)
NEW TUNNEL B⁴ N°131
HEAD-O-TH-LANE
HARECASTLE TUNNELS
GOLDENHILL
GOLDENHILL
RAVENSCLIFFE
PITTS HILL

CHATTERLEY
Turnover B⁴ N°130
TUNSTALL
Towpath Bridge
Tunstall B⁴ N°129
TUNSTALL
Peakes B⁴ (Private)
Brownhills B⁴ N°128
Top B⁴ N°127
Longport B⁴ N°126
LONGPORT
Porthill B⁴ N°125
Bridge Inn Footbridge N°2
Newport Lane B⁴ N°123
WOLSTANTON
Footbridge
Footbridge (Private)
BURSLEM
Burslem Turnover B⁴ N°122
COBRIDGE
Grange B⁴ N°121
Macaroni Foot B⁴ N°120
High B⁴ Shelton
Ry B⁴ Shelton Cᵒ
NORTHWOOD
Loop Line Ry B⁴
BURSLEM
SMALLTHORNE
FORD GREEN
NORTON IN THE MOORS
NORTON GREEN
ENGINE LOCK
Engine Lock B⁴ N°17
Daisy Bank B⁴
Downfield B⁴ N°18
Junction B⁴ N°17
MILTON
CARSIDE
Redhills B⁴ N°16
Abbey Rᵈ B⁴ N°15
ABBEY HULTON

From Market Drayton
SILVERDALE
GRANVILLES WEIR
Turnover B⁴
Lord Street B⁴ N°118
ETRURIA
ETRURIA CHECK LOCKS
Etruria Yard B⁴
JOHNSONS LOCKS
Newcastle Rd B⁴
TWYFORD LOCKS
COCKSHOTT LOCK
NEWCASTLE UNDER LYME
Etruria Drawbridge N°1
ETRURIA DOUBLE LOCKS
Russell B⁴ N°14
HANLEY
Ivy House
Ivy House B⁴ N°12
BUCKNALL
BUCKNALL & NORTHWOOD

STOKE BOTTOM LOCK
Stoke Road B⁴ N°114
Copeland St B⁴
CLOSED IN 1938
Abandoned by Stoke Corporation Act 1935
CLAYTON
Globe St B⁴ N°113
STOKE ON TRENT
Stoke Basin B⁴ N°111

Abandoned by N.S.Ry Act 1921

High St B⁴ N°112
T.Path B⁴
Footbridge
MOUNT PLEASANT
FENTON
TRENT VALE
Boothen B⁴ N°110
Sideway B⁴ N°109
Ry Bridge (Michelin Cᵒ)
LONGTON
HANFORD
Lyme Meadows B⁴ N°108
Aqueduct
TRENTHAM PARK
Aqueduct

Continued on Sheet 3
TRENTHAM

Maximum Size of Boats		
	Feet.	Ins.
Length	72	0
Width	7	0
Headroom	7	0
Draught	3	6
- on Caldon Branch	3	0

Level of water above Ordnance Datum shewn thus 408

— Scale — Approximately 2 inches to 1 mile —

T&M.C.   Sheet 2

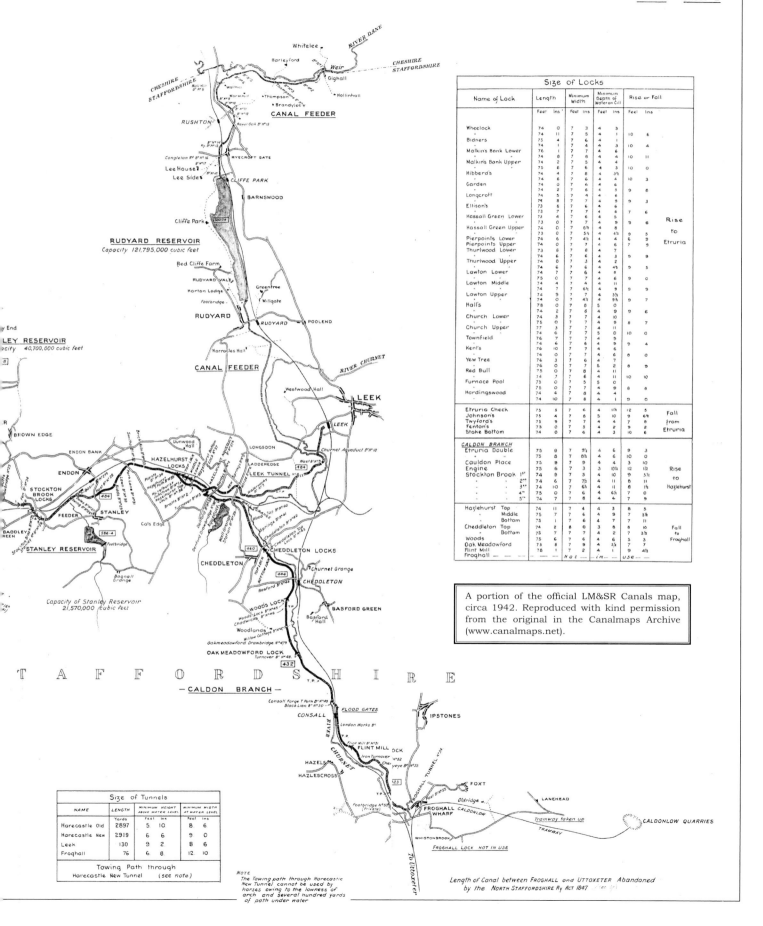

A portion of the official LM&SR Canals map, circa 1942. Reproduced with kind permission from the original in the Canalmaps Archive (www.canalmaps.net).

A delightful photograph of Stevens' other corn mill at Shardlow circa 1930, showing the Stevens' motor lorry in the centre being loaded with sacks of corn and a horse-drawn cart waiting with a load of baled hay. On the right can be seen the canal. The Stevens business in Shardlow was longstanding and he was also the local agent for the NSR (later LM&SR) wharf. *Shardlow Heritage Centre*

The initial focus of the Royal Commission recommendations was to be the improvements made to the navigation of the River Trent to Nottingham but no further consideration was paid to any other ideas because of the outbreak of War. After the First World War ended, the Ministry of Transport concluded that one scheme at a time should be proceeded with, the first being the Midlands to Mersey route referred to above. The cost of this was now estimated at £6,593,627 but the route was to bypass the T&M until Aston-by-Stone and then to make a new cut between Middlewich and Winsford to join the Weaver Navigation. This would involve the replacement of ninety-two locks by twenty-four lifts. Between 1923 and 1925, a group of local authorities, led by the County Borough of Stoke-on-Trent, unsuccessfully sought Government approval and financial assistance for a scheme between the Midlands and the Potteries that could accommodate 100-ton barges; there is no indication of any LM&SR interest in these proposals. A later 1943 scheme, which did not involve the T&M, was also not progressed.

During the LM&SR era, engineering work on the T&M Canal concentrated on four main areas of activity. First were the canal repairs linked to subsidence, since the T&M passed through areas where the extraction of coal took place (for example at Sideway and Etruria) and salt (*e.g.* at Rookery, Croxton, Middlewich and Wheelock); indeed, subsidence as a result of brine pumping at Sandbach forced the reconstruction in 1945 of Elton canal viaduct, at the considerable cost of £38,691. Secondly, there was the need to meet the requirements of incoming industrialists, who wished to extract water from and return water to the canal; these included Pirelli at Burton, Michelin Tyre at Burton, The India Rubber & Gutta Percha Telegraph Works at Burton, Stoke Corporation, and the British Soda Company at Elton (Sandbach). Thirdly, following the Road & Rail Traffic Act 1933, there was the need for bridge widening and reconstruction throughout the length of the T&M – for example, at Shardlow, Swarkestone, Willington, Middlewich, Croxton and Acton Bridge, and on the Caldon Canal at Milton.

Fourthly, following the passing of the Reservoirs (Safety Provisions) Act 1930, improvements were carried out at the Knypersley and Stanley reservoirs that fed into the Caldon Canal.

With the retirement of the NSR Canal Engineer in 1925, his replacement was designated Canal Engineering Assistant to the District Engineer. In 1925, he was provided with a motor bicycle and side car to inspect the canal system, superceded in 1943 by the provision of a 7hp motor car.

In 1942, the LM&SR carried out a major review of its canal operations, which took place as a result of the inheritance of a substantial network of canals from its constituent companies. For the most part, they had come into railway ownership during the railway boom of the mid-1840s, when companies formed to build railways bought them up, as a means of overcoming the likely opposition from canal proprietors to Bills before Parliament. The former NSR canals, of course, fell into that category.

Since the 1922-23 Grouping of the railways, the LM&SR had modernised its network during a period of economic recession, whilst fighting the growing threat of road competition through making cuts in both rail and canal provision. From 1918 to 1929, the recovery of traffic on the inland waterways after the war was hindered by the depression and the early stages of the development of the road transport system. The downward trend in traffic volumes reflected both the dominance of road transport and the economic depression. Whilst the pottery industry relied heavily on the movement of clay by canal from Runcorn (itself promoted as 'The Potteries Port') and the return working of crated pottery, services elsewhere on the T&M went into decline. For example, the carrying service by Gandy from Horninglow and Rugeley ceased in the mid-1930s, whilst that of Fellows, Morton & Clayton to London and Liverpool from Rugeley ceased circa 1930, though its service from Shardlow continued at least into the mid-1940s. The former NSR wharves at Lawton, Wheelock and Middlewich had all closed by 1939.

However, with the outbreak of the Second World War, the

Willington, just north of Burton, a location where the T&M runs parallel to the former Midland Railway main line to Yorkshire. These two interesting views of locomotive workings were both taken on Saturday 20th May 1933. Above, former Midland Railway Johnson/Deely 4-4-0 No. 1001 at the head of eleven coaches comprising the northbound 'Devonian', the crack Restaurant Car holiday express that ran between Kingswear/Paignton/Torquay and Leeds/Bradford. The second view, below, is looking north, with Beyer Garratt 2-6-0+0-6-2 No. 4985 at the head of a 99-wagon coal train from South Yorkshire. Built by Beyer, Peacock in 1930, it is seen here fitted with a 9-ton rotating bunker. The T&M can be seen on the left. *Both E.R. Morten*

Government sought to increase the use of the canal system and this led to the establishment of a Central Canal Committee. The Government appointed Frank Pick to report on the canal system and, as a result, the LM&SR decided to review the position of its canal system; because of Pick's death, this was concluded by Ashton Davies, LM&SR Vice-President. In the context of the Trent & Mersey system, its tonnage had fallen from 423,276 tons in 1930, to 300,735 tons in 1934, before decreasing further to 285,870 tons in 1938. Competition for through traffic with the railways was intense, whilst improved road transport competed with the waterways for short-distance traffic.

Tonnages carried between 1938 and 1947 were as follows:

Year	Tonnage
1938	285,870
1940	237,981
1941	236,846
1942	225,950
1943	240,056
1944	237,039
1945	198,136
1946	186,020
1947	155,866

Following on from this, the next table shows the increasing losses incurred by the Trent & Mersey Canal system between 1938 and 1941, the period covered by the Government review:

Year	Receipts £	Expenditure £	Net Deficit £	Tonnage
1938	27,478	40,081	12,603	285,870
1940	24,617	39,571	14,954	237,981
1941	24,939	41,890	16,951	236,486

The ensuing report recommended that nine LM&SR canals, or sections thereof, be abandoned and the Company saw this as a great opportunity to get rid of the liability of these unprofitable routes. One of the waterways that Davies recommended for abandonment was the Leek Canal, on which the annual traffic of 1,000 tons of tar from Leek to Milton had ceased in 1939. Under the LM&SR (Canals) Act of 21st December 1944, the Leek Canal was abandoned as unnecessary.

Ashton Davies also looked at the possible amalgamation of the T&M with the Shropshire Union Canal but could not see any operational or commercial advantage being obtained from such a merger. In the case of the T&M, its own commercial links were in the Potteries and the Engineer was located in Stoke, whilst the Shropshire Union's administration was located in Chester. Another option proposed, at the same time, centred on the possible advantage of the western canals of the L&NER – the Ashton, the Peak Forest and the Macclesfield – being taken over by the LM&SR. Davies found that there was no advantage to the national effort, nor commercially, for greater possibilities for traffic development, nor would the amalgamation of management enable staff economies to be effected. The long term decline in traffic over the T&M is reflected in the following table:

Year	Tonnage
1888	1,139,098
1898	1,215,140
1924	534,821
1930	423,276
1938	285,870
1946	186,020

Under the 1947 Transport Act, the T&M system, like most British canals, was taken over on 1st January 1948 by the British Transport Commission. Subsequently, with effect from 25th July 1948, the BTC transferred the functions of the T&M from the Railway Executive to the Docks & Inland Waterways Executive.

ABOVE: The basin at Horninglow Wharf, Burton-on-Trent, certainly has a derelict feel in this 1950 view looking towards Willington and Shardlow. The wharf was located about half a mile from the centre of Burton and, in earlier years, there was also an important warehouse located here for timber. However, as Burton and the breweries became more and more dependent on their extensive railway networks, the economic importance of the T&M diminished. Note the crane on the wharf, whilst the building straddling the canal on the right gives an indication of the 13ft 6ins width of the canal bridge holes from Derwent Mouth, near Shardlow, to Horninglow; the width of the T&M from here to Middlewich is 7ft 6ins. *C.A. Moreton*

RIGHT: Horninglow in the 1950s, the sign on the wall proclaiming this building to have been the salt warehouse of the North Staffordshire Railway, and promoting rock salt, agricultural salt and butter salt. It was located alongside the canal. The 'hump' is the former L&NWR bridge carrying the road over its Dallow Lane Branch. *Author's collection*

ASK FOR

MARSTON'S

FAMOUS

BURTON ALES

THE BREWERY
BURTON-ON-TRENT.

A fine aerial view, probably taken in the 1930s and looking south, showing the brewery of Marston, Thompson & Evershed Ltd at Burton-on-Trent. The T&M Canal can be seen running right across the top of the picture, with the branch railway serving Marston's brewery crossing over it by means of the bridge on the extreme left of the picture. The handsome archictecture of the main buildings should be noted; like many other breweries around the country, it was built in a distinctly Bavarian style, reflecting the popularity of so called Bavarian ales – what we know today as lager – as well as lending the business an 'authentic' air. Under the Marstons name, this brewery remains in operation today, producing the various Marstons beers, as well as draught Bass under licence. Just visible beyond the canal are the Shobnall Maltings of Wm Bass & Co. Ltd, to the right of which are the same company's Klondyke Sidings. Barely visible centre bottom are Allsopp's Shobnall Maltings, served by another branch of the extensive network of brewery railways which existed in Burton. This view was an advertising postcard, the reverse of which is reproduced inset right. *Author's collection*

LEFT: Fradley Junction looking west circa 1920, from a painting by Alan Firth, with the lock in the foreground. The junction with the Coventry Canal is to the left. Fradley was an important location for the T&M, which had a warehouse and maintenance yard there, as well as the famous pub, The Swan. One of two T&M Canal Inspectors was also based there. The LM&SR sold the pub and a nearby residential property in 1940 for £1,050. *Author's collection*

ABOVE: Stone was the headquarters of the Trent & Mersey, being a central location for the canal as a whole. This aerial view, looking east, was taken in the late 1920s. Across the centre of the picture from left to right, is a timber yard, warehouse, dry dock and boat building yard, and the canal maintenance yard. On the far right is the Star Lock and the Star Inn, whilst bottom centre can be seen the hospital. The cast milepost opposite the T&M offices below Star Lock is 46/46, Shardlow/Preston Brook. *Roy Lewis collection*

RIGHT: A rare postcard view from the late 1920s of the British Alabaster Bowl Company's works at Weston, where alabaster bowls were manufactured. It was located on an arm off the T&M (where previously there had been a salt works), as was its sister firm, the British Alabaster & Marble Co., stone carvers for ecclesiastical and domestic use. These works were established by 1925. In the left foreground can be seen a tennis court, presumably for the use of employees. *Author's collection*

British Alabaster Bowl Coy's Works, Weston, Stafford.

Stoke Basin had been an important location for commercial activity that pre-dated the coming of the railways. In the LM&SR era, the Head Office of The Anderton Carrying Company Ltd was in Wharf Street, whilst the Mersey Weaver & Ship Canal Carrying Co. Ltd operated out of Imperial Wharf, also on Wharf Street. Also based there during this period were Alliance Sanitary Earthenware Ltd, Tatton Bros Ltd (earthenware manufacturers), W. Vernon & Sons Ltd (flour millers); and John Aynsley (flint grinders). On Lytton Street were Earthenware Millers Ltd (potters' millers), and Smith & Jones (coopers).

ABOVE: These two views of Stoke Basin were probably taken in 1935 and are looking south. With the gasholder towering in the background, china clay is loaded on the wharf.

LEFT: A few yards further north, this busy scene shows china clay being barrowed off. This load has travelled from Runcorn Docks at Weston Point. *Both E.J.D. Warrilow, Keele University collection*

BELOW: Shelton Wharf at Stoke circa 1950, with the Salvation Army boat *Salvo* in the foreground. Behind is the long-established timber yard of F.G. Chambers. In the background can be seen the tall signal gantries of the Down and Up main lines and behind those are the bottle ovens of the Winton Pottery. *Author's collection*

RIGHT: An interesting picture, probably taken in the 1930s, which shows the off-loading of china clay into the canalside works of Thomas Twyford's Cliffe Vale Potteries, which were situated on the T&M a few hundred yards north of Stoke station. The narrowboat was owned by Potter & Son, coal and clay merchants of Runcorn, who operated a fleet of about thirty boats, the name of each one starting with the letter 'S'. The firm had traded at Runcorn since 1821 and commenced its carrying operations, of Gravesend flints, along with Newhaven and French boulder flints, from Runcorn and Weston Point docks to the Potteries around 1896. Potter's fleet numbers diminished sharply with the contraction of the canal carrying trade in the mid and late 1940s. This view is looking south towards the station, with the tall LM&SR signals clearly visible. Note the two compartments of the boat and also the wide towpath. *Author's collection*

MAIN PICTURE: A detailed aerial photograph, looking south and taken in 1943, which shows the Etruria Junction of the T&M and Caldon canals. Bottom left can be seen the white roofs of the two warehouses belonging to the Mersey Weaver & Ship Canal Carrying Co. at Weaver Wharf, across the canal from which is the Albion Foundry. Just above this and veering to the left is the start of the Caldon Canal, whilst the T&M heads straight on, with Stoke station in the distance. At the start of the Caldon there was a repair dock and wharves occupied by The Anderton Company, whilst between the canal and the road is the flint mill belonging to G. Mellor & Co. Ltd. As the Caldon climbs through double locks, the distinctive bottle ovens of Ridgway's Bedford Street Works can just be seen (indicated by the corner of the inset view). The canal then curves round to Hanley Park and the disused works of Cauldon Potteries Ltd can be made out (the site by this time was used for civil defence training). Looking south along the route of the T&M, the intense industrialisation along either side of the canal is clear. The Toll House, with its roof over the waterway, is visible at the junction, beyond which is the short arm serving the bone and flint mill of Jesse Shirley & Son. In the distance, just before the T&M Canal passes under the main line at Cockshott Lock, Cliffe Vale Potteries (Twyford's) is passed, to the right of which is the enlarged Cockshute Sidings. To the right of these sidings can be seen the three former NSR carriage sheds, with the Market Drayton line heading off picture, centre right. Beyond Cockshott are the enlarged sidings leading to Stoke Yard and on the far right is Etruria Gas Works. Incidentally, for anyone wondering what they might be missing, the inset picture hides a major blemish in the main photograph. *E.J.D. Warrilow, Keele University collection*

LEFT: Looking west towards Newcastle in 1946, with the spire of Hartshill church peeping out behind the Etruria gas holders. Foreground bottom is Etruria Hall, headquarters of the Shelton Iron, Coal & Steel Co. and immediately behind which can be seen the Loop Line, going from Etruria (right) to Hanley (left). Running across the centre of the picture is the T&M and the 1864 diversion through the works can be clearly seen. Behind this is the pottery works of Josiah Wedgwood & Sons Ltd, part of which had sunk below the level of the canal. By the date of this view, some of their manufacturing activities had migrated (in 1940) to the Barlaston Garden Factory and this site was sold to Shelton in 1943. Beyond the gas holders runs the NSR main line *E.J.D. Warrilow, Keele University collection*

BELOW: Just north of the elevated internal railway at Shelton Works, which connected with the NSR's Grange Branch, Anderton boat *Rose* No. 1097, registered at Runcorn in 1911 and re-registered at Stoke in 1939, cuts a lonely figure with its northwards cargo of coal as it negotiates the enormous slag banks on either side of the canal. The view dates from around 1930. *E.J.D. Warrilow, Keele University collection*

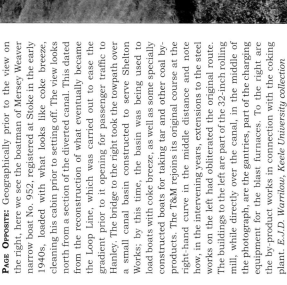

Copyright E.J.D. WARRILLOW HOCKEY.

PAGE OPPOSITE: Geographically prior to the view on the right, here we see the boatman of Mersey Weaver narrow boat No. 952, registered at Stoke in the early 1940s, loaded with what looks like coke breeze, cleaning his cabin prior to setting off. The view looks north from a section of the diverted canal. This dated from the reconstruction of what eventually became the Loop Line, which was carried out to ease the gradient prior to it opening for passenger traffic to Hanley. The bridge to the right took the towpath over a small canal basin constructed to serve Shelton Works; by this time, the basin was being used to load boats with coke breeze, as well as some specially constructed boats for taking tar and other coal by-products. The T&M rejoins its original course at the right-hand curve in the middle distance and note how, in the intervening years, extensions to the steel works on the left had obliterated the original route. The buildings to the left are part of the 32-inch rolling mill, while directly over the canal, in the middle of the photograph, are the gantries, part of the charging equipment for the blast furnaces. To the right are the by-product works in connection with the coking plant. *E.J.D. Warrilow, Keele University collection*

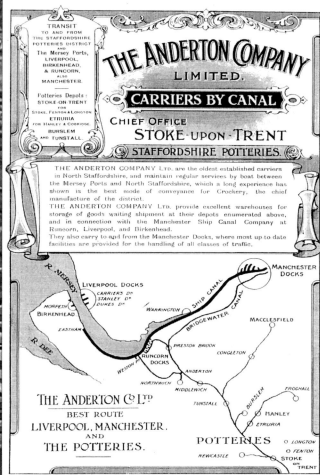

ABOVE: A 1920s advertisement for The Anderton Company Ltd, showing the routes they traded between the Potteries and the various docks at Manchester, Runcorn, Liverpool and Birkenhead. *Author's collection*

LEFT: This outstanding aerial photograph, taken in the late 1940s, shows the industrial complex of the Shelton Iron, Steel & Coal Company and of the surrounding area; the view is looking north-east towards Congleton. Forge Lane, Shelton, is bottom right, Smallthorne is top right, Newport Lane, Burslem, is top left, and Etruria is bottom left. The Trent & Mersey Canal can be seen coming in on the right, into the 1864 canal diversion (which allowed the easing of the Loop Line gradient) and it then snakes through the works, going from right centre and passing the 32-inch rolling mill on its left, beyond which on the left the canal passes the blast furnaces. The waterway then turns sharply left, passing under the 1916 private line from the former NSR Grange Branch Sidings into the works, with the Sinter plant adjacent to the sidings. The canal next passes the power station and makes an 'S' bend before, at the top of the photograph, the Burslem Canal departs to the left. Next comes two flint mills alongside Newport Lane, the one on the left belonging to Oliver & Son (Burslem) and the one on the right to the North Staffordshire Pulveriser Co. The top left of this picture corresponds with the bottom picture on page 119; the newly built Burslem Co-op Bakery can just be made out here. Two dirt tips of the former Racecourse Pit can be seen, top right, below which are the coking plant and the chemical by-products plant, with Etruria Hall just visible on the right. In the bottom third of the picture, from left to right, there is a slag mound, the NSR Loop Line between Etruria and Hanley, the hot metal mixer buildings, the slag recovery plant and the melting shop (steel furnaces) adjacent to the 32-inch mill. Finally, the Wedgwood Works appear in the angle of the Loop Line and the canal diversion, in the centre right foreground. *Photography courtesy The Potteries Museum & Art Gallery, Stoke-on-Trent*

There were two boatyards situated on this section of the Trent & Mersey. The first, the Mersey Weaver boatyard seen here, was located at the junction of the T&M and the Burslem Canal (Burslem Arm) and had probably been established in the early 1940s. In the background is the rising skyline of the town of Burslem, whilst the entrance to the short (660 yards) Burslem Canal can is on the far right. At this time, with the decline in traffic on the canal system, activity at the boatyard was concentrated on boat repairs. *Author's collection*

OPPOSITE PAGE BOTTOM: The section of the T&M which passed through from the Burslem Canal to Middleport and to Longport was extremely busy with industrial activity, both alongside and adjacent to the canal. There were numerous wharves and earthenware factories receiving raw materials and despatching crated pottery to all parts of the country. This aerial view of the Newport Lane area of Burslem, taken in the mid to late 1920s, is looking towards Furlong Lane at the terminus of the Burslem Canal. Running across the bottom is the T&M, left to Middleport and Longport, and right to Shelton. Centre left, alongside the canal, is the Royal Staffordshire earthenware works of A.J. Harrison, to the right of which is the Newport Pottery Company Works, where the famous Clarice Cliff pottery was manufactured. Bottom right, and also alongside the canal, is the flint mill of Oliver & Son (Burslem). Directly above this is the newly built bakery of the Burslem Industrial Co-operative Society, in front (on the far side) of which passes the Burslem Canal. Fronting on to this canal are Malkin Brothers, corn millers, then the warehouses formerly occupied by the Shropshire Union, leading to the terminus of the canal, the Anderton Wharf and, at the top, Trent & New Wharf Potteries and the tall chimney of Furlong Mills. Finally, running diagonally from top left to bottom right is Newport Lane, with its various potteries, tile works and flint millers. *Photography courtesy of The Potteries Museum & Art Gallery, Stoke-on-Trent*

LEFT: A rare view of the Burslem Canal or Arm in 1946, with the Bunn family aboard *Swan*, a narrowboat registered at Stoke. The vessel was owned by Potter & Son, referred to earlier. On the right is the warehouse built in 1880 for the Shropshire Union Railways & Carrying Company; when this company ceased carrying in 1921, the buildings and wharves passed to the Mersey Weaver & Ship Canal Carrying Co. Behind can be seen the separate clay wharves, whilst in the background is the actual terminus of the Burslem Arm, from where The Anderton Company traded. The bottle ovens on the left are part of the Lincoln Pottery of Samuel Ford & Co. (Burslem), whilst the bottle ovens to the right belong to the Trent & New Wharf Pottery of Wood & Sons Ltd. The single storey building facing on to the wharf is the 1843 Furlong Mills, which carried out flint-grinding and was owned by Alfred Meakin (Tunstall) Ltd. *David Salt collection*

ABOVE: A view of the Burslem Canal, looking north towards its terminus, with the former Shropshire Union Railways & Canal Company (owned by the L&NWR) warehouse in the centre; this building was taken over in the LM&SR era by Mersey Weaver. In the background is an open warehouse used for china clay and beyond that is the Anderton Wharf. The tall building on the left is a corn mill, which received supplies by the canal, as did the 'model bakery' of the Burslem Co-operative Society, which was located nearer the junction with the T&M. The bottle ovens behind the 'Shroppie' warehouse belong to the Dale Hall Pottery of Keeling & Co. Ltd and the road climbing to the right, towards the centre, was Navigation Road, which carried the 1805 Burslem tramroad to the centre of the town. *The Waterways Trust*

A few hundred yards further along the T&M towards Longport was to be found the second of the two boatyards, the distinctive facility of The Anderton Company at Middleport. This boatyard was established here in the 1890s but, by 1948, activity was concentrated on boat repairs. In the middle distance can be seen the tall Port Vale Mills (flour) belonging to Fitton & Pidduck and Pidduck Street Bridge over the canal. On the skyline in the right background is the dirt tip at Shelton. *Author's collection*

A 1940s aerial view, looking east, of the pottery factory of Burgess & Leigh. Across the centre of the photograph runs the T&M, which brought in the raw clay from Cornwall and along which were despatched the finished wares to Liverpool and Hull docks. This pottery was built in 1888 and had its entrance on Port Street, at the rear of the picture. Burgess & Leigh called their products Burleigh Ware, and a sign bearing this name appears on the roof of the main building, above the title Middleport Pottery. The Company manufactured general earthenware, as well as Jet and Rockingham pottery. The total area of the site was approximately 1½ acres and the factory was known locally as the 'Seven Oven Works', a nod to the fact that the pottery boasted four glost and three biscuit ovens. A Boulton & Son Lancashire boiler drove all the work's machinery. To the left of the pottery factory is the Colonial Wharf of Mersey Weaver and to the right the Anderton dockyard; bottom left can be seen a collection of allotments. *Burgess & Leigh Archives*

LEFT: Looking north along the Trent & Mersey Canal circa 1927, showing from right to left the T&M goods warehouse at Longport, the open air clay warehouse belonging to Mersey Weaver and then the other Mersey Weaver warehouses. On the right are piles of clay stone in front of Albion Pottery. In the background, in the centre, is the Top Bridge Pottery of Price Brothers, then the Keeling Pottery and lastly, on the skyline with their name painted at the top, the distinctive building of John Maddocks & Son Ltd, manufacturers of hotel tableware. *Author's collection*

RIGHT: A later view of the Mersey Weaver warehouses at Longport, with one of the buildings being supported by a new retaining wall. Moored alongside are a couple of Mersey Weaver boats, the nearest of which is *Empire*, built in 1926. *Author's collection*

BELOW: Just beyond Trubshawe Cross in the late 1920s with the former Longport Pottery, now occupied on the left by Thomas Hughes & Son Ltd and in the background by Arthur Wood & Son (Longport) Ltd. Note the rising towpath on the right as the canal veers to the left to Longport Wharf. *Author's collection*

The Pot Works, Stoke-on-Trent.

Harecastle Tunnels

The first canal tunnel at Harecastle was started in 1766, in connection with James Brindley's Grand Cross scheme to link the rivers Severn, Thames, Trent and Mersey. It took eleven years to construct and was probably the smallest but longest tunnel of its day, being only 9 feet 3 inches wide, 12 feet high and 2,897 yards long. There was no towing path and this meant one-way traffic only, with the boats being legged through.

The increased volume of traffic necessitated a second tunnel being built and this one, engineered by Thomas Telford, took three years to construct, opening in 1827. It was 14 feet in diameter, had a 5 foot wide towing path and was 2,926 yards long. Boats were allowed to use both tunnels, one for northbound and the other for southbound traffic. Settlement and roof falls lowered the headroom in both tunnels over the years. As a prelude to the closure of Brindley's tunnel in 1918, the NSR had taken Parliamentary powers in 1904 to operate an electric tug service through the tunnel and,

RIGHT: The electric tug in the Etruria dry dock circa 1948, towards the end of its working life. It was of bulk steel plate construction, with wooden fenders, and was 40 feet in length. On the deck were a deck house and two 5 foot drums powered by a pair of 15hp Royce electric motors, acting upon a 2 inch thick steel cable of 11 tons breaking strain. Note the wire rope laid on the bow and the spring loaded base of the trolley pole. *Author's collection*

BELOW: The southern end of the Harecastle Tunnels at Chatterley in 1931, a view looking south towards Stoke. Note the trolley poles for the electric tug on either side of the entrance, still awaiting wires to be connected. In the centre of the picture is one of the two battery accumulator boats that were attached to the tug, one being recharged whilst the other was operating. The storage batteries took the form of 115 chloride cells and weighed 18 tons, the cells being manufactured by the Chloride Electrical Storage Co. Ltd. The battery boats were 72 feet long and built at the NSR boatyard at Etruria. Recharging took place at a power station, seen here on a plot of land between the old and new tunnels, the canal being widened to accommodate boats alongside; the accumulator boats were dispensed with in 1931. *E.J.D. Warrilow, Keele University collection*

The same location about twenty years later, with the tug using the electric wires and towing a small train of boats. Note the timber baulks on either side to guide the boats into the tunnel. In the centre right background is the approach to Brindley's original tunnel and beyond is the NSR main line to Chatterley Junction and Stoke. *Bill Jack per Manifold collection*

in 1914, this tug service commenced through the Telford tunnel. By this means, up to thirty boats, each with a load of 20 tons, could be hauled through at a time, though in practice, fifteen to eighteen boats was the normal load. Traffic in the tunnel was worked at a speed of 2mph and there were six trains a day each way passing through. The method adopted was to provide a tug with an electric motor towing a boat with batteries, with the tug pulling its way through on a wire rope that was anchored at each end of the tunnel. By 1926, between 16,000 and 17,000 boats per annum were worked through each tunnel and estimates of the cost to repair the towpath under water amounted to £16,000.

The first tug was built at the Etruria dockyard in 1914 at a cost of £1,563 and in 1926 was described as being in poor condition. A second tug was built, at a cost of £1,359, in 1933, to allow maintenance work to be carried out on the first tug without disrupting the flow of traffic. When the batteries began to break down, it was decided to place an overhead tram wire through the tunnel, fit the tug with a pick up pole and work it as an electric tramcar. This was installed in 1931 and the two accumulator barges were dispensed with. The condition of the tunnel continued to deteriorate and, by 1942, the official LM&SR advice was that '*the towpath can not be used by horses owing to the lowness of the arch and several hundred yards of path under water.*' By 1950, there was a more severe warning: '*Towpath of the new tunnel is no longer usable having crumbled away in the centre. Subsidence has lowered the headroom and many craft can not use the waterway as they were constructed to pass under the statutory headroom and until repairs are affected some difficulties may arise in navigating the tunnel. Draught of the tunnel is given as 3ft only as many sections of the canal are in need of dredging.*'

The entrances to the two northern portals at Harecastle probably in the late 1940s, with Telford's tunnel on the left, and Brindley's original tunnel, by this date disused and inaccessible for traffic, on the right. The tug is about to enter the tunnel and the trolley pole is now positioned for the journey, with the wires clearly visible at the top of the picture. However, note the severe subsidence damage to the arch; closure could not have been far off when this picture was taken. The timber baulks for guiding the boats can again be clearly seen. *E.J.D. Warrilow, Keele University collection*

ABOVE: The canal at Harecastle in 1935, a view looking south, with the entrance to the new tunnel just visible on the left, beyond the railway bridge carrying the main line from Macclesfield to Stoke. This particular wharf was one of several on the T&M that connected the NSR (LM&SR) railway system with the canal; others included Cockshute Sidings (at Etruria) and Rookery Bridge (at Sandbach). Five boats, all owned by The Anderton Company, are waiting to be towed by the tug through Harecastle Tunnel. That second from the right bears the name *Daisy* (first registered in Runcorn in 1910), with the legend 'BRIDGEWATER NAVIGATION ROUTE'. Note in the centre the 5-ton crane located in the sidings of Harecastle station goods yard, behind which can be seen Harecastle Junction signal box. *E.J.D. Warrilow, Keele University collection*

Two tunnel tug tickets, Chatterley to Harecastle and Harecastle to Chatterley. *Author's collection*

LEFT: Wheelock looking north in the 1930s, with all the dereliction and waste of the former Wheelock Old Salt Works on the right-hand side. Many of the salt and chemical works between Sandbach and Middlewich had the advantage of being located on land between the T&M and the NSR Sandbach Branch and were served by wharves and railway sidings. The building in the background is the former Silk Mill. *Author's collection*

Left: This aerial view shows the flatness of the Cheshire Plain just south of Middlewich and also contains interesting detail of the salt and chemical industries here, which were served by both the T&M and by the former Northwich Branch of the L&NWR. The canal runs from bottom right to centre, whilst the railway runs from centre right to top left. In the centre of the picture is the Verdin-Cooke & Middlewich Salt Works, which later became Cerebos and then Rank Hovis McDougal. Behind this is the clutch of buildings that formed the Electrolytic Alkali Co., which opened in 1899 and closed in 1930. In the background can be seen the open salt pans of the 1887 Murgatroyd's Salt Works, whilst to the left of it, and just off the picture, is the Brunner Mond alkali works. In the top of the picture can be seen one of the many flashes in the area that were caused by subsidence arising from brine pumping. *Middlewich Canal & Salt Town Project*

Above: A busy scene just north of Middlewich circa 1930, looking north. In the centre of the picture is the alkali works of Brunner Mond, established here in 1892 as the Murgatroyd's Ammonia & Salt Syndicate to manufacture sodium carbonate; it was sold to Brunner Mond around 1894. Note the two boats tied up at the wharf in the centre, whilst on the far right are the railway sidings serving the works. In the background can be seen the King's Lock public house and the canal arm into the works. *Author's collection*

Right: A view of Middlewich looking south towards Sandbach in the 1930s, from the footbridge just south of Town Bridge. On the left and running parallel to the canal is the River Croco, behind which is the Brooks Lane Salt Works, established in 1889 and subsequently taken over by local salt manufacturer Henry Seddon. Beyond it, in the right background, is the Murgatroyd Salt Works, established in 1889, and owned by the Levinstein family after 1894. In the foreground on the right is the Wych House Lane Salt Works, established in 1892 and also owned by Henry Seddon. Immediately behind this is the brick entrance to the former Newton Salt Works, by this date demolished. *John Ryan collection*

Canal, River and Chemical Works, M...

MDH.I.

RIGHT: The original Town Bridge, Middlewich in 1929, shortly before rebuilding and looking north towards Lostock. On the left is Town Wharf and the River Croco is visible on the right. Beyond the bridge on the left is the Navigation Inn. *A.L. Earl collection*

BELOW: A major reconstruction of Town Bridge took place in 1929 and 1930, which involved its widening over the canal and the River Croco. This view of the reconstruction work also includes The Anderton Company's boat *Violet* on the right, moored at Town Wharf. The cost of this work was born by the local authority and amounted to £8,387. *A.L. Earl collection*

BELOW: An evocative scene on the T&M in the mid 1920s, showing a log jam of nine narrowboats queuing near the top of the Anderton Lift, either waiting to descend or having just ascended. Most of the boats are empty, bound perhaps for Runcorn to load material for the Potteries. Two of the boats are sheeted, however, indicating they are probably loaded with cargoes of pottery. The houses in the background were built by the NSR and are still there today. *Author's collection*

LEFT: Whereas most of the cargoes from the T&M would descend by the Anderton Lift, salt, from the various salt works at Middlewich belonging to Henry Seddon & Sons, would be unloaded by labourers in to handcarts. It was then barrowed across the wharf and tipped on to chutes which dropped it down straight in to the hold of a steam packet, moored on the Weaver Navigation below. It was hot and perspiring work, hence each member of the gang is wearing a neckerchief. *The Salt Museum Northwich*

BELOW: The Anderton Boat Lift in the 1930s, seen from the Brunner Mond works across the Weaver. The nearest point of these competing waterways, the Weaver and the T&M, was at the village of Anderton and for nearly 150 years, they co-operated in establishing facilities for exchanging traffic between them. The boat lift was built by the Trustees of the Weaver Navigation in 1875 and operated by them. The lift raised and lowered boats a height of 50ft 4ins by means of a hydraulic mechanism which used counter balancing caissons, that would each hold two narrow boats. However, the hydraulics suffered as a result of the briny nature of the local water, the salt ironically proving the lift's *raison d'etre* and greatest enemy. The hydraulics were replaced in 1908 by an electrically operated pulley and hoist system, supported, effectively, on a new lift built over the top of the old one. The site here in the 1930s was a shadow of its former self, with several of the salt warehouses and salt works on either side of the lift having closed and been demolished. Two of the salt chutes mentioned above can be seen on either side of the lift. On the left is the wharf belonging to The Anderton Company. The volume of traffic using the lift in the LM&SR era was a good barometer of waterways traffic. Recorded tonnage of cargo passing through was 97,805 tons in 1922, 112,596 tons in 1930, 74,153 tons in 1935, 45,025 tons in 1940, and 32,624 tons in 1947. Closed on safety grounds in 1983 and left to decay for nearly two decades, today the fully restored lift is now used by pleasure craft and a new visitor centre has been opened alongside. *Author's collection*

Anderton Lift.

ABOVE: A delightful 1930s postcard view of the Trent & Mersey Canal near Chute Bridge, Barnton. *Marston*, a member of the Mersey Weaver fleet, is seen about to pass Soot Wharf as it heads from Barnton towards the Anderton Lift. *Marston* was first registered at Stoke in January 1904 and was acquired from The Salt Union, a holding company established in 1888 for numerous salt companies throughout England. The boat is horse-drawn, the smoke presumably coming from the stove in the cabin. *Author's collection*

ABOVE: There were three canal tunnels between Anderton and Preston Brook: Barnton (572 yards long), Saltersford (424 yards long), and Preston Brook (1,239 yards long). The T&M was not required under statute to provide a towing service but there were good operational and commercial reasons for doing so and a steam tug was used for working boats through each of these tunnels. In the heyday, boats were worked in trains by the tugs, nine a day each way between the south end of Barnton Tunnel and the north end of Saltersford Tunnel, and through Preston Brook Tunnel. As traffic declined on the canal and as the tugs got older and in need of replacement, they were withdrawn from service, the first in 1943 and the second in 1944, until finally the tug service was withdrawn in July 1946. This is a view between Barnton and Saltersford tunnels, showing a steam tug at work. The leader of the tow is an Anderton boat and the second appears to be a Thomas Clayton tank boat. *The Waterways Trust*

The T&M terminates at the northern portal of Preston Brook Tunnel where, from here on, it becomes the Bridgewater Canal, shortly to split in two heading west to Runcorn and north-east to Manchester. This view, looking south, shows the toll keeper's cottage and the canal exiting the tunnel mouth. *The Waterways Trust*

TUG TICKET
NOT TRANSFERABLE
BARNTON To
SALTERSFORD
6D.
4627

Tug ticket Barnton to Saltersford. *Author's collection*

NSR HOTELS

The LM&SR inherited five hotels and pubs from the North Staffordshire Railway, as well as the Cliffe Park Estate at Rudyard. The Hotel Rudyard was sold in auction in August 1927 for £6,350, along with adjacent land holdings, whose ownership dated back to 1797 and the building of Rudyard Reservoir by the T&M. The nearby Cliffe Park Estate and Hall, acquired by the NSR in 1904 for leisure development purposes, remained in LM&SR ownership throughout their era, with the lease of the hall to the Youth Hostels Association eventually covering the period from 1933-1969. The Yew Tree Inn, at Caldon Low, purchased in 1922, was sold in July 1947 for £3,000 to Ind Coope & Allsopp, whilst the Bulls Head Inn, Hanley, continued to be leased to Worthington & Co. throughout the LM&SR period. The Churnet Valley Hotel, adjacent to Leek station, was sold in 1938.

The flagship hotel of the NSR was the North Stafford Hotel, which had been leased for a fourteen year period, from January 1919, to the Home Counties Public House Trust Ltd. During the end of that period, the Controller of LM&SR Hotels described it as: *'The worst hotel that I have visited during the past 10-15 years'*. This in turn triggered off a major review by the LM&SR Hotel & Catering Committee in June 1932, who felt that the annual receipts should be in the region of £30,000 and the annual working profit £5,000.

Approval was given in November 1932 for a major capital programme of refurbishment and modernisation, at a cost of £45,600. This programme consisted of a new restaurant, an attractive American bar near a new banqueting entrance, a new banqueting suite, a new ballroom, a new passenger lift and the complete modernisation of the eighty bedrooms, with all of them having central heating and running water. The lease was given up to the LM&SR on 5th January 1933, the hotel was temporarily closed on 29th July 1933 and was then officially reopened on 16th October 1933 with great ceremony. However, the subsequent trading results, whilst showing an improvement, did not reach expectations:

Year	Receipts £	Expenditure £	Profit/(Loss) £
1933	11,735	14,330	(2,595)
1934	18,479	19,723	(1,244)
1935-37 average	22,327	20,529	1,798

From 1933, the North Stafford was one of a group of thirty LM&SR hotels that were promoted nationally. The Company graded its hotels in three classes; the North Stafford was in Class II: *'of less extensive appointments than Class 1 but high-class accommodation for travellers and tourists and for local business needs.'*

Hotel Rudyard.

A 1924 postcard of the front of the Hotel Rudyard, whose origins went back to 1851, shortly after the opening in 1849 of the Churnet Valley line. Initially, the water bailiff's house had been used and subsequently there were several extensions, the last one prior to this photograph taking place in 1907, as the NSR sought to exploit commercially the attractions of Rudyard Lake as a tourist attraction. At that time, a top floor was added to provide additional accommodation and the facilities downstairs were enhanced, including the provision of a Chicago-style bar. *Author's collection*

TELEGRAMS:
"RELIABLE. STOKE-ON-TRENT."

TELEPHONE:
CENTRAL 1251.

North Stafford Hotel, Stoke-on-Trent.

LEFT: A North Staffordshire Railway 'official' postcard, published circa 1913, promoting the North Stafford Hotel. *Chris Knight collection*

BELOW: An LM&SR advertising leaflet of 1934, detailing the Company's hotels. The North Stafford Hotel is second from last in the England and Wales list. *Author's collection*

NORTH STAFFORD HOTEL

ONE OF THE LMS HOTELS

STOKE-ON-TRENT

ARTHUR TOWLE   CONTROLLER   LMS HOTEL SERVICES

...RAVEL ...EASY

...RVE YOUR SEAT

SEATS MAY BE RESERVED IN MANY

LMS

TRAINS ON THE FOLLOWING TERMS :—

SINGLE SEATS

1/=

(in addition to fare)

may be reserved at the Principal Stations (with certain exceptions) for passengers joining at the STARTING point of the trains, or the STARTING point of any Through Carriage running in connection therewith.

STAY AT
LMS HOTELS

ENGLAND AND WALES

LONDON (St. Pancras), N.W. 1 *Tel. : Midstel London.*	Midland Grand Hotel *Phone : 7000 Terminus*
LONDON (Euston), N.W. 1 *Tel. : Nearest London.*	Euston Hotel *Phone : 3000 Museum*
BIRMINGHAM (New Street Station) *Tel. : Bestotel Birmingham.*	Queen's Hotel *Phone : 2740 Midland*
BRADFORD *Tel. : Midstel Bradford.*	Midland Hotel *Phone : 4475 Bradford*
CREWE *Tel. : Bestotel Crewe.*	Crewe Arms Hotel *Phone : 2401 Crewe*
DERBY *Tel. : Midstel Derby.*	Midland Hotel *Phone : 994*
FURNESS ABBEY *Tel. : Hotel Furness Abbey Stn.*	Furness Abbey Hotel *Phone : 58 Barrow-in-F.*
HOLYHEAD *Tel. : Bestotel Holyhead.*	Station Hotel *Phone : 24 P.O.*
LEEDS *Tel. : Midstel Leeds.*	Queen's Hotel *Phone : 21501*
LIVERPOOL *Tel. : Midstel Liverpool.*	Liverpool Royal Exchange Hotel *Phone : 4400 Central*
LIVERPOOL (Exchange Station) *Tel. : Station Hotel Liverpool.*	Midland Hotel *Phone : 3440 Central*
MANCHESTER *Tel. : Midstel Manchester.*	Midland Hotel *Phone : 1994 Central*
MORECAMBE *Tel. : Midstel Morecambe.*	Park Hotel *Phone : 770*
PRESTON *Tel. : Bestotel Preston.*	North Stafford Hotel *Phone : 56026*
STOKE-ON-TRENT *Tel. : Midstel Stoke-on-Trent.*	Welcombe Hotel *Phone : 48581 Hanley.*
STRATFORD-UPON-AVON *Tel. : Welcombe Stratford.*	*Phone : 477*

SCOTLAND.

AYR *Tel. : Station Hotel Ayr.*	Station Hotel *Phone : 3268 and 3269*
DORNOCH* *Tel. : Dornoch Hotel Sutherland.*	Dornoch Hotel *Phone : 28*
DUMFRIES *Tel. : Station Hotel Dumfries.*	Station Hotel *Phone : 363 and 364*
EDINBURGH *Tel. : Luxury, Edinburgh.*	Caledonian Hotel *Phone : 25012 Edinburgh*
GLASGOW (Central Station) *Tel. : Lartrue Glasgow.*	Central Hotel *Phone : 9680 Central*
GLASGOW (St. Enoch) *Tel. : St. Enoch Hotel Glasgow.*	St. Enoch Hotel *Phone : 9310 Central*
GLENEAGLES * *Tel. : Gleneagles Hotel Perthshire.*	Gleneagles Hotel *Phone : 70 Auchterarder*
INVERNESS *Tel. : Station Hotel Inverness.*	Station Hotel *Phone : 267*
KYLE OF LOCHALSH* *Tel. : Kyle 2*	Station Hotel *Phone : Kyle 2*
STRATHPEFFER* *Tel. : Highland Hotel Strathpeffer.*	Highland Hotel *Phone : 27*
TURNBERRY *Tel. : Turnberry Hotel Ayrshire.*	Turnberry Hotel *Phone : Turnberry 2*

*—Open during Summer only.

IRELAND.

BELFAST *Tel. : Midstel Belfast.*	Midland Hotel *Phone : 4181 and 4182 Belfast*
LARNE † *Tel. : Midstel Larne.*	Laharna Hotel *Phone : Larne 28*
PORTRUSH ‡ *Tel. : Midstel Portrush.*	Northern Counties Hotel *Phone : Portrush 164*

†—Open June to September.
‡—Open Easter to September.

Tariffs and full information can be obtained at any of the Hotels, or for Hotels in England, Wales and Scotland, on application to Arthur Towle, Controller LMS Hotel Services, St. Pancras, London.

Fo der F 1 B   (E.R.O. 53392)   Printed in England by McCorquodale & Co., Ltd., London and Newton-le-Willows.

ABOVE: The striking art deco poster issued in October 1933 promoting the recently refurbished and re-opened North Stafford Hotel, now back under the management of the LM&SR. *Chris Knight collection*

LMS
HOTEL
SERVICES

RIGHT: The promotional official postcard published in 1934 promoting the North Stafford Hotel as '*The latest LMS Hotel*'. *Author's collection*

NORTH STAFFORD HOTEL
STOKE-ON-TRENT

THE LATEST
L.M.S. HOTEL

The changing style offered by the North Stafford Hotel is reflected in this selection of contrasting photographs. Those on the left were taken circa 1920, around the time the Home Counties Public House Trust entered into its lease with the NSR; those on the right were taken at the end of the substantial LM&SR refurbishment scheme in 1933. **Top:** A bedroom; **Centre:** The dining room; **Bottom:** The reading room/lounge. **Bottom Right:** Brochure cover. **Left:** *All National Monuments Record;* **Right:** *All author's collection*

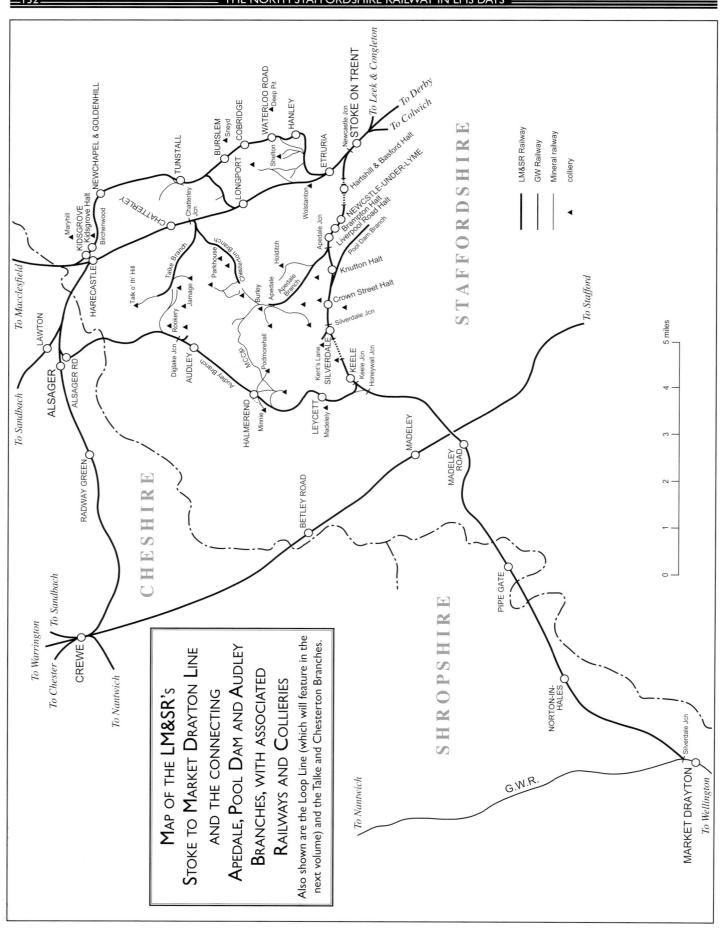

MAP OF THE LM&SR's STOKE TO MARKET DRAYTON LINE AND THE CONNECTING APEDALE, POOL DAM AND AUDLEY BRANCHES, WITH ASSOCIATED RAILWAYS AND COLLIERIES

Also shown are the Loop Line (which will feature in the next volume) and the Talke and Chesterton Branches.

7
The MARKET DRAYTON LINE and CONNECTING BRANCHES

The North Staffordshire Railway line from Stoke (Newcastle Junction) to Market Drayton (Silverdale Junction) was one of strategic importance to the Company for two main reasons. Firstly, it provided a link to the Great Western Railway network at Market Drayton, and beyond to Shrewsbury and the Welsh Borders; secondly, it was a spine route from which lines were built to connect to the vast coal and ironstone reserves of the western section of the North Staffordshire coalfield, specifically the Madeley/Leycett district and the Audley/Harecastle district.

The line to Market Drayton had a very mixed parentage. The first section to Knutton (just west of Newcastle) opened in September 1852, with a branch to Apedale, where extensive coal and iron workings and furnaces existed. The NSR leased the Newcastle to Silverdale Railway in 1863, from the Sneyd family. This was a private line which, from 1854, connected the Newcastle-under-Lyme Canal to Silverdale Colliery and Ironworks. Finally, the last section consisted of the NSR line from Silverdale to Market Drayton, which opened in February 1870. Running off this route, the important branch line to Apedale opened in July 1853 and that from Keele Junction to Alsager Junction (the Audley line) in July 1870. The railway to Market Drayton was 16 miles 336 yards long and, once it had left

coal and ironstone areas, it passed through sparsely populated agricultural country. The line was on climbing gradients of 1 in 102, 1 in 82 and 1 in 104 to Keele, and then on falling gradients of 1 in 126 and 1 in 84 to Madeley, before a steady descent from Pipe Gate to Market Drayton. There were three long tunnels, at Newcastle (650 yards), Silverdale (686 yards) and Keele (316 yards), as well as two very short tunnels at Newcastle and Keele.

Inevitably, the bulk of the traffic between Stoke and these branch lines was mineral traffic – on the Apedale Branch, for the Midland Coal, Coke & Iron Company Ltd, Burley, and Brymbo/Holditch collieries, whilst on the Audley lines west of Silverdale, it went from and to the numerous collieries and small pit villages such as Leycett, Halmerend and Audley.

In the LM&SR era, the branch line to Market Drayton reflected, in a microcosm, what was happening on the LM&SR system as a whole – reductions in passenger and goods services on branch lines, the need to reduce operating costs through station closures, through line singling, through rationalisation of signalling and through the closure of engine sheds, and from competition from the expansion of bus services. On a more positive note, the introduction of the Country Lorry Services for Farms and Villages

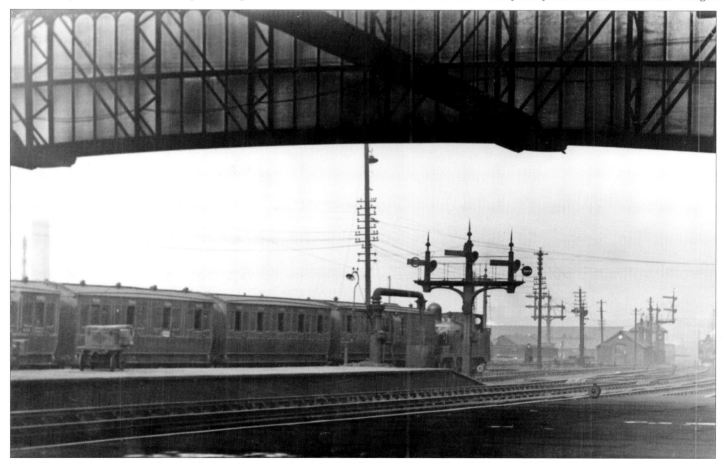

The Newcastle bay at the north end of Stoke station, sometime in the late 1920s, with an unidentified former 'D' Class waiting to depart with a rake of old NSR 4-wheeled and 6-wheeled carriage stock on a working to Market Drayton. What an evocative NSR scene this makes, before the creeping effects of the LM&SR era had begun to make its impact – the NSR water column, a fine array of signals and, in the background, Stoke North Outlet signal box, with an unidentified former 'B' Class locomotive alongside, on the very edge of the picture. *Author's collection*

LEFT: In the early evening of 11th July 1932, former L&NWR 'Precedent' Class 2-4-0 No. 5011 *Director*, off Rugby shed, is leaving for Market Drayton with the evening milk empties train; the locomotive will return with the milk train for Rugby. This working to and from Rugby, introduced at the start of the LM&SR era, lasted through until the late 1930s, before falling victim to the national decline in rail-borne milk traffic. At the time of the photograph, the locomotive was the regular pilot from Rugby for 'The Mancunian', the crack mid-afternoon express from London to Manchester. *Gordon Walwyn*

BELOW: Looking west towards Newcastle circa 1944, as Stanier 2-6-2T No. 156 approaches Newcastle Junction with a mineral train from the Audley line. This locomotive was allocated to Stoke shed in November 1937 as part of the roll out of the class from 1935 onwards. At the time of Nationalisation, it was still in the North Staffordshire Section, at Uttoxeter. *John Birchenough*

in 1928, and of the Town Cartage scheme in 1932, brought the benefits of the railway to a much wider community.

The impact of the Second World War resulted in declining output from collieries as men were diverted to the armed forces. However, there were also numerous Unadvertised Workmen's Trains, which took male workers to the construction of Ordnance Factories at Swynnerton, near Stone, and Ford Houses, near Wolverhampton, and subsequently, male and female workers to Cold Meece, the newly built LM&SR station for Swynnerton.

At the time of Grouping, there were seven passenger trains daily each way between Stoke and Market Drayton, with extra trains on Saturdays and Wednesdays, eleven shuttle trains daily between Stoke and Newcastle, with extra trains on Saturdays, and seven trains daily to Silverdale plus an extra train on Saturday. In addition, there were three trains via the Audley line to Halmerend and three to Harecastle, with extra trains on Saturdays. All in all, parts of the line were very busy at that time. The only surviving rail motor workings on the line were two trains each way on Sundays between Stoke and Newcastle, in the late afternoon and early evening; these workings ceased in the spring of 1923. In 1935, there were five passenger trains daily each way between Market Drayton and Stoke.

At Grouping, freight duties between Stoke and Market Drayton

were performed by the heavier NSR 0-6-0 goods locomotives, the 'E' Class, the '159' Class and the '100' Class; down to the mid-1930s, these were increasingly replaced by the 'New L' Class and after that by the 2-6-4Ts. The passenger locomotives used for many years were the NSR 'A' and 'B' classes, until they were mostly withdrawn in the late 1920s and early 1930s; they were followed by Stanier 2-6-4Ts and 2-6-2Ts. There was a gradual reduction in locomotive allocations to the NSR Market Drayton shed, which had three engines in 1912 (six loco men), two in 1925 and none by 1929. At the time of Grouping, the freight workings totalled three between Stoke and Market Drayton, a Stoke to Wellington and a GWR Stoke to Coleham working, along with shorter trips from Stoke to Brampton and to Silverdale. The workings from Stoke to Shrewsbury and to Coleham ceased after Grouping. By 1924, a milk train empties service from Rugby to Market Drayton had been started; the return working in 1928 called to collect milk at Pipe Gate, Keele, and Newcastle but only called at Pipe Gate by 1934, serving the newly erected dairy of Henry Edwards & Son Ltd. This train continued until the late 1930s. In 1935, there were only three goods trains each way. The 1938 local trip and shunting engines roster comprised Class '4F' 0-6-0s for Stoke Yard to Hartshill workings, and 2-6-2Ts and 2-6-4Ts for Market Drayton to Silverdale, Brampton, and Stoke goods workings. Although the Market Drayton NSR engine shed was formally closed

Bird's Eye View of the Potteries.

ABOVE: In the first of two views looking east across the Vale of Trent in the late 1940s, St. John's Church, Hanley, is prominent in the centre background, whilst numerous banks of bottle ovens can be seen on the left. The line from Stoke to Newcastle can be seen running across the centre of the picture and the three Cockshute carriage sheds are immediately behind, beyond which is the main line and marshalling yards. *Author's collection*

BELOW: Looking from above Hartshill Sidings with the Hartshill Brick & Tile Works, whose siding dated back to 1872, in the foreground. The vast Shelton Iron, Steel & Coal Co. Works is in the background and Etruria Gas Works can be seen on the right. The Market Drayton line is just to the right of and behind the photographer and where it passes here was the site of Hartshill & Basford Halt, located 1,100 yards west of Newcastle Junction, opened in 1905 and closed in 1926. Immediately beyond the tile works is Shelton New Road. *Author's collection*

LEFT: An NSR ticket for Stoke to Hartshill & Basford Halt, issued on 24th January 1923. *David Geldart collection*

N.S.R.—THIRD CLASS.
Available by Rail Motor only
STOKE-ON-TRENT To
HARTSHILL & BASFORD HALT
Available for one journey on day of issue only
Turn over Hart^l & B. 72 Fare 2d.

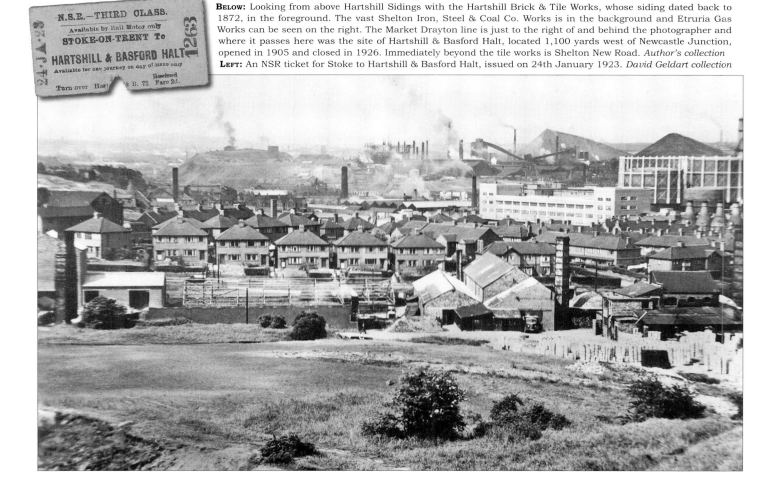

The Stoke to Market Drayton train in the early 1930s, picking up the tablet at Harts Hill signal box (note the two word spelling); this permitted access to the single line between here and Newcastle station. The train is headed by former 'New L' Class 0-6-2T No. 48, now LM&SR No. 2273. This engine, which was not yet ten years old when seen here, was in the last batch of locomotives to be built at Stoke Works early in 1923; it was withdrawn from service in February 1937. The box controlled Hartshill Sidings and the connection in to the brick works (previous page) is just behind the engine, whilst in the background is smoke from Shelton Works. The location of the (closed) halt and the entrance to the tunnel was a few yards behind the photographer. Around this time, additional siding accommodation was provided here for Unaphalt (Granite) Ltd. *E.J.D. Warrilow, Keele University collection*

on 27th April 1931, demolition was not finally approved until January 1937 and was eventually carried out for a mere £41.

In line with the LM&SR policy of closing little used country stations, especially where replacement bus services were available, Madeley Road station was closed with effect from 20th July 1931. This station only handled passenger traffic and there had been a decline in recent years; bus competition from Crosville Motor Services (initially partially owned by the LM&SR) had made the viability of the station worse. Savings from Madeley Road's closure amounted to a mere £92 pa.

Again, in line with the policy of cost reduction, the LM&SR Traffic Committee approved the conversion to single track of the double track line from Silverdale Junction at Market Drayton to Silverdale and along the Audley Branch from Keele Junction to Alsager Road. The cost of these works was estimated at £6,639, with estimated annual savings of £3,882 but, in the event, the actual costs amounted to only £1,084, mainly as a result of increased income from the recovery of materials. There were two block sections, Silverdale to Pipe Gate (approximately seven miles) and Pipe Gate to Silverdale Junction (about five miles), with a passing loop at Pipe Gate and a new LM&SR-style signal box at Silverdale.

The availability of Workmen's tickets on the branch was initially determined by the existence of several halts, introduced in May 1905 along with the Beyer, Peacock-built rail motors, to enable the NSR to maintain its share of Workmen's traffic in the face of bus and tram competition. The halts, sometimes located only a few hundred yards from each other, were designed to accommodate a single coach and most were sited on this branch. The first of these to close (and on the NSR network) was Basford Halt on 2nd April 1923, to be followed by Knutton Halt and Hartshill & Brampton Halt on 26th September 1926 (the Knutton Manor Mining Co. Ltd, employing 135 people, closed around the same time). Both Crown Street Halt and Liverpool Road Halt lasted into BR days. Unlike the rest of the NSR network, the availability of Weekly Workmen's tickets to other locations was considerable – from Hartshill, Newcastle, Brampton, Liverpool Road, Knutton, Crown Street, Silverdale and Keele to numerous destinations. There was also limited availability of Workmen's Daily tickets to Newcastle from Fenton, Longton, Meir, Hanley and Stoke. This pattern remained largely unchanged in 1924 but had expanded by March 1929, with tickets available from Market Drayton to Norton-in-Hales and from Pipe Gate to Silverdale. There was the widespread introduction by 1929 of Workmen's Daily tickets, available from Newcastle to eleven destinations, from Silverdale to nine destinations and from Keele to three destinations.

The Second World War saw the introduction of Unadvertised Workmen's trains, taking workers to and from munitions factories and other factories engaged on munitions work. By October 1941, there were three trains daily and two on Sunday from Silverdale to Cold Meece, one to Norton Bridge and Badnall Wharf (for construction traffic for Cold Meece Royal Ordnance Factory) and another to Ford Houses (north of Wolverhampton) for construction traffic. The Workmen's traffic for the construction phases ceased at both factories in 1942 and thereafter such services continued only to Cold Meece throughout the war. It operated on a reduced scale in October 1947, when there was just one Workmen's train daily from Silverdale to Cold Meece, and none on Sunday.

In the autumn of 1943, as part of the war effort, the British Thomson-Houston Co. Ltd, electrical engineers, opened a factory at Milehouse Lane, Newcastle, and this was served by a short spur off the line at Apedale Junction.

The LM&SR Town Cartage scheme, for collecting and delivering goods and parcels, was introduced in 1932, with Stoke goods depot serving Hartshill, and with Newcastle goods depot serving Chesterton and Basford. The Stoke arrangements continued through until 1939 (the latest date for which information is available) but the service from Newcastle depot expanded to Silverdale, Westlands, May Bank, Knutton and Cross Heath in 1935, and further to Clayton and Seabridge in 1938. Villages served in 1939 by LM&SR Country Lorry Services included Butterton, Scott Hay, Mucklestone, Woore and Betton.

RIGHT: Looking west at the short section between the two tunnels required to pierce the hill between Stoke and Newcastle, one 96 yards long and the other 650 yards. Note the steep slopes to the cutting, which needed regular repair in order to prevent slippage. In the late 1920s, major repairs to the longer tunnel were required in the form of 110 yards of substantial cast iron lining to the brick work, at an estimated cost of £18,000. This remedial work necessitated the line being closed for many months, finally reopening in February 1930. The concrete retaining wall, seen here on the right, was completed at the same time. *Author's collection*

BELOW: Newcastle station in 1952 looking towards Stoke. The main station buildings are on the right and the signal box is also on the platform on the right-hand side. In the background, the line becomes single for the section through the two tunnels until Hartshill. *Newcastle Museum Archives*

INSET ABOVE: LM&SR Workman's ticket, Newcastle-Stoke. *Author's collection*
RIGHT: NSR tickets issued at Newcastle for journeys to Stafford and Stoke on 15th and 19th January 1923 respectively. *David Geldart collection*

LEFT: Brampton Siding signal box in the 1930s, looking south with Enderley Street behind. There was a halt at this location between May 1905 and April 1923. Indeed, it was the first NSR passenger station to be closed in the LM&SR era, albeit before the formal legal ownership of the NSR had passed to the LM&SR on 1st July 1923. The halt, opened as part of the rail motor service established between Trentham and Silverdale, was located 418 yards west of Newcastle station and 396 yards east of Liverpool Road Halt. There were extensive sidings at Brampton (coal) Wharf to the right, off picture. In pre-Grouping days, there was a daily goods service between here and Stoke. In 1930, numerous goods and mineral trains stopped here, including three from Market Drayton and two mineral trains from Leycett, and there was a return working to Pool Dam. In 1945, two mineral trains from Holditch Colliery called here, as well as the Pool Dam working. The Madeley Coal Coke & Brick Co. Ltd traded out of Brampton Wharf in the late 1920s and the Shelton Iron, Steel & Coal Co. Ltd in later years. *Author's collection*

LEFT: Liverpool Road Halt, seen here on 13th June 1953, was also opened in May 1905 and, because of its proximity to Enderly Mills (army clothing manufacturers), was able to sustain a Workmen's railway service for many years, before finally closing on 2nd March 1964. The short length of the platform was intended to accommodate the coach of the rail motor and served trains to Market Drayton. Note the modest and crude waiting shelter. *F.W. Shuttleworth* **INSET:** An LM&SR Stoke to Liverpool Road Third Class ticket. *Author's collection*

BELOW: Apedale Junction looking west to Silverdale in 1964. In the centre is the line to Market Drayton and, in the fork with the Apedale Branch, can be seen the hip roofed McKenzie & Holland signal box. The line off to the right is the Second World War siding leading to the British Thomson-Houston Works. *Newcastle Museum Archives*

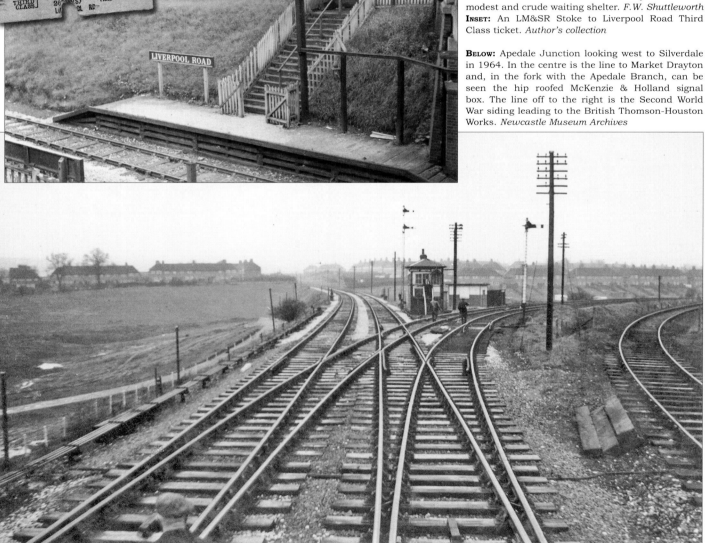

LIVERPOOL ROAD

L. M. & S. R.

STOKE TO LIVERPOOL ROAD

THIRD CLASS   FARE -/4

The Apedale Branch

The Apedale Branch was one mile 1,012 yards long at the time of Grouping. It had opened in November 1853 and was built to connect Apedale Ironworks and Burley Pit with the Newcastle to Silverdale railway at Apedale Junction, 1,327 yards west of Newcastle station. The Midland Coal, Coke & Iron Co. Ltd acquired Apedale Ironworks in 1890. Originally with six blast furnaces but latterly four, it dominated the Apedale Valley. In this area, the company operated 82 coke ovens, a power station, a by-product recovery plant and several collieries. In 1923, Burley Pit employed 976, the footrail at Apedale 387, and the Podmorehall, Minnie and Halmerend pits 570. However, this vast complex was a victim of the depression of the mid and late 1920s, and, following the appointment of a receiver in November 1929, the entire plant was purchased by Thomas W. Ward Ltd, scrap merchants, with iron manufacturing and coal extraction ceasing in April 1930.

Freight traffic to and from MCC&I reflected the level of that company's activity. At the time of Grouping, there were four goods trains daily each way. In addition, MCC&I had running powers for its engine over nearby NSR lines, and there was one goods train daily each way between Apedale and Newcastle, and also one between Apedale and Knutton daily each way. To all intents and purposes, goods traffic ceased in 1930 with the liquidation of MCC&I and its acquisition by Ward. In 1932, the NSR siding agreement with Apedale & Tar Macadam Ltd was transferred to Tarmac, whilst Ward assumed responsibility for the numerous sidings worked by MCC&I. The 1938 trip workings show that '4F' 0-6-0s and 2-6-2Ts worked the Apedale Branch.

The MCC&I also worked three passenger ('Paddy') trains for its employees between Halmerend station, on the Audley Branch and Newcastle, via the MCC&I private line and the NSR Apedale Branch. This train, nicknamed 'The Nigger', made three return workings each day; it ceased to run on 19th July 1926.

The other significant user of the Apedale Branch was Holditch Colliery. Shafts for coal and ironstone were sunk by the Brymbo Steel Co. Ltd just before the First World War, on land leased from Ralph Seedy, and a half mile spur off the Apedale Branch was completed in the autumn of 1919. The colliery became a subsidiary of the Shelton Iron, Steel & Coal Co. Ltd. From very modest beginnings, employment increased from 53 in 1923, to 565 in 1928, 810 in 1938 and to 1,485 in 1946. It was worked initially as an ironstone mine but coal output increased from 84,756 tons in 1930 to 552,938 tons in 1940. In 1947, at the time of the handover to the National Coal Board, coal output amounted to 403,632 tons. NSR and, later, LM&SR locomotives carried out shunting duties at the colliery. At the time of the Grouping, there was one mineral train daily from the colliery to Stoke. In 1930, there were four daily trains to Newcastle Junction and in 1945 there were two daily to Stoke and one to Ford Green for the Norton Ironworks.

ABOVE: The MCC&I Company operations only lasted seven years into the LM&SR era and these photographs reflect different aspects of those final years. This view of MCC&I Co. wagons dates from 1930, at the time of liquidation and is taken from the sale catalogue of Thomas W. Ward Ltd. The wagons carry the instructions 'EMPTY TO APEDALE LMS (N.S. SECTION)'. *Allan Baker collection*

LEFT: Burley Pit at Apedale after its closure in 1930. This view is looking down the route of the rope-hauled narrow gauge tubway from Watermills Colliery to Burley, which served the Burley screens but which had been lifted some years prior. The pit was one of many owned by the MCC&I Co. in the Apedale and Halmerend areas; these between them in 1929 employed 1,729 above and 497 below ground, and produced 600,000 tons of coal annually. *Bill Jack*

ABOVE LEFT: A closer study of the headframe at Burley Pit taken around the same time.

ABOVE: Manning Wardle 0-6-0ST *Podmore* (Works No. 870) arrived new at Silverdale Ironworks in 1883 but was later sold to the MCC&I, probably in 1902 when Silverdale closed. The engine is seen here circa 1925 at the Burley screens. Along with seven other MCC&I engines, it was sold to Thos W. Ward Ltd following the company's liquidation in 1930. *David Dyble collection*

RIGHT: *Audley* was another Manning Wardle 0-6-0ST (Works No. 542) which went new to Silverdale in 1875. The Apedale Slag & Tar Macadam Co. Ltd, which had close working relationships with MCC&I, operated a slag reduction plant at the Apedale Ironworks from 1920. This engine was transferred over from Thos Ward to Apedale S&TM Co. in the summer of 1930, following the MCC&I closure. Scrapped in March 1937, it is seen here on shunting duties at the slag plant, with some of the firm's private owner wagons in the background. *Author's collection*

LEFT: An aerial view of Holditch Colliery on 2nd July 1937, showing some of the activity following a series of two underground explosions in which 30 lives were lost. This disaster was one of the worst in the North Staffordshire coalfield in the 20th century and was doubly tragic, as a number of lives lost in the second explosion were of the rescue party. They included Mr John Cocks, Joint Managing Director and Mining Director of its owners, the Shelton Iron, Steel & Coal Co. Ltd. The left-hand headgear is the downcast shaft, whilst that on the right is the upcast one, the coal drawing shaft. Note the new screening plant under construction to the extreme left and the locomotive shed in the middle foreground. *The Sentinel Newspaper Group*

The Pool Dam Branch

With the consolidation of the railway system following the opening of the line from Silverdale to Market Drayton, the short spur from Newcastle (Brook Lane) to Knutton Junction (a one mile 638 yards long single goods line) became known as the Pool Dam Branch. Pre-Grouping workings consisted of a mineral train from Silverdale to Pool Dam and a goods working from Pool Dam to Stoke. There was also the use of the line from Silverdale to Canal Wharf (Brook Lane) by Shelton locomotives and men (a practice that continued well into the LM&SR era) and of the use of the line from Apedale to Canal Wharf by the Midland Coal, Coke & Iron Co. Ltd but this latter use did not last long into LM&SR days.

The Knutton Iron & Steel Co. Ltd, wholly owned by the Midland Company, owned and worked Knutton Ironworks and forge, which was accessed from this branch as well as the Stoke to Market Drayton line. With the closure of this works in 1931, the LM&SR entered into an agreement with John Cashmore & Co. Ltd in April 1932 for a siding at Pool Dam, which enabled Cashmores to remove slag from the ironworks site; this was a new facility which replaced the original ironworks siding. Trip working in 1938 consisted of one freight working each way daily and this lasted throughout the LM&SR period; the working was performed by a 2-6-4T. Newcastle Gas Works had a siding and there was a succession of coal merchants at Pool Dam, such as Enoch Delves and the Silverdale Equitable Co-operative Society, and also at Brook Lane, including Lew Timmis, Margaret Meaden and Berry Hill Collieries. The Penmaenmawr & Trinidad Lake Asphalt Co. Ltd also traded from Brook Lane.

Above: The Pool Dam Branch in July 1927, a view looking towards Knutton. Note the absence of crossing gates on the wide Blackfriars Road, although the post on the left suggests that gates had been provided here at one stage. *Manifold collection*

Left: A view taken further along the branch in the late 1940s, looking towards the terminus and showing the gas holder and buildings of Newcastle-under-Lyme Corporation Gas Works behind the fencing on the left. *Author's collection*

Right: Brook Lane Wharf at Newcastle, the termination of the Canal Extension Railway on 4th May 1956. The Newcastle-under-Lyme Canal was to the far left, behind the concrete posts and wire fence. *Author's collection*

This view southwards, taken from the gas holder of Newcastle-under-Lyme Corporation Gas Works in the mid or late 1930s, is looking towards Brook Lane and the terminus of the Pool Dam Branch. The main buildings belong to the gas works, as well as the siding and headshunt bottom left. In the background, where the sidings finish was the site of the terminus of the Newcastle-under-Lyme Canal, whilst on the right is Lyme Brook, to the right of which are the new buildings of Priory Garage. This was the base for the Princess Bus Services operated by Thomas Duggins, who ran stage services to Silverdale; a bus can just be seen to the right of the garage. Also on the right is the Pool Dam Branch and the gated level crossing protected the approach to Brook Lane. This line was the original, half mile long, 1854 Newcastle Canal Extension Railway from the canal to Pool Dam, the start of the private line to the Silverdale Colliery and Ironworks. *Author's collection*

The Newcastle-under-Lyme Canal

The coming of the railways from the 1850s onwards in the Newcastle area led to the four-mile long Newcastle-under-Lyme Canal losing its economic and industrial importance. This canal was established through an Act of Parliament in 1797; it was never owned by the NSR but, under the Newcastle-under-Lyme Canal Act 1864, the NSR leased it, paying a perpetual rent and this requirement continued right through the LM&SR era. In the early part of the 20th century, there was very little canal traffic but what existed was carried over a short section from its connection with the T&M at Stoke. As the remaining part of the canal was hardly used at all, the NSR promoted the use of a section of its bed, between Hanford and Brook Lane, Newcastle, for the proposed Trentham, Newcastle-under-Lyme & Silverdale Light Railway. However, this scheme was abandoned by the NSR in 1921, thus leaving the canal increasingly derelict. Part was filled in under the 1921 NSR Act, whilst nearly all of the rest was abandoned under the 1935 Stoke-on-Trent Corporation Act as being redundant, because, for some years, it had not been used for navigation. The rest of the route in the centre of Stoke was in-filled in 1938.

PORTION OF NEWCASTLE BRANCH CANAL

Plan for the abandonment of the Newcastle Branch Canal between Copeland Street and Church Street/High Street in 1938, under the 1935 Stoke-on-Trent Corporation Act. W.T. Copeland & Sons Ltd was the last user of this short section from the T&M. The canal was filled in to its termination at Aqueduct Street, the only part that remained being a short stub of 100 yards. This was used as moorings by the Stoke-on-Trent Boat Club until 1972, when it was finally buried under the Potteries 'D' road. *David Salt collection*

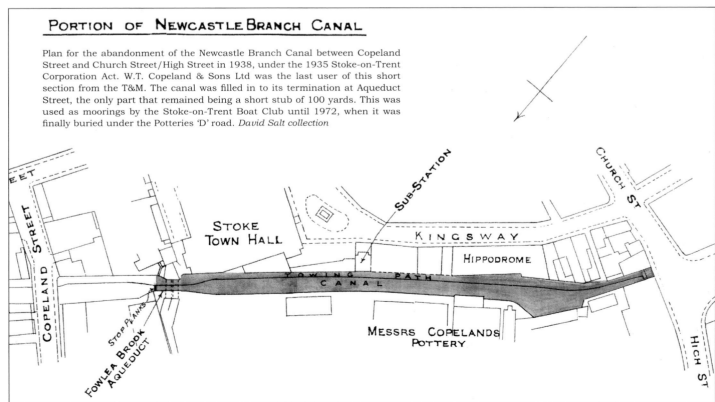

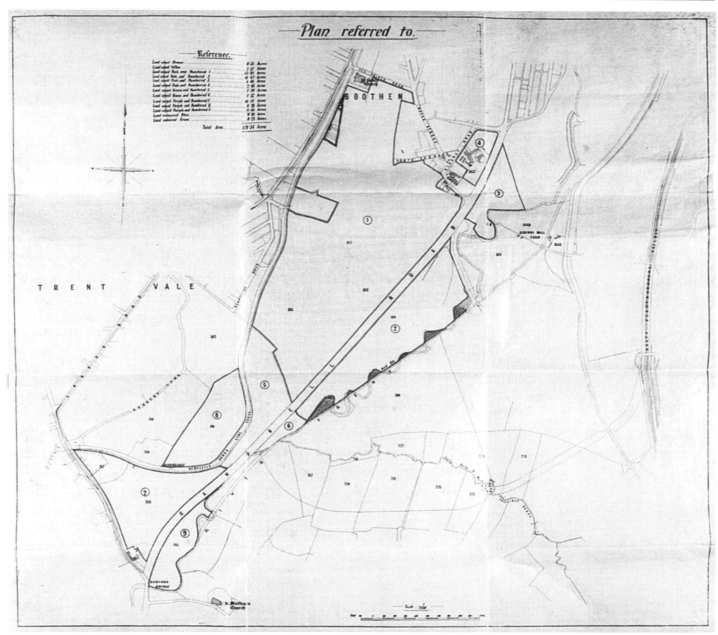

ABOVE: Plan of the site of the Michelin Works, which formed part of the conveyance in 1926 for its purchase. The total acreage of the various plots amounts to 128. On the left is the abandoned bed of the Newcastle-under-Lyme Canal, which formed the site boundary on the western side for some distance. In the centre is Campbell Road, which formed another site boundary, On the right-hand side are, firstly, the Trent & Mersey Canal and then the Main Line South railway line. *Michelin Tyres PLC*

RIGHT: A 1930s view of the long boundary wall built by Michelin along London Road, Stoke-on-Trent, in front of which is the route and filled in former bed of the Newcastle-under-Lyme Canal. *E.J.D. Warrilow, Keele University Library*

RIGHT: A mid-1920s aerial view of Knutton Forge, operated by the Knutton Iron & Steel Co. Ltd, which was situated between Newcastle and Silverdale, at the junction of the Market Drayton line with the Pool Dam Branch; rail access to the forge was from both lines. The branch can be seen curving behind the works and was part of the 1853 Silverdale & Newcastle-under-Lyme Railway, privately built by Francis Stanier. The Market Drayton line can be seen running across the centre of the picture, on the right of which can just be made out the platform of Knutton Halt; the village of Knutton can be seen top right. Knutton Forge was part of the MCC&I empire and closed in 1931. The three chimneys were not felled until the Second World War, when they were considered to be a landmark for enemy aircraft. *Author's collection*

Silverdale signal box and level crossing in 1950, with the station in the background. The signal box is to an LM&SR design, replacing an earlier NSR box at the same location when the line was singled between here and Market Drayton in 1935. This is a view looking west towards Keele; the private line to No. 17 Pit at Kent's Lane is just visible on the right, with two industrial locomotives hard at work. The station was the starting point during the Second World War for the Unadvertised Workmen's services that went to Royal Ordnance Factory No. 5 at Cold Meece. *Author's collection*

LEFT: No. 17 Pit at Silverdale Colliery, a 1930s view showing the coal winding shaft. Coal and iron workings on the Silverdale site dated back to the late 18th century but Kent's Lane Colliery, acquired by Shelton in 1918, was the pit that lasted through the LM&SR period, eventually closing in December 1988. In 1923, there were 482 workers, and in 1930 1,250 workers produced 202,909 tons; output fluctuated due to the war, dropping from 360,319 tons in 1939 to 177,227 in 1945, picking up to 262,720 tons in 1948. Numbers employed in 1946 were 738. In 1930, there were two mineral trains calling at Silverdale and three freight trains daily. By 1938, there were five daily trip workings calling at Silverdale, one locomotive being rostered from Alsager and four from Stoke. *Author's collection*

L.M.&S.R. For conditions see Back
THIRD CLASS SINGLE
Silverdale(Staffs)
Silverdale (Staffs.) To
NEWCASTLE (STAFFS)
NewcastleStaffs

L.M.&S.R. For conditions see Back
THIRD CLASS SINGLE
Silverdale@Staffs
NewcastleStaffs

-/5 P   FARE   6

ABOVE: Silverdale station on 12th June 1948, looking east to Newcastle, with a Market Drayton train about to depart. The Stanier 2-6-4T, with its 5D shed plate, now has a British Railways number, 42676, although the locomotive still retains LM&SR livery. Following the withdrawal of NSR locomotives, the Fowler and Stanier 2-6-4Ts were the mainstay of passenger workings on the line. The Stanier 2-6-4Ts started to arrive at Stoke in January 1936 but this particular locomotive did not come until November 1945. Note the water tank on the right. *W.A. Camwell*

INSET ABOVE: An LM&SR Silverdale to Newcastle Third Class single ticket. *Author's collection*

ABOVE: Silverdale on 21st June 1944, with Stanier 2-6-4T No. 2668 shunting the yard. This locomotive arrived new at Stoke in December 1942 and, at Nationalisation, was one of twenty-three of the class based there. Following the 1935 singling and resignalling, the single track to the left was dedicated to the Market Drayton line and that on the right to the Audley line. This is reflected in the two starter signals on the bracket post immediately behind the locomotive. In the background is the imposing station master's house. *John Birchenough*

LEFT: Silverdale station master's house, seen here in 1924, was built in 1870 when the line opened and, as can be seen, was substantial. An architectural feature was the wooden crossbeam above the window, a design feature that appears in similar station masters' houses built by the NSR at the same time, such as Wall Grange and Hanley, both of which have survived. *Peake family collection*

RIGHT: A Leycett to Stoke mineral train, powered by Fowler Class '3F' 0-6-0 No. 7416 off Crewe South shed, is seen between Keele and Silverdale in 1944. This locomotive was built at Vulcan Foundry in 1926 and, by 1933, was shedded at Crewe South. The class was a very populous one in the North Staffordshire Section and, in November 1945, there were eleven of them based at Stoke and four at Alsager. *John Birchenough*

LEFT: Fowler 2-6-4T No. 2316 was photographed banking a Market Drayton freight on the 1 in 100 gradient between Silverdale and Keele on 25th March 1944. This locomotive was transferred to Stoke in March 1942 but was based at Willesden at the time of Nationalisation. *John Birchenough*

BELOW: An aerial view, looking north and taken in the early 1930s, showing Silverdale Tileries, which were located half-a-mile to the west of Silverdale station; the line is just off picture top left. This firm were established by the 1820s and were one of several tileries in the area that were served by the Stoke to Market Drayton line, the others being T.E. Walley Ltd, Rosemary Hill Tileries and Knutton Tileries. Each of these tileries had their own marl hole producing clay. This photograph was used as an advertising card by the Company, hence the name painted onto the roof of one of the buildings (not there in reality) and the lettering at the bottom. *Newcastle Museum Archives*

ABOVE: Keele was a small country station and the station nameboard, to the traditional NSR style, can be seen on the right of this view, taken from a passing train on 30th April 1933, before the line to Market Drayton was singled. *H.C. Casserley*

BELOW: Keele station on 21st May 1948, as the 7.05pm Market Drayton to Stoke stops to pick up an occasional passenger. It is hauled by one of the ubiquitous 2-6-4Ts, still in faded LM&SR livery, which has made identification of the locomotive difficult. Note the replacement LM&SR hawkseye nameboard on the left and the disused platform, following singling of the route, on the right. A goods passing loop was left in place here.

INSET: LM&SR Dog ticket for use from Keele station. *Author's collection*

The Audley Branch

The Audley Branch was an important one for the North Staffordshire Railway, as it opened up the substantial coal fields to the north and west of Newcastle to rail traffic. It was seven miles 977 yards long and ran from Keele Junction, on the Stoke to Market Drayton line, to Alsager East Junction on the Crewe to Harecastle line. The Audley Branch opened in July 1870 for freight, and for passenger traffic in July 1880; spur lines went from it to collieries at Madeley Bignall Hill and to Jamage. It passed through open countryside, with a handful of small mining communities and stations were opened at Leycett, Halmerend, Audley and at Alsager Road & Talke. The line climbed steeply from Keele Junction to Audley (mainly on gradients of 1 in 50, 1 in 41, and 1 in 66), before descending from Jamage Junction to Alsager East Junction on falling gradients of 1 in 53 and 1 in 111.

The line served two parts of what was called the Western Anti-clinal Region of the North Staffordshire coalfield; this region took in the Madeley/Leycett area and yielded the highly bituminous gas and coking coals, which were heavily in demand; the Audley/Harecastle section, with Apedale in between, yielded non-coking coals.

The economic depression of the late 1920s and early 1930s saw the closure of several collieries served by the Audley Branch, as they become worked out or less suitable for mechanization, with some of the mixed coal and ironstone seams becoming completely exploited. The LM&SR era saw a significant run down of mining activities with the following colliery closures: Jamage Main in June 1928, Podmore Hall (Minnie) in May 1930, Jamage in 1941 and Bignall Hill (Rookery) in 1947. This had the inevitable impact on mineral traffic, whilst the line was also singled in 1933-35, at the same time as the section from near Market Drayton to Silverdale.

At Grouping, there was one goods train daily between Alsager Junction and Silverdale calling at Halmerend and Alsager Road. The collieries were served by three shunting engines from Alsager shed; all three worked at Jamage, whilst Halmerend and Leycett were worked by the No.1 shunting engine from Chatterley. Until their withdrawal, the locomotives used were the heavier NSR goods engines, such as the 'H' Class. In July 1930, there were two mineral trains daily from Leycett to Stoke and in October 1945 there was one freight train daily from Leycett to Stoke. In 1938, there were four trip workings serving the Audley line, three from Alsager shed and one from Stoke shed. Three of the locomotives used were Class '3' 2-6-2Ts, generally on lightly loaded trains and returning empties, whilst the '4F' 0-6-0s worked the heavier loads at Diglake, Jamage Colliery, Audley, Leycett, Halmerend and Silverdale.

At Grouping, passenger services went from Stoke either to Halmerend (three times daily and an extra train on Saturday) or to Harecastle (three times daily and three extra trains on Saturdays); this was not a bad service for a country line. On Sundays, there were two trains via the line to Harecastle. In September 1930, there were two trains to Halmerend and one on Saturdays, whilst three went to Harecastle with two additional trains on Saturdays. This was the pattern of service when the line closed for passenger traffic in the following year. Ex-NSR 'B' Class locomotives provided the motive power.

The decision to close the Audley Branch for passenger traffic was agreed by the LM&SR Traffic Committee on 25th March 1931, to which it was reported that: *'passenger traffic originating on the Audley branch has diminished since 1923 because of the institution and development of competitive omnibus services. Therefore there is no prospect of the Passenger Traffic Services on the branch becoming competitive.'* Passenger services ceased on 27th April 1931, although parcels and miscellaneous traffic continued to be handled at Leycett, Halmerend and Audley & Bignall End (renamed in April 1923), with a motor lorry working from Longport. Operating costs were estimated at £3,176 pa and revenue losses were estimated at £1,625 pa; net savings from ceasing passenger traffic was estimated at £1,240 pa. The line closure was considered by the LM&SR Board as an excellent illustration of: *'the co-ordination of road and rail transport, in order to effect economy by the withdrawal of unremunerative train services and closure of stations, leaving the traffic to rely on the services of the Associated Road Companies covering the area concerned.'*

Madeley Collieries consisted of four pits, Harrison and Woodburn, which were located to the north of the Audley Branch, and Bang Up and Fair Lady to the west of the line. These collieries were the only ones in the North Staffordshire coalfield that were connected to the L&NWR, at Madeley, via a standard gauge private line some 3½ miles long. The vast majority of the output from Madeley Collieries thus went via the L&NWR line. By the time of the Grouping, both Harrison and Woodburn pits had ceased to draw coal but were retained for ventilation and pumping purposes. This is an early 1930s view of the Harrison Pit upcast shaft; note the timber construction and the two private owner coke wagons with their distinctive bold white lettering. Also just visible is a narrow gauge tubway and wagon. In 1920, the Madeley Coal, Coke & Brick Co. (1905) Ltd was acquired by Robert Heath & Low Moor Ltd and a 50% stake was sold to Brunner Mond & Co. Ltd (later ICI), for whom coking coal was essential. Following company reconstruction in January 1925, Brunner Mond retained its 50% stake, the remaining 50% being acquired by coal factors Montague Higginson (Cardiff) Ltd; output at that time was 260,000 tons from the four pits. In 1935, Madeley Collieries employed 1,150 workers. *Bill Jack*

Two of the locomotives seen working at Madeley Collieries in the 1930s.

RIGHT: *Madeley*, an 0-6-0ST built by Robert Stephenson in 1904, came to the collieries in 1933. It also transferred to the NCB in 1947.
BOTTOM: *Hesketh*, an 0-6-0ST, was built by Peckett & Sons Ltd. in 1905 and came to the collieries new. It was transferred to the NCB on Nationalisation in 1947. *Both H.W. Robinson*

BELOW: LM&SR period wagon label for Madeley Collieries Ltd, Leycett. *Author's collection*

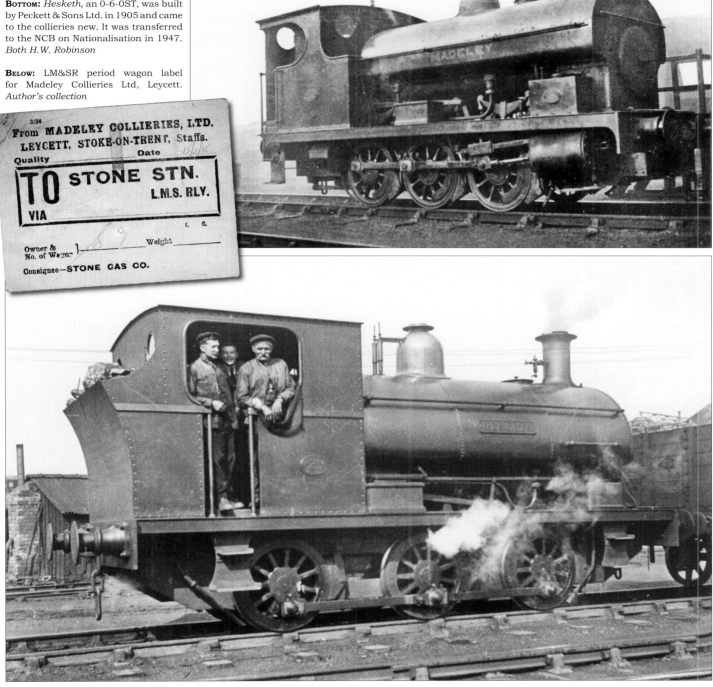

3/34
From MADELEY COLLIERIES, LTD.
LEYCETT, STOKE-ON-TRENT, Staffs.
Quality   Date
TO STONE STN.
                 L.M.S. RLY.
VIA
Owner & No. of Wagon }   Weight
Consignee—STONE GAS CO.

The availability of Workmen's Weekly tickets to and from stations on the Audley Branch was limited to Leycett. In October 1922, such tickets were available from Crown Street Halt, Keele, Knutton Halt, Liverpool Road, Newcastle and Silverdale. By September 1924, tickets to Halmerend were available from Newcastle and Silverdale, and these arrangements still applied in March 1929. There were no Workmen's tickets issued from stations on the Audley Branch. Following the withdrawal of the longstanding MCC&I Workmen's trains in September 1926, the LM&SR replaced them with a daily early morning return service between Stoke and Halmerend, a Saturdays only mid-day service between Stoke and Halmerend, a Saturdays excepted early afternoon service between Stoke and Halmerend, and a Saturdays excepted evening service between Stoke and Leycett. These workings presumably coincided with shift patterns but the service did not survive the closure of the pits at Halmerend in 1930.

The development of the LM&SR Country Lorry Services led to villages on the Audley Branch being served, such as Leycett, Alsager's Bank, Foxley and Wood Lane but this area was not served by the LM&SR Town Cartage system.

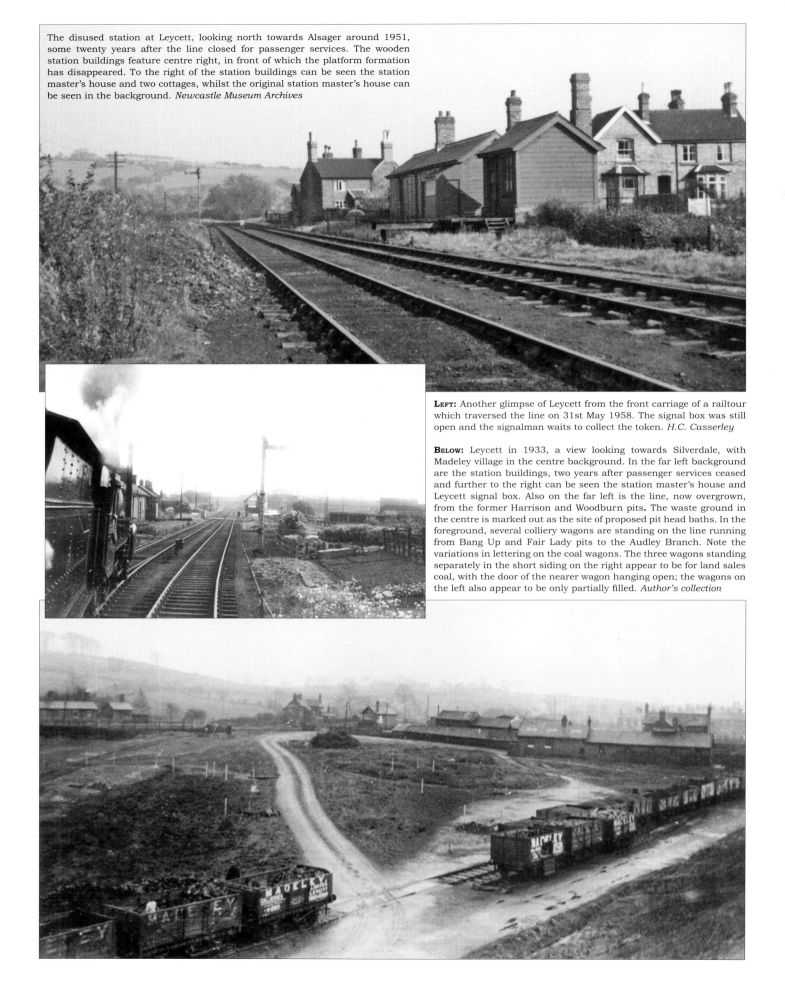

The disused station at Leycett, looking north towards Alsager around 1951, some twenty years after the line closed for passenger services. The wooden station buildings feature centre right, in front of which the platform formation has disappeared. To the right of the station buildings can be seen the station master's house and two cottages, whilst the original station master's house can be seen in the background. *Newcastle Museum Archives*

LEFT: Another glimpse of Leycett from the front carriage of a railtour which traversed the line on 31st May 1958. The signal box was still open and the signalman waits to collect the token. *H.C. Casserley*

BELOW: Leycett in 1933, a view looking towards Silverdale, with Madeley village in the centre background. In the far left background are the station buildings, two years after passenger services ceased and further to the right can be seen the station master's house and Leycett signal box. Also on the far left is the line, now overgrown, from the former Harrison and Woodburn pits. The waste ground in the centre is marked out as the site of proposed pit head baths. In the foreground, several colliery wagons are standing on the line running from Bang Up and Fair Lady pits to the Audley Branch. Note the variations in lettering on the coal wagons. The three wagons standing separately in the short siding on the right appear to be for land sales coal, with the door of the nearer wagon hanging open; the wagons on the left also appear to be only partially filled. *Author's collection*

ABOVE RIGHT: Halmerend in the late 1940s, south of the station, showing the railway bridge carrying the privately-owned MCC&I line from the Audley Branch to the former Podmorehall Colliery, which had been closed in May 1930. *Author's collection*

ABOVE: Halmerend signal box circa 1920, a poor condition view but worth including because of its rarity. *Author's collection*

RIGHT: Minnie Pit at Halmerend opened in 1881 and was part of the Halmerend group of collieries which belonged to MCC&I, the others being Hayeswood Colliery, Podmorehall Colliery and Sandpit footrail. In 1929, and immediately prior to closure, MCC&I employed 1,729 workers below ground and 497 above, with an annual output of around 600,000 tons. This view showing the head gear dates from around 1925. *Author's collection*

BELOW: Minnie Pit on 1st May 1930, with miners leaving the cage at the end of the last shift. The cage also brought coal tubs to the surface and, in the foreground, are two of the narrow gauge lines worked by rope haulage. *Author's collection*

Lined up outside Audley & Bignall End station in the early 1920s is this fine fleet of five new buses belonging to Johnsons of Audley. This was the era of expansion for bus transport but Johnson overreached himself and his business was put into liquidation in 1924, to be acquired by Mainwarings of Audley, a firm that ran local bus services for many years. Just visible are two destination boards, one for Halmerend, Audley and Newcastle, and one for Newcastle, but it is known that Johnson also provided services to Crewe and Market Drayton. All these services were in competition with the Potteries Electric Traction Co. Ltd, which provided a frequent bus service between Newcastle, Chesterton and Audley. With this intense competition from buses, it was no wonder that the Audley Branch railway passenger services struggled and soon closed. Above the roof of the first bus can be seen the steps to the station platform. *Newcastle Museum Archives*

Right: Diglake signal box was to an LM&SR design and replaced an earlier NSR box situated on the Up side of the line. The new box was located on the Down side, 760 yards north of Audley & Bignall End station, being put in when the line was singled in 1934-35. It is seen here in the early 1950s. *National Railway Museum*

Bottom Right: *Bignall Hill No. 2*, an 0-6-0ST, was built by Andrew Barclay in 1911 and came to Bignall Hill Collieries new. It was later re-named *Jamage Colliery No. 2* and transferred to the Stafford Coal & Iron Co. Ltd in 1944. *H.W. Robinson*

Above: The Bignall Hill Colliery Co. Ltd owned three collieries, Jamage, Jamage Main and Rookery, as well as several footrails. It was served by the Jamage Branch of the NSR, 1,188 yards long and opened on the same day as the Audley Branch. In 1923, the combined output of the BHCC was 339,731 tons by 1,367 colliers; following the closure of Jamage Main the workforce fell to 1,132. This number had dropped in 1938 to 660 workers, with output some 200,000 tons. Only Rookery Colliery remained after the closure of Jamage Colliery in late 1941, to be subsequently transferred to the National Coal Board on 1st January 1947, at which time it employed 381. These pictures (and on the following two pages) illustrate the changing fortunes of BHCC in the LM&SR era. This is Jamage Main Colliery circa 1925, looking north, with the former Jamage Branch out of sight between the colliery engine house and the dirt tips. Note the selection of private owner wagons on view, for Bignall Hill Colliery, Settle Speakman and Fenton Collieries. Jamage Main ceased winding on 9th June 1928 and never resumed; it was abandoned in 1931. Settle Speakman acquired BHCC from representatives of the Wedgwood family in December 1927 but its links with the BHCC dated back to 1902, when Joel Settle installed a Luhrig coal washer at Jamage and, as a result, washed coal for the other BHCC collieries as well; subsequently Settle, and then Settle Speakman, acted as their selling agents. In the LM&SR era, through acquisition, Settle Speakman became one of the largest colliery owners in North Staffordshire, acquiring Mossfield Colliery in December 1927, Fenton Collieries in June 1931 and the Stafford Coal & Iron Company in 1934. *Bill Jack*

LEFT: One of the Jamage locomotives at Bignall Hill, an 0-6-0ST, built by Beyer, Peacock in 1870, which had transferred here from Talk o' th' Hill Colliery in the late summer of 1928. It was scrapped in the autumn of 1937. *H.W. Robinson*

BELOW: The remains of the 1886-built beehive coke ovens at Jamage Main in 1943. When they were constructed, they were only the fourth set of regenerative by-product ovens to be erected in Great Britain and they were followed by the construction of a chemical plant. These ovens remained in use until 1st September 1941, by which time, as well as being completely worn out, they were some of the oldest working by-product ovens in this country. *Bill Jack*

BELOW: A general view over Jamage Main Colliery and the chemical works site, looking towards the end of the Jamage Branch, in the late 1940s, with some of the ancillary buildings of Jamage Main on the extreme left. Disused track can be seen in the foreground and a water tank is on the right. The village of Red Street is on the horizon. *Bill Jack*

Rookery Colliery, seen here in the 1930s, was part of the Bignall Hill Colliery group. It was sunk in 1898 and was located alongside the Audley line. At Grouping, it had 467 employees, in 1932 there were 475, and in 1940 the total was 480, with an output of 145,000 tons. At the time of Nationalisation in January 1947 there were 381 employees but it was shortly afterwards that the pit was considered to be uneconomic and it closed at the end of that year. *Bill Jack*

BELOW: An overall view of the wagon repair and engineering works of Settle Speakman & Co. Ltd at Alsager in the late 1940s; note the war-time camouflage paint still extant on the buildings. Modest work shops had been established in Alsager in 1901. However, as a result of the substantial expansion of its business between 1924 and 1938, by which time the firm owned some 3,420 main line wagons, new facilities became necessary. In 1938, the entire wagon works was reorganised, and extensively rebuilt and equipped. The new workshops were opened in September 1939 and comprised two repair sheds, a machine shop and smithy, a paint shop, and stores. During the Second World War, the railway wagons, together with all other fleets, were requisitioned for the war effort; subsequently, under Nationalisation, the British Transport Commission acquired the firm's 3,003 wagons, paying compensation of £173,398. The railway line coming in on the right is the Audley Branch, whilst Alsager Road station, closed on 27th April 1931, was situated on the far right. *Author's collection*

ABOVE: After 1928, Settle Speakman ceased to construct new wagons and all new builds came from outside contractors. An example is this newly built 12-ton wagon, one of a batch of 200 (No's 3176-3375) which came from the Birmingham Railway Carriage & Wagon Co. in May 1937. *Author's collection*

RIGHT: Madeley Road station, looking east in 1929 towards Newcastle and showing the main building on the left, with waiting shelter, station nameboard and greenhouse just in front of the NSR signal on the right. The smoke in the background has come from a locomotive passing on the nearby ex-L&NWR Crewe to Stafford West Coast Main Line. Madeley Road station closed on 20th July 1931, its rural isolation never creating much traffic. *Claude Moreton*

LEFT: A similar viewpoint in the 1940s, with the line having been singled, the platform on the right removed and replaced by a garden allotment, with the station building now used as a residence. Although trains no longer called, note the white lining on the platform and the protective barrier to prevent people from stepping on to the track. Interestingly, the line through here was to be doubled again in the early 1960s, in conjunction with the construction of the Madeley Chord and the diversion of traffic during the electrification of the West Coast Main Line. *Author's collection*

RIGHT: Pipe Gate station yard looking east in the 1940s. This was after the route had been singled, although double track remained through the station. On the left is the goods shed with its corrugated and curved awning, an NSR design feature, whilst in the centre can just be seen two NSR ground disks. On the right is the processing plant of Henry Edwards & Son Ltd, built in 1934-35 for milk and dairy products, and the construction materials for which were delivered here by rail. The LM&SR signed a private siding agreement with the firm in February 1935 and contributed £476 to installing the siding. *Author's collection*

ABOVE: Pipe Gate station, seen here in the early 1950s but presenting a scene which would not have changed since LM&SR days. The view is again looking east, with 2-6-4T No. 42119 pausing with a three coach train bound for Market Drayton. *Author's collection*

BELOW: Norton-in-Hales station was situated between Pipe Gate and Market Drayton, in an area otherwise almost devoid of population and probably as a consequence, it was rarely photographed, certainly in the LM&SR era. It is seen here from the window of a service bound for Market Drayton on 28th August 1954. The main building was identical to those provided at Pipe Gate and Silverdale, and there is a glimpse of the signal box which was sold privately when the station closed. *H.C. Casserley* **INSET:** An LM&SR Norton-in-Hales to Silverdale Third Class ticket. *Author's collection*

RIGHT: Smartly turned out LM&SR Fowler 2-6-4T No. 2347 pictured at the south end of Market Drayton station whilst running round on 30th April 1933. Note the metal rim of the smokebox door and its hinges have been brightly burnished, a practice more reminiscent of Scottish enginemen of the pre-Grouping era. No. 2347 was new in to service from Derby Works in May 1929. *H.C. Casserley*

ABOVE: A short while later, No. 2347 waits to depart Market Drayton with the 10.21am service to Stoke. Note the train is not using the 'Stoke bay' platform on the right. Trains leaving from this platform had to cross both running lines to take the Stoke line at Silverdale Junction. The architecture and station furniture is pure Great Western. *H.C. Casserley*

LEFT: GWR 'Barnum' Class 2-4-0 No. 3223 about to head north from Market Drayton to Crewe with the 9.40am train from Wellington on 30th April 1933. Silverdale Junction was sixteen chains north of the station and the branch to Stoke can just be seen heading off to the right in the background. The wooden posted signals are worthy of study. Note the fish-tailed distant arms and the starter for the 'Stoke' platform marked 'BAY'. Built in December 1889, No. 3223 had just three years left in traffic when pictured here, being withdrawn from Wellington shed in May 1936. The Crewe Branch was to be the final outpost for the 'Barnums' and only two of the class outlived No. 3223, No's 3210 and 3222, both being withdrawn from Wellington in March 1937. *H.C. Casserley*

Above: Early morning sunshine conveniently lights up 2-6-4T No. 42235 as it stands, more conventionally, in the bay platform with the 8.42am working to Stoke on 27th August 1954. Six years after Nationalisation, nothing in this scene will have changed from 'Big Four' days, apart from the locomotive's number. The engine was one of the LM&SR-built Fairburn tanks, emerging from Derby Works in 1946 as No. 2235. By the date of this picture, the passenger service to Stoke had less than two years left to run, the last trains operating on Saturday 5th May 1956, the service being officially withdrawn from Monday 7th. The passenger service on the ex-GWR line through Market Drayton station closed on 9th September 1963. *H.C. Casserley*

Inset Above & Right: Two unusual tickets for Market Drayton line services. Above is a Third Class Weekly Season ticket for journeys between Newcastle and Market Drayton. Issued in 1943, it is possible that the holder worked at the Second World War British Thomson–Houston Works near Newcastle. First Class travel on this line was a rarity indeed, so the fact that the NSR First Class ticket, right, for a journey all the way from Stoke to Market Drayton, was not issued until 1934 (by which time, as the handstamp indicates, the fare had been revised upwards!) is not a surprise. *Both author's collection*

A thin line between the hour and minute figures indicates p.m.

STOKE-ON-TRENT, NEWCASTLE, HARECASTLE (VIA AUDLEY) AND MARKET DRAYTON.

	Week Days	Sundays.

(Detailed passenger timetable grid showing departure and arrival times for Stoke-on-Trent, Newcastle, Liverpool Road Halt, Crown Street Halt, Silverdale, Keele, Leycett, Halmerend, Audley & Bignall E., Alsager Road, Harecastle, Madeley Road, Pipe Gate, Norton-in-Hales, Market Drayton, and G.W. Rly. connections to Tern Hill, Hodnet, Peplow, Wellington and Shrewsbury, with return workings and columns marked "Saturdays only", "Saturdays excepted", etc.)

G—Calls by signal to pick up passengers on notice being given at the station, and to set down on notice being given to the guard at Pipe Gate.

SO—Saturdays only.

LEFT: LM&SR passenger timetable for services on the Market Drayton and Audley branches in 1930. Note that from Market Drayton, onward connections to stations on the GWR line as far as Shrewsbury are also shown, whilst trains on the Audley Branch worked to and from Harecastle. Anyone actually travelling between Harecastle and Stoke, however, would have used the Main Line North, not the roundabout route via Audley. *Author's collection*

BELOW: Another view of the 8.42am to Stoke waiting to depart from the bay on 27th August 1954. Note that the starting signals had been replaced since the 1933 picture. *H.C. Casserley*

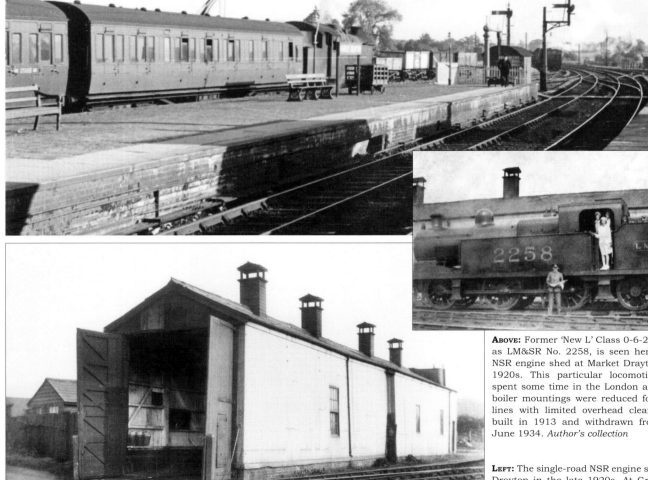

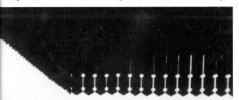

ABOVE: Former 'New L' Class 0-6-2T No. 89, now as LM&SR No. 2258, is seen here outside the NSR engine shed at Market Drayton in the late 1920s. This particular locomotive previously spent some time in the London area, where its boiler mountings were reduced for working on lines with limited overhead clearance. It was built in 1913 and withdrawn from service in June 1934. *Author's collection*

LEFT: The single-road NSR engine shed at Market Drayton in the late 1920s. At Grouping, there were three NSR locomotives allocated here but by 1929, under the LM&SR, there were none. The shed was closed officially on 27th April 1931 but not demolished until 1937. *Author's collection*